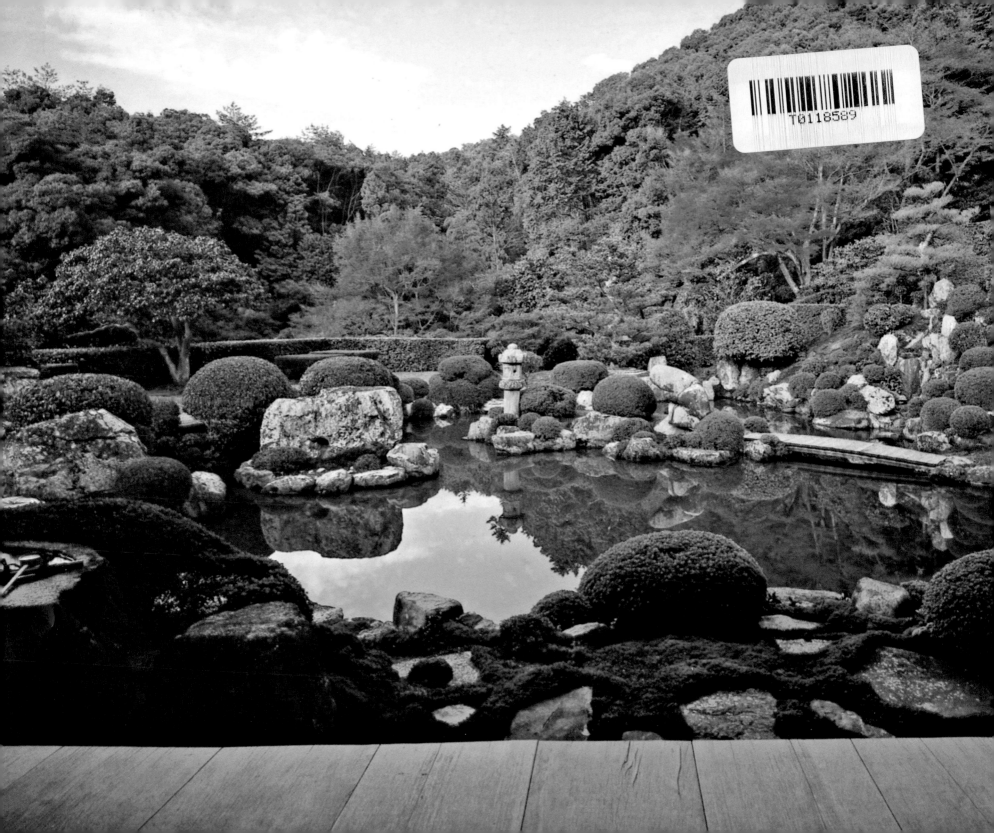

Published by Tuttle Publishing, an imprint of Periplus Editions

www.tuttlepublishing.com

LCC card no. 96061007 Hc
ISBN 978-0-8048-3856-6 Hc
ISBN 978-4-8053-1425-8 Pb

Distributed by
North America, Latin America & Europe
Tuttle Publishing
364 Innovation Drive
North Clarendon, VT 05759-9436 U.S.A.
Tel: 1 (802) 773-8930; Fax: 1 (802) 773-6993
info@tuttlepublishing.com; www.tuttlepublishing.com

Japan
Tuttle Publishing
Yaekari Building, 3rd Floor
5-4-12 Osaki, Shinagawa-ku
Tokyo 141-0032
Tel: (81) 3 5437-0171; Fax: (81) 3 5437-0755
sales@tuttle.co.jp; www.tuttle.co.jp

Asia Pacific
Berkeley Books Pte Ltd
61 Tai Seng Avenue, #02-12
Singapore 534167
Tel: (65) 6280-1330; Fax: (65) 6280-6290
inquiries@periplus.com.sg; www.periplus.com

Hc   14 13 12 11 10   6 5 4 3 2
Pb   22 21 20 19 18   6 5 4 3 2

Printed in China   1801RR

Front cover photo: Japanese Garden at Kennin-ji Temple,
Kyoto. Spine photo: Sanbō-in, Kyoto. Back cover photo:
Fall foliage at Ryoan-ji Temple, Kyoto.

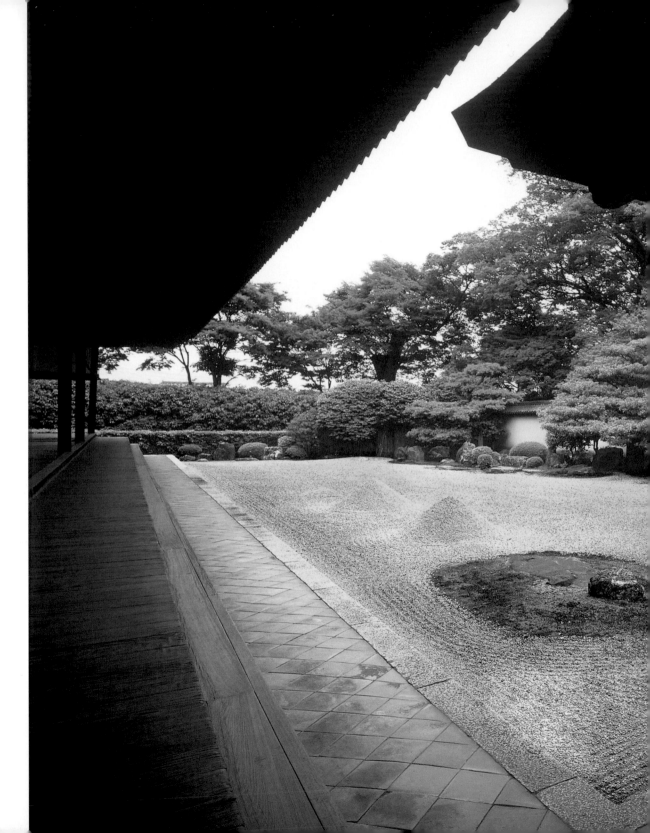

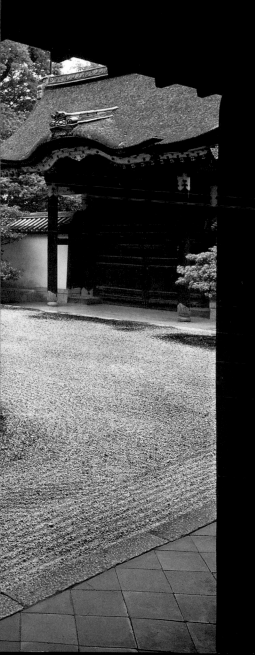
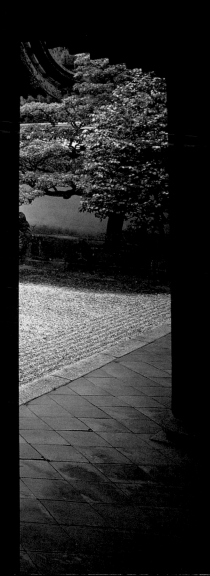

JAPANESE GARDEN DESIGN

MARC PETER KEANE

Photographs by **Haruzō Ōhashi**

Drawings by the author

TUTTLE Publishing

Tokyo│Rutland, Vermont│Singapore

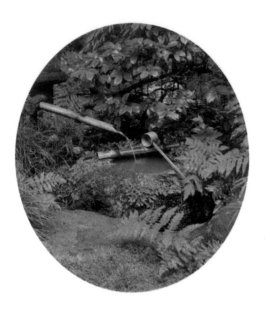

For my mother
    who showed me the beauty of art

    and for my father
        who led me to nature

CONTENTS

CREATIVE INSPIRATION

DESIGN

FOREWORD Preston L. Houser

Tourists are insatiable creatures. There are basically two kinds, pilgrims and shoppers, and, in their mobile element, they assiduously seek and devour. Literally thousands of tourists visit Kyoto every day from different parts of Japan as well as from the far corners of the globe, and they mostly visit temples and gardens—sacred places. The pilgrims come to gain a sense of artistic heritage which will expand and enrich their cultural identities. They temporarily occupy spaces that artisans, aristocrats, and Zen masters of prior ages have occupied as if, by sharing the same "view," a more enlightened perspective of the soul and the world will be achieved. For the shoppers, on the other hand, traveling is a kind of consumption called "doing," such as doing New York or doing the Louvre, as if cultures can be done as one would do an amusement park or a shopping mall—profane places. The shoppers seem to revel in the hollowness of such misadventure, and their proclamation of experience invariably betrays an exaggerated sense of *mal de siècle*: "Been there, done that."

Most tourists who come to Kyoto, however, are pilgrims. For them, the rewards of travel are more profound than simply being there and doing that —or so they would prefer to think. For pilgrims, Kyoto remains the city of choice for its cultural wealth and its abundance of tourist destinations— again mostly temples and gardens. The original designers of Kyoto City, by imposing an ancient Chinese civic scheme upon its streets and borders, conceived of the capital as a kind of noble garden. Unlike cities that grew outward from a military center, Kyoto was deliberately, artistically planned, and the gardens throughout the city display the same mindful concern with design. The pilgrim's impetus to come to Kyoto is likewise characteristically noble: one seeks to participate in a highly charged cultural environment if only for a few days and bring an insight gained in a garden back to one's home territory— thus indirectly enhancing one's own community, if not one's country. The tourist's nightmare, consequently, is that one looks upon a temple garden with only half-sight, without penetrating the subtleties of the landscape, esteeming only the superficial, mistaking the obvious for the sublime. Pilgrims risk short-changing themselves as well as their home neighborhoods if they have not fully grasped the significance of the sights they have seen. For such tourists, to return spiritually empty-handed from a journey, none the better for their discoveries or without a newly acquired perspective on the universe, is tantamount to community treason. Misapprehension, therefore, is an unprofitable experience to be avoided at all costs— although it is often as unavoidable as the occasional bout with malicious amoebae.

The Japanese garden defies quick and easy apprehension. More than a quaint arrangement of stones and shrubbery, the Japanese garden delights the senses and challenges the soul—a majestic enigma. We gaze at a Japanese garden with the nagging sensation that we could be seeing more, understanding more. Frustrated, we reprehend our lack of connoisseurship because we know that we are never farther from self-realization than when we misunderstand the external world. Since to understand art is to understand our souls (and vice versa), we believe—correctly—that proximity with one will bring us into proximity with the other. For many, nothing so manifests that spiritual proximity as the Japanese garden.

All art is collaborative. True, a novel or a piece of music is usually the result of individual effort, but the influences upon the artist are manifold. Most artists acknowledge artistic debts of influence; those who claim to create in a vacuum are liars. Today this simple aesthetic truth is often buried under the mountain of adulation we heap upon an individual talent. Even in Japanese landscape gardening, the desire to assign the composition of a particular garden to a particular artist is great. This garden was designed by Sōami, that one by Enshu Kobori— we seem to demand that one person be representative of all influences and talents of an age, as if that were possible or even desirable. But gardens are more like poetic epics than novels in that many successive generations of designers and artisans have contributed to the garden's composition. Like the Bible, *The Odyssey*, or *The Mahabharata*, the Japanese garden is a distillation of many hands and

hearts spanning many generations. Poetic epics and Japanese gardens reveal qualities of the human spirit rather than a single individual personality. The gardener, therefore, subsumes personality in deference to the garden, thus contributing to an artistic immortality that can be shared by all.

As a landscape architect and teacher, Marc Keane is less concerned with speculating upon those individuals responsible for a certain garden style and more concerned with depicting what the designers were probably thinking when laying out a garden. With this shift in emphasis, Mr. Keane has united us with our cultural ancestors, articulated their "view" and their consciousness; in the process he has enhanced our own appreciation for what we are seeing.

Lest we forget, gardens, like their distant theme-park cousins, are fictitious environments in that they are not wild. A garden's reality is of a different order; we enter a garden for different reasons than when we take a hike or go camping. The visitor to a garden participates in an illusory environment that often represents, ironically, a psychological reality

richer than our daily experience. This is the paradox of all art. A garden may be contrived but the truths it speaks are as real as those spoken by a Hamlet, a Don Quixote, or a Faustus. Like literary characters, gardens speak to us but in a language of image: oceans, mountains, rivers, waterfalls, turtles, cranes. Garden designers manipulate these cultural emblems to create a three-dimensional sculpture. The garden becomes, therefore, a kind of anthology of symbolic images and patterns; but the defining images of a garden, like aspects of fictional characterization, must be learned.

In the pages that follow, Mr. Keane illustrates how these cultural images have been utilized in the development of the Japanese garden. Lacking television monitors, for example, the aristocracy of the Heian court created a visual entertainment not unlike current video projections. Sitting in a room particularly made for the purpose, they would gaze out upon a garden that evoked images of mythology and literature—usually from China. Sometimes there was musical accompaniment or poetry recitation. After a time, not content with a static perspective, the people moved out into the garden and interacted with the images—from a boat at first, then by strolling around the garden to achieve the optimum visual effect. The aristocracy inserted themselves into the garden scene in a way that modern interactive computer toys have yet to match; for them, entering a garden was like stepping into a myth and taking an active role. Contemporary tourists—a transient aristocracy—can do the same; indeed, Jungian analysts claim we have been doing it since time immemorial.

These days we are continually reminded that we live in a material world. Gardens are a representation of our material world at its best, in contrast to the invisible, ideological worlds of nirvana, heaven, hell, or cyberspace. Mr. Keane has shown how the garden becomes an extension of our communities, our planet; then he shows how it turns around and becomes a metaphor for our innermost thoughts. The book you are holding represents years of careful study and experience in the art of Japanese garden design. With it, Mr. Keane promotes connoisseurship in the original sense of the word—a cultivated familiarity with the Japanese garden. As readers and pilgrims, what we finally learn is this: The garden manifests a pattern of collective psychic energy; our apprehension of that pattern enables us to participate in nothing less than a spiritual dance of paradise.

At the end of his life, American poet Ezra Pound, who struggled with poetic and political ideologies alike, realized that it is impossible to replicate paradise here on earth. In one of his final cantos he wrote: "Let the wind speak. That is Paradise." The Japanese garden designer, like the poet, creates a theater for the wind to speak, and to our delight we find that the wind has words. In listening, we participate in more than just a pleasant garden scene; we participate in our own immortality. With *Japanese Garden Design*, Mr. Keane provides an etymology, grammar, and lexicon for deciphering just what the wind has to say.

Introduction Marc P. Keane

Looking back, I can see that this book began with another book—six small books in fact, all neatly packed into a clothbound case that fastened snugly shut with tiny ivory tongs. The books were Japanese children's stories, printed around the turn of the century, in English no less. They were from a series called *chirimen-bon*, privately published in Tokyo by a certain Takejiro Hasegawa, who wanted to introduce Japanese culture to the world. One set of the books found their way to my bedroom nighttable via my father who brought them back from Japan just after the end of World War II.

All the classics were included: "Momotaro," the heroic quest of a brave young man and his companions; "The Tongue Cut Sparrow," which taught that good hearted folk and evil-doers get their just rewards; and "The Old Man Who Made Dead Trees Flower," a poignant tale of an old man who creates beauty where there was none. It was not the stories, however, that left an impression on me; it was the feel of the books themselves. Printed on *chirimen* paper—a crinkled blend of Japanese paper and

silk—they were, despite all the years, still supple to the touch. Each book had been carefully bound with hand-stitching, giving them a quality altogether unlike that of the other books I knew at the time. The colors and the balance of the graphics, the texture of the pages, and their tidy packaging instilled in me the first inklings of a new aesthetic. Not that I thought so at the time. It was a seed planted, and only now in quiet reflection can I hear the sound of that most potent seed falling.

In a way, those books drew me to Japan where I found that the same aesthetics that were in the books were to be found in the gardens too. This was my first lesson: The forces that shape a society's culture are complexly interwoven and the aesthetics found in one aspect of a culture are present in all other aspects as well. The study of the garden, I discovered, can be enhanced by watching a Noh play, listening to a *shakuhachi* flute, or even eating Japanese food.

My next lesson was that there is no one definitive "Japanese garden." Instead, over the course of a 1,500-year history, various gardens were created by

people inspired by different turns of events—a new religion, philosophy, or shift in social structure. By considering those periods of creative inspiration we find hints of ways to perceive what a garden *is*—not only what was unique about the Japanese garden historically, but also kernels of knowledge for garden designers now.

Over the course of the next ten years, designing gardens in Japan and talking with the many gardeners I met along the way, I began to get a *feel* for the design of a Japanese garden—the aesthetics, the rhythms and balance, the structure that lies behind the rocks and carefully pruned pines. This then is the final lesson that I will attempt to impart through this book: There is something more essential to the gardens than the materials they are made of—that the essence of the garden lies in the way it is designed, not in what it is designed of.

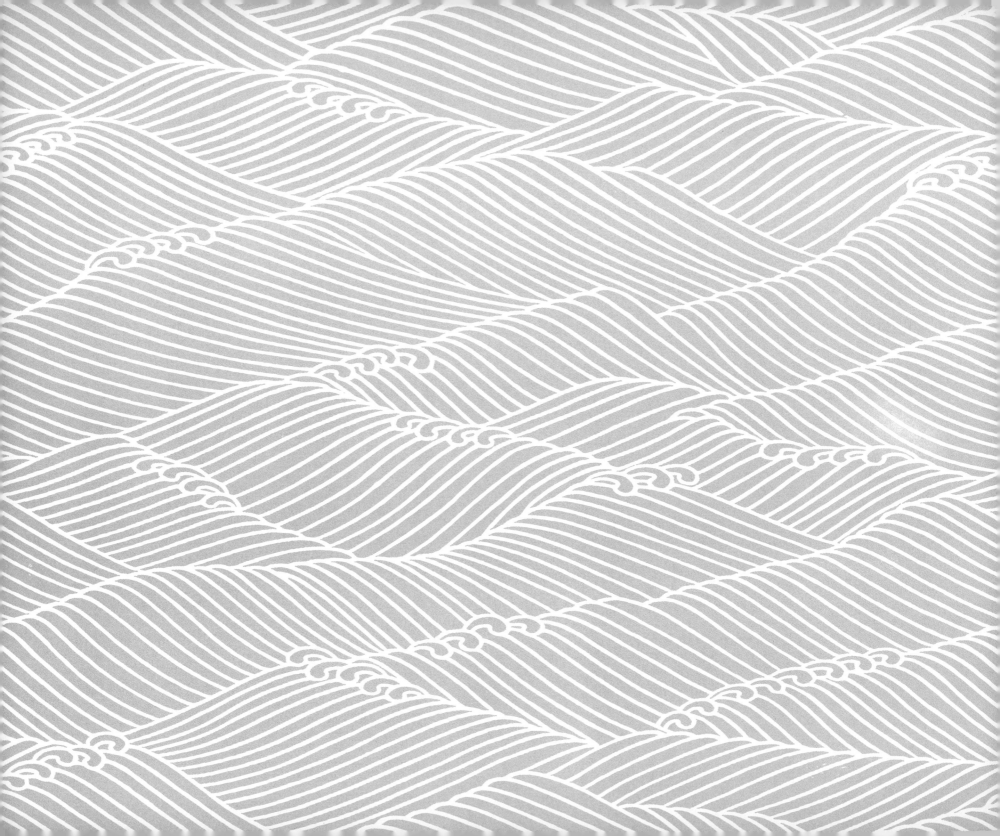

CREATIVE INSPIRATION

THE DEVELOPMENT OF THE ARTS IN JAPAN, INCLUDING GARDEN DESIGN, HAS EVOLVED CONTINUALLY OVER THE PAST MILLENNIUM. NEVERTHELESS, WITHIN THAT LONG HISTORY, THERE HAVE BEEN CERTAIN SPECIAL TIMES WHEN DRAMATIC SHIFTS HAVE TAKEN PLACE. AT THOSE TIMES, THE CONFLUENCE OF COMPLEX CHANGES IN SOCIETY, POLITICS, RELIGION, ARCHITECTURE, AND AESTHETICS GAVE RISE TO A NEW CULTURAL ENVIRONMENT. UNDER THE INFLUENCE OF THOSE CHANGES, GARDEN DESIGNERS WERE INSPIRED TO CREATE NEW FORMS OF GARDENS AND, MORE IMPORTANTLY, NEW WAYS OF PERCEIVING WHAT A GARDEN **IS**—PERCEPTIONS FROM WHICH WE CAN DRAW INSPIRATION FOR OUR OWN CREATIVE WORKS.

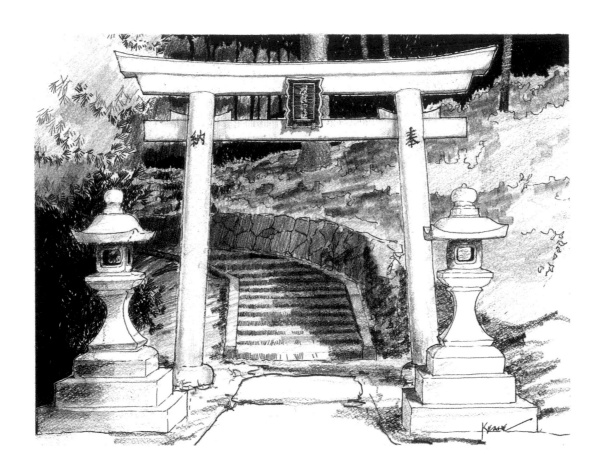

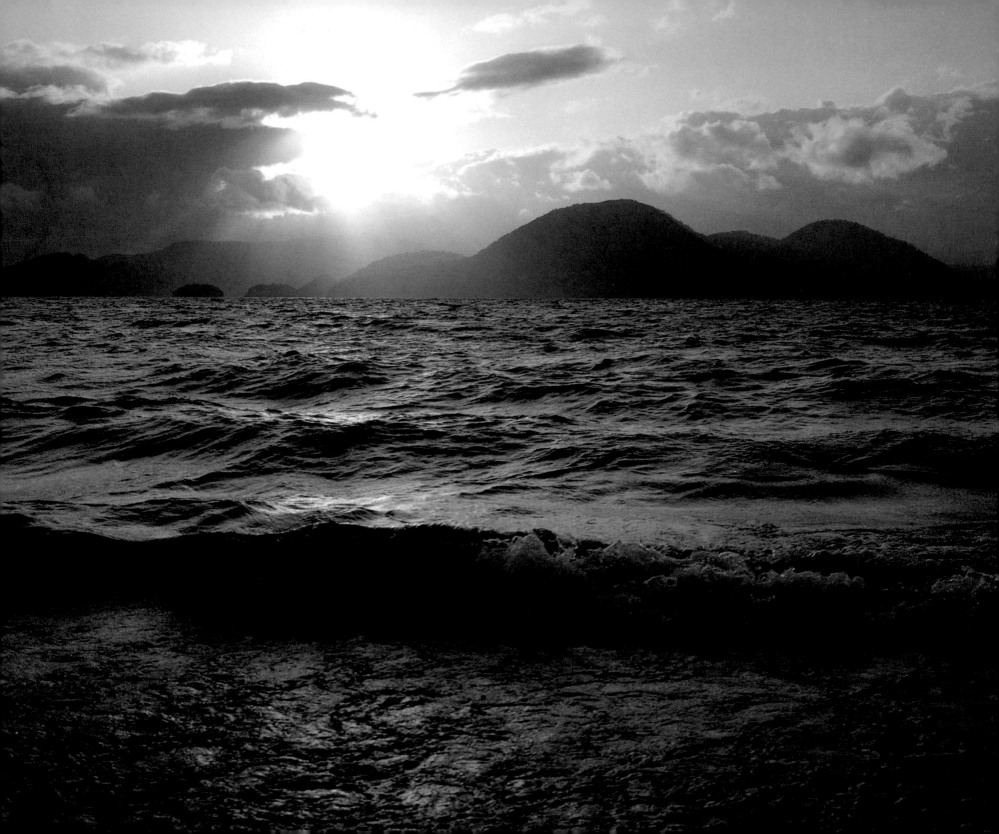

PREHISTORIC ORIGINS

Gardens are an expression of our relationship to the natural world. Begun in prehistoric times, this relationship was perceived over the course of time in increasingly spiritual, aesthetic, and intellectual manners. Eventually, this heightened awareness led to the creation of gardens through which designers expressed an idealized vision of nature and our place in it. In order to understand the Japanese garden, therefore, we must first look at the land and the people as they first inhabited it.

Left: Mountains and water:
The prototypical image for the Japanese garden.

Below: A figurine from the Jōmon period.

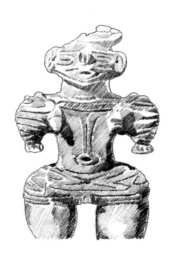

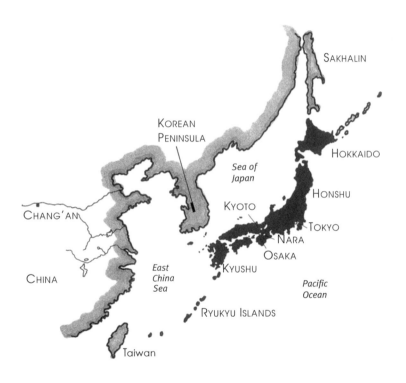

VOLCANIC CRESCENT

SAKHALIN

KOREAN
PENINSULA

Sea of
Japan

HOKKAIDO

HONSHU

CHANG'AN

KYOTO

TOKYO

NARA

CHINA

OSAKA

East
China
Sea

KYUSHU

Pacific
Ocean

RYUKYU ISLANDS

Taiwan

THE LAND

The crescent of islands in the Japanese archipelago from Hokkaido to Kyushu and on through the outlying Ryukyu Islands sits on the eastern edge of the tectonic plates that form the Asian continent. As the opposing plates that lie under the Pacific Ocean push down under the continental plates, the intense heat turns rocks to magma which forces its way up to the surface forming the volcanic mountains that are the backbone of Japan. Of some 850 active volcanoes throughout the world at least fifty are to be found in Japan alone.[1] Seventy-five percent of Japan's landmass is mountainous (over fifteen percent slope); the rest is primarily narrow mountain valleys and coastal plains. The constrictive nature of the landscape was a primary force in shaping the development of Japanese society in general and with regard to garden design in particular, it can be said that the primary prototypical image for the garden derived from the physical structure of Japan, in short, mountains rising abruptly from the sea.

The lowered sea levels caused by the last Ice Age gave rise to land bridges that connected the Japanese archipelago with the mainland. Two routes were created, a southern one connecting the Korean peninsula and China to Kyushu, and a northern route through what is now the island of Sakhalin. At that time, the Sea of Japan was a large enclosed body of water. As animals migrated out and across the land bridges, people followed and settled. A general warming trend beginning around 10,000 B.C. signaled the end of the Ice Age and changed the very nature of the archipelago. What was an extended peninsula became a series of islands as the exposed coastal shelves were inundated by released glacial waters. Warm waters and winds heavy with rain flowed up from the south breathing new life into the islands—deciduous forests in the north and broadleaf evergreens in the south. The most recent examination of seed types found in archeological sites shows that there were broad areas of meadow as well. The ecology we know today with its rich variety of flora—the image of which was the basis for the gardens themselves—originated at this time.

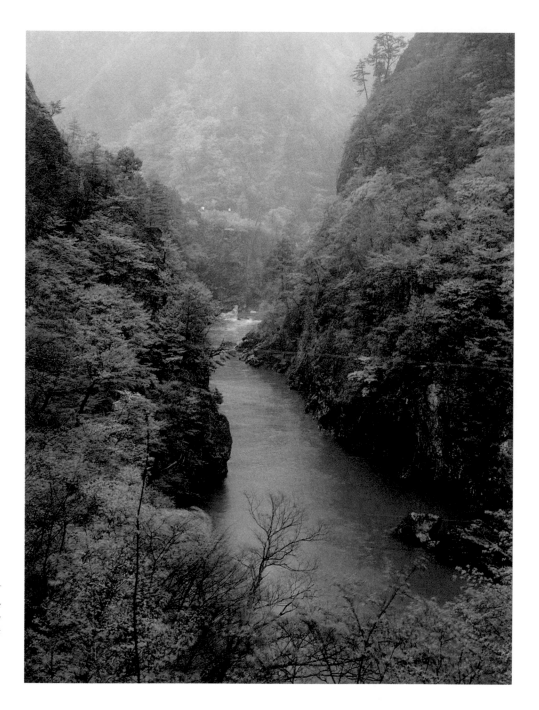

*The constrictive nature
of the landscape was a primary
force in shaping the development
of Japanese culture in general.*

THE PEOPLE

The period of time starting roughly after the Ice Age is known as the Jōmon period (10,000–300 B.C.), which is distinguished by pottery making, a technical innovation that may have been imported from China or Korea but is thought by many to have developed independently in Japan. Jōmon literally means "cord-mark" and refers to the distinctive patterns made by impressed rope that are found on the pottery of this period. Hunting and gathering in the inner hills was the primary means of subsistence in the early Jōmon period, but as the climate warmed, the newly flooded continental shelves allowed for the easy collection of shellfish and marine life. Settlements shifted accordingly to the coastal areas, and the piles of discarded shells that mark these sites indicate the importance of marine life in the diet of the people. While recent archeological evidence hints at the existence of a rudimentary agriculture using slash-and-burn techniques, it is believed that inland foraging for grains and game continued as well. Life would go on in much the same way until the third century B.C.

The next important phase of the prehistoric period is the Yayoi period (300 B.C.–A.D. 300), named for a site near Tokyo where Yayoi pottery was first discovered. This period is marked by the full development of wet-rice farming and a shift from a hunter-gatherer society to an agrarian society.[2] Kyushu marks the point of initial introduction of the new farming technique which spread widely within a few hundred years. The sudden appearance of bronze at this time, and soon afterward iron implements, together with the new farming techniques, clearly points to a massive cultural influence from the larger Asian continent. Undoubtedly there was a new migration, this time by boat, and it is not unreasonable to suggest that the Japanese people and their culture as it exists today derive from an overlapping of the Yayoi-period immigrants and the aboriginal peoples. In the early Yayoi period, settlements were clustered about lowlands where the marshy conditions provided natural paddy fields, making it possible to farm there without the need to create complex irrigation systems. By the end of the period, though, farming techniques had developed sufficiently to allow upland valleys to be cultivated. By the second century A.D. Yayoi culture could be observed as far north as northern Honshu. Many of the customs that guided the daily lives of the Japanese people until the middle of this century—the seasonal rites and social value system—have their roots in the Yayoi agricultural communities.

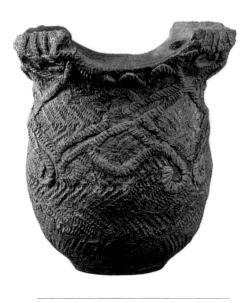

Distinctive cord-marks on a Jōmon vessel.
Kyoto National Museum

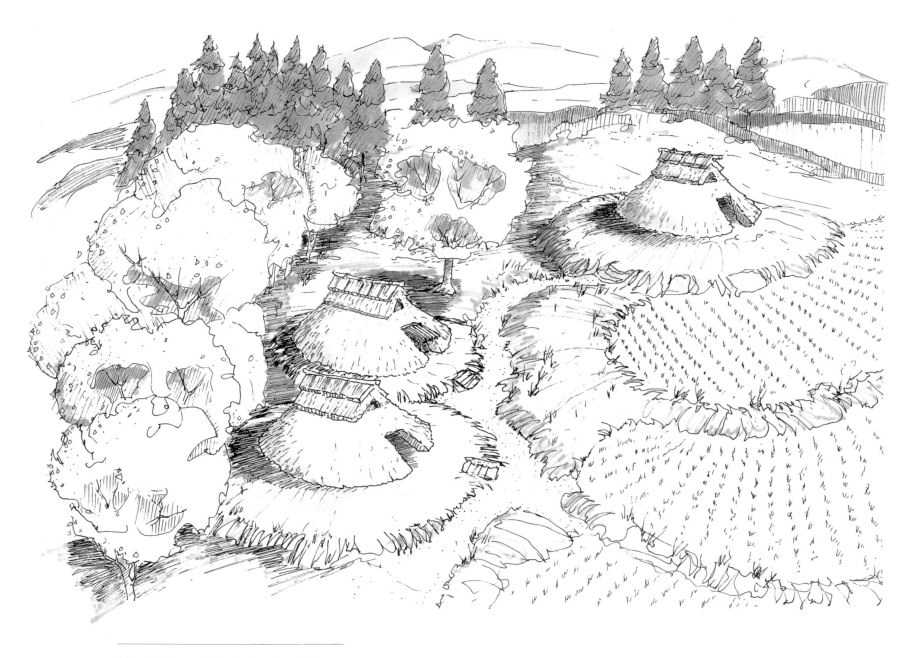

A Yayoi village and the beginnings of agriculture.

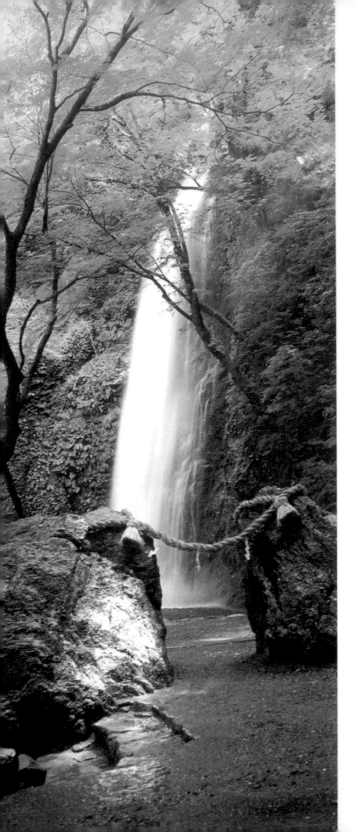

ORIGINS OF THE GARDEN

Gardening as a fully developed art form was introduced from China and Korea in the sixth or seventh century A.D., nevertheless, several aspects of Japanese garden design can be traced back to prehistoric years. The first aspect of the garden that can be said to have evolved from ancient times is the balance of natural and man-made beauty—a guiding principle that forms the aesthetic basis of all Japanese gardens. This aesthetic grew out of the cultural transitions that occurred during the Jōmon and Yayoi periods as an agrarian society developed in Japan. Evidence of this transition is revealed in the etymology of two of the most common words for garden, *niwa* and *sono*.[3]

NIWA

During the Jōmon period, a crude form of architecture—a thatched roof built over a shallow pit —had already developed. From settlements of these pit-dwellings the Jōmon people gathered food along the coast as well as foraged inland. They were not exclusively nomadic, as the existence of built settlements shows, but it is thought that they traveled over a wide range in search of food and materials for tools. Although there are no written records from this time, we can assume, by tracing the use of the word back through the ages that the name for this extended territory was *niwa*.

The earliest written record that includes the word niwa is the *Man'yōshū*, an anthology of poems from the eighth century A.D., which associates niwa with the broad open sea and fishing grounds found there.

Left: Because of the particular character or spirit they embody, certain places in the landscape, like this waterfall, are considered sacred.
Yōrōnotaki, Gifu

Right: Boulders along the Japanese coast were the inspiration for the rocky shores in pond gardens.
Tosa shoreline

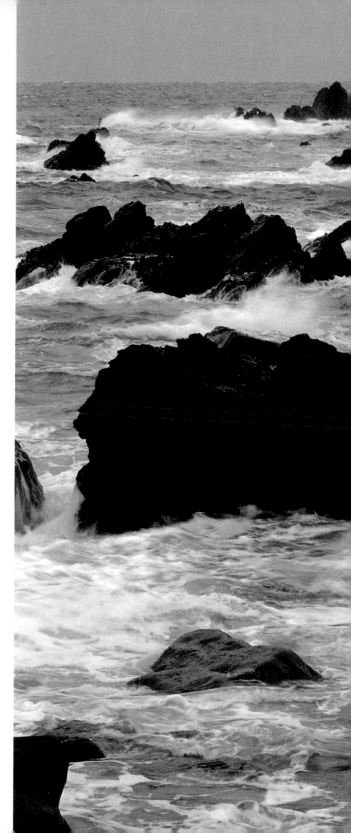

*The **fishing grounds** at Kehi*
must be yielding their riches today;
scattering about on the waves,
like freshly cut reeds, I can see
the boats of fishermen [4]

kehi no umi no
niwa *yoku arashi*
karikoma no
midarete izumiyu
ama no tsuribune [5]

Hunting ranges, *kari-niwa,* have the same etymology, as do places for events to take place, like *sa-niwa* or *yu-niwa*, purified spaces used for prayers. By the middle ages in Japan the word niwa was being used by traveling minstrels and actors as the term for the area they worked in, still maintaining the quality of territory.[6] Even to this day, the term *uri-niwa* (sales area) exists and is used by modern "foragers" in neckties and suits. Niwa also had the implication of being an ownerless area thus distinguishing it somewhat from the English word territory, which implies a captured or controlled area. It is easy to believe that, until the advent of agriculture through which nature is subdued for mankind's benefit, the human community and the natural world were not perceived as being separate entities. The Jōmon period, being primarily pre-agricultural, was just such a time of unification. In light of this, the word niwa represents humans in nature as an inherent and indivisible part of it.

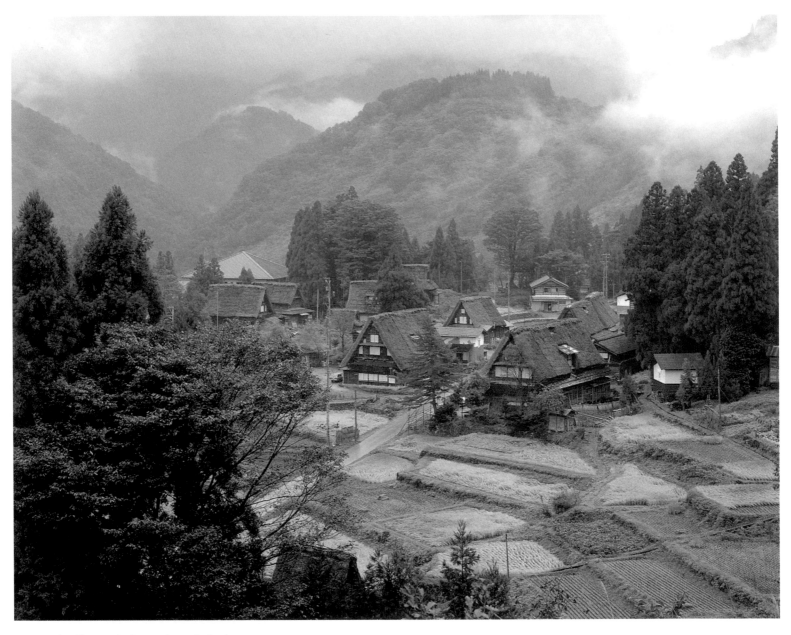

A mountain village: agriculture reshapes the landscape.

The introduction and development of wet-rice farming during the Yayoi period would irrevocably alter man's relationship to nature. Wet-rice farming, much more than raising other grains, requires a dramatic restructuring of the landscape. Within a relatively brief period the landscape changed as much of the land around settlements was reshaped for agricultural purposes. Gardens for growing medicinal herbs, plots for raising crops, orchards, pens for animals, and rice fields were all such restructured, agricultural landscapes and originally they also shared a common name—*sono*.[7] An early use of this word in literature, also found in the *Man'yōshū*, refers to a "garden" with plum flowers.

I would have the plum flowers
always in my **garden**
    never falling
like the ones
   that bloom before me now [8]

Ume no hana
ima sakeru goto
chiri sugizu
waga e no **sono** *ni*
arikosenu kamo [9]

Sono can be interpreted as a pastoral, agricultural landscape and as such represents the control of nature by man—the antithesis of niwa.

TEIEN

Both niwa and sono are used today to mean garden in one way or another. Interestingly, they can be used together to form a compound word that not only means garden but also succinctly expresses a guiding principle of garden design—the balance of natural and man-made beauty. Almost all words in the Japanese language have multiple pronunciations depending on context and so it is with niwa and sono. One pronunciation is the ancient Japanese; the other is an approximation of the Chinese pronunciation that came with the writing system in the sixth century A.D. When two or more characters are used in combination to express a single idea the Chinese pronunciation is usually used. Niwa has the alternate pronunciation of *tei* and sono can be pronounced *en*. When written together, rather than saying niwa-sono, the pronunciation becomes *teien* (pronounced "tay-ehn"). Although there are many words in Japanese that mean garden (*niwa, niwa-saki, sono, teien, sentei, senzai, sansui, chisen, gyoen*), teien is perhaps the most commonly used.

Written character	庭	園
"Chinese" pronunciation	TEI	EN
Japanese pronunciation	*niwa*	*sono*
Original meaning	territory (wild nature)	bordered fields (controlled nature)

Although the original meaning has been somewhat lost in the modern word, teien represents two opposing characteristics—*wildness* and *control.* It is in the exquisite balance of these two fundamental qualities that the Japanese garden finds a universal voice. Sitting quietly on the veranda of a temple and looking out into the light of the garden, one can still feel the sensory world of the Jōmon period although it has been transformed through the controlled art of the gardener into a spiritual, aesthetic, or even intellectual expression.

STONES AND PONDS

Another aspect of Japanese garden design that can be traced back to prehistoric times is the use of stones and ponds—two of the most fundamental elements of the garden—which derive from sacred spaces that predate the first gardens by at least 1000 years. The native Japanese religion, now called Shintō, is an animistic religion.[10] *The Chronicles of Japan* (*Nihongi*), a record of Japan's ancient history compiled in the early eighth century, depict the most ancient period as being a time when rocks and plants had human qualities, a perception revealed in passages like "the very rocks, trees, and herbs were all given to violence" or "there were also trees and herbs all of which could speak."[11]

The use of stones and ponds in Japanese gardens is connected to those ancient animistic religious practices. According to one interpretation, the native gods of Japan, known as *kami,* can be divided into two groups, those that descend from above, *ama-kudaru kami,* and those that come from over the sea, *tōrai kami.*[12] In these early years there was no religious architecture, no shrines or temples, only the natural world. It was believed (and still is by many) that certain places in the natural landscape, because of the particular spirit they hold, were likely spots for the gods to inhabit. Islands, waterfalls, huge ancient trees, or prominent boulders jutting from the landscape or sea all were such places. In order to communicate with the gods, to pray to them, appease them, and entice them to bestow their blessings, sacred spaces were created at those natural "spirit places." The same interpretation that divides the gods in two groups also holds that these sacred spaces fall into two types: sacred stones for the gods from above and sacred ponds for those from beyond the sea. Whether this interpretation is correct or not is beyond proof, but the sacred stones, called *iwa-kura,* and the sacred ponds, *kami-ike,* exist even to this day.

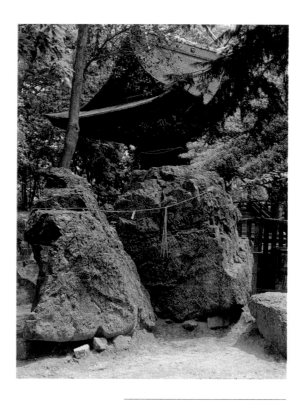

Iwakura: *Touchstones for the gods.*
Achi Jinja, Okayama

IWAKURA

The iwa-kura (written "boulder seat" as in "seat of the gods") are found throughout Japan, hidden in the hills near towns and villages. In order to signify their respect for the kami, the ancient people delineated and purified the area around the iwa-kura. They delineated the area by tying straw ropes (*shime-nawa*) around it and physically purified the area by clearing it, and in later years, covering it with a layer of sand or gravel, per-

THE FIRST GARDENERS

The Asuka (A.D.552–710) and Nara (710–794) periods were marked by active contact with Korea and China, resulting in the wholesale importation of continental religion and culture. A variety of craftsmen and scholars were invited to Japan—or found their way on their own in order to seek their fortunes. There were sizable resident Korean communities in Japan and undoubtedly friends and relations followed each other over.[15] Considering that during the Asuka and Nara periods the cultures of China and Korea were far more advanced than that of the Japanese, it is understandable that the first gardens in Japan would have been made by foreign craftsmen for Japanese clients, namely, the Imperial line or other powerful families. One such craftsman was the Korean immigrant Michiko Takumi, who is recorded in *The Chronicles of Japan* as having built a garden in Japan in the early seventh century A.D.

There were, as well, Japanese who showed an interest in garden building and may have guided the construction of their own gardens—for example, Soga no Umako and Otomo Tabito. Umako had a pond and island built in his garden which made such a social impression as to gain him the name Minister of the Island. Tabito, a famous poet whose work is amply recorded in the *Man'yōshū*, built a garden with his wife, who figures prominently in many of his poems.

haps white.[13] This demarcation was called *kekkai*, the "boundary zone"—in this case, between the secular world and that of the gods. Once the physical space was prepared, prayers to the gods could then commence.

The iwa-kura were at first natural stones; as religious practices developed, stones were set upright for the purpose of creating ritual spaces. Among these artificial constructions there are *iwa-saka* and "stone circles." To create the iwa-saka ("god boundary") twin rocks were placed side by side forming a gap or slit which suggested an abstract image of female genitalia. "Stone circles" were made of horizontally laid, pillar-shaped stones which are built in a broad circular shape encircling a central stone. These stone circles demarcate a sacred area the way shime-nawa do. The amount of thought and work required to create iwa-saka and stone circles indicates that they were a later development in the process of using stones to communicate with the gods.[14]

KAMI-IKE

The sources of water for many of the ponds used to create kami-ike seem to be natural springs. "Water is life," thus a wellspring of water is the source of life itself. By this interpretation, the kami-ike is a shrine to the gods that inhabit that wellspring. In addition the kami-ike can be seen as shrines to tōrai-kami—the gods from beyond the sea. It would not be out of keeping with the pantheistic nature of Shintō if both explanations were true. The gods that come from over the sea were believed to reside on islands collectively called *haha-guni*, the mother country, or ancestral land. There are traditionally three islands in this group, each with its own prime goddess. It is possible that ancient peoples recreated this image by building islands in a pond. To what degree these ponds were natural or man-made is uncertain. Most likely the builders used an already existing pond in the creation of a kami-ike—deepening it and adding the central islands. In the course of time they built shrines on the islands to honor the gods.

Kami-ike and iwa-kura were not created for aesthetic reasons. They were sacred places meant for prayers and rituals. They do contain, however, powerful aesthetic components that would later be "discovered" and brought to the fore in the creation of gardens. The kami-ike has a planar, horizontal beauty derived from the surface of the water—original-

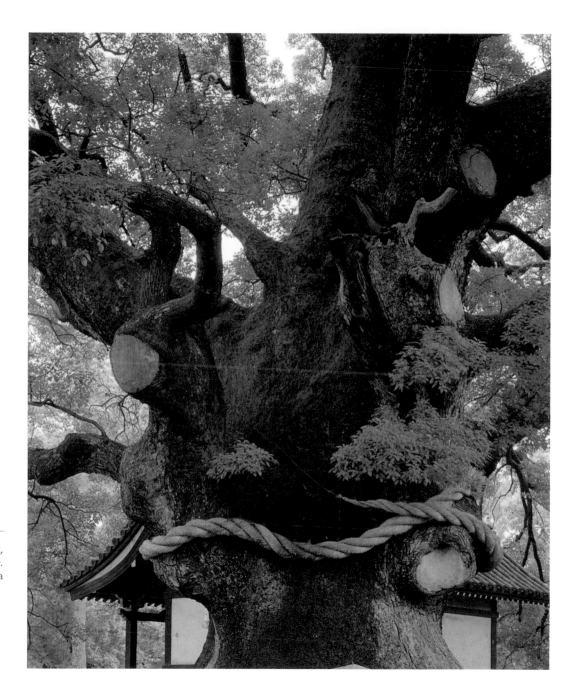

A straw rope, called a shime-nawa, *denotes a sacred tree.* Zentsū-ji, Kanagawa

ly the vast surface of the sea. This is referred to in some texts as "bird's-eye beauty" (*fukan-bi*) implying that the principal aesthetic is found in the two-dimensional ground plane. On the other hand, the beauty of the iwa-kura is sculptural, volumetric beauty (*ritai-bi*). One of the fundamental design techniques used in the creation of all Japanese gardens, perhaps most clearly seen in the dry rock gardens of the medieval period, is the harmonic interplay between planes (flat, raked sand, walls, and fences) and volumes (rocks and clipped plants).

During the sixth and seventh century A.D., the incipient Japanese aristocracy began to imitate Chinese and Korean culture in an attempt to "civilize" themselves. At that time, gardens were a requisite part of civilized life on the mainland and consequently the nobles incorporated gardening into their new life style. Garden design, as it was imported from the continent, was a fully developed art form, replete with myriad symbolic images—some of which were associated with stones and ponds. Because of the ancient rituals regarding iwa-kura and kami-ike, however, the early Japanese garden builders undoubtedly found these "foreign" ideas somehow familiar. It is easy to believe that, while embracing these imported ideas, the early Japanese garden designers also maintained as an essential element of their garden design the ancient, animistic perception that natural objects—rocks, ponds, and islands—are not inanimate but shelter sacred spirits.

Kami-ike: *An image of the sea, and distant, sacred islands.*
Ryūsenji, Osaka

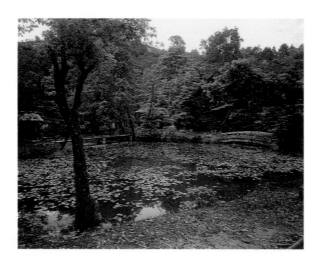

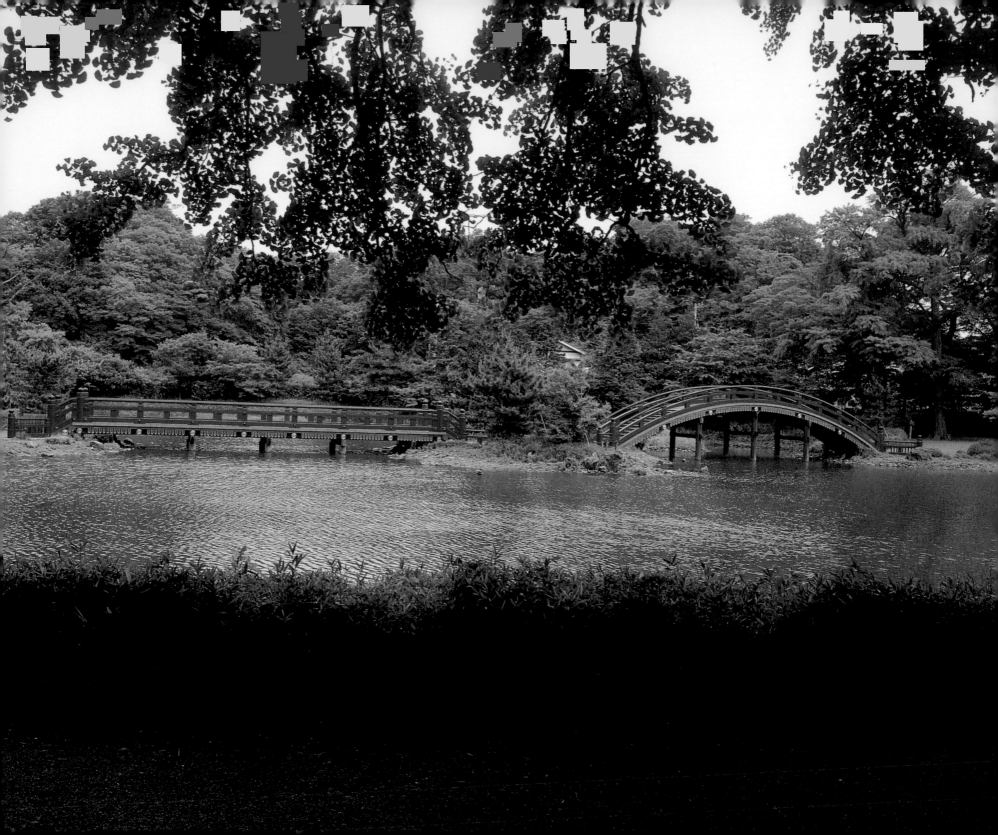

GARDENS OF THE

HEIAN ARISTOCRATS

The transformation from a hunter-gatherer society to an agrarian society during the Yayoi period was followed by a growing tendency of the Japanese people toward settlement, the development of permanent structures, and centralized socio-political systems based on Chinese and Korean examples. This shift eventually led to the development of the highly sophisticated Heian aristocratic court in which the garden as an art form would thrive. In order to understand the gardens of the Heian period (794–1185)—how they were perceived at the time and, in turn, what inspiration we can draw from them now—it is necessary to look at the development of society in general: first, the socio-political arena with the establishment of the imperial line, its court, and the successive influence of the Fujiwara regents; second, the development of the cultural environment under the influence of continental ideas: Confucianism, geomancy, Buddhism, poetry, and of course the art of gardening itself. The development of the physical setting, the city of Heian-kyō (modern-day Kyoto) and the *shinden* residences at which the gardens were built, are also of importance.

Unfortunately, there are no extant gardens from the Heian period. What we know of them can be surmised from images preserved in literature and paintings and from recent excavations. The gardens of the Heian period do not resemble traditional "Japanese gardens" that are based on gardening styles which developed from the middle ages onward. In fact, most of what is emblematic of Japanese culture—Noh and Kabuki theater, tea ceremony, flower arrangement, samurai, Zen Buddhism, tatami, and sushi—did not exist in Heian times; those images must be set aside in order to garner a sense of what life in the ancient capital was like during the tenth and eleventh centuries.[1]

Left: The central island of Heian pond gardens was connected to shore by vermilion bridges, linking the world of man to paradise.
Shōmyō-ji, Kanagawa

SOCIETY AND POLITICS

The Kofun period (300–c. 550), which immediately followed Yayoi, is named for the large burial mounds the clan leaders had built for themselves. It was during the Kofun period that the imperial household was established. Claiming descendency from the Sun Goddess, Amaterasu Omikami, they achieved a superior position among a number of warring clans and created the Yamato Court. They not only established themselves as head of the nation, but also as chief priests, with a direct link to the gods of the land. Other clans were assigned particular tasks in relation to the court regarding the provision of goods and services. From the Kofun period on, the imperial court would be an integral part of Japanese history and culture.

The imperial court gradually consolidated its power by emulating existing Chinese and Korean systems of government—delegating to the other clans certain titles, rights, and responsibilities which would bind them to the imperial hierarchy. In the seventh century one of these clans, the Nakatomi (court liturgists), founded a new family line called the Fujiwara. By cleverly associating themselves with the imperial line through marriage, the Fujiwara rose to a position of great power at court. By the tenth century they effectively usurped power from the imperial line by appointing child emperors and wielding power in their stead as regents (*sesshō*). The last three centuries of the Heian period are commonly referred to as the Fujiwara epoch not only because the family effectively controlled the government but also for the distinct culture that pervaded the court during the time of their supremacy.

The political and cultural ideals that led to the development of the Fujiwara epoch were imported from China and Korea. Whether they came through the kingdoms in Korea or directly from China, they were of Chinese origin. To this degree Japanese culture was, until the Heian period, influenced by Chinese models. The Heian period is significant in that the Japanese aristocracy broke off official relations with China at that time. The T'ang dynasty in China was in decline, which caused the Japanese to feel that, having reached a level of cultural maturity, they need not imitate Chinese society any longer. Although the occasional private vessel still sailed to China and some Chinese ships still came to Kyushu, by 894 official embassies were halted. This hiatus allowed for a period of introspection during which the cultural imports of the previous centuries were distilled and from which grew a uniquely Japanese culture—including a form of garden design that was truly Japanese.

Cultural Development

Tradition holds that two Korean scholars, Achiki and Wani, came to Japan in A.D. 404 and 405 respectively bringing with them knowledge of Confucian thought which had penetrated the Korean peninsula from China in the fourth century A.D. Confucius (551–419 B.C.) was a Chinese philosopher of the late Zhou dynasty (1027–256 B.C.).[2] Longing to revitalize the harmonious society of the early Zhou, Confucius formulated guidelines for an ideal society. These rules were not to be legally enforced, but were supposed to be observed voluntarily by all people in society. Appropriate behavior for one's social status, especially the moral example and altruism of those in leadership positions, constituted the basis of a Confucian society. Central to the development of moral behavior was the concept of filial piety, in which a child gives unquestioned respect and obedience to parents (in practice the father). The Japanese imperial line, believing that the hierarchical order of Confucianism was key to the success of the Chinese dynasties, accepted it as a model for their own country. Confucianism also stressed the ideal of education and self-cultivation as a meaningful end to itself, setting in motion a positive social attitude toward scholarship that reached a pinnacle with the Fujiwara epoch. Although Confucian ideals are not reflected in Japanese gardens directly, they were the foundation for the erudite, artistic society that created gardens.

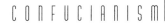

CONFUCIANISM

Confucian thought developed extensively within China before it was introduced to Japan. Of particular interest to the development of the Japanese garden was the admixture during the Han dynasty (A.D. 206–220) of a complex cosmology we now call geomancy. There are two Japanese expressions for geomancy: one is *eki*, which is often translated as divination, and the other is *fūsui* (wind and water).[3] In short, geomancy is a theory of universal structure based on the opposing yet complementary principles of Yang (the positive, active force) and Yin (the negative, passive force) and their mutual effects on the five basic elements: wood, fire, earth, gold (metal), and water. In Japanese Yin and Yang are, respectively, *in* (sometimes *on*) and *yō*. These elements have conjunctive qualities as well, including a cardinal direction, a color, and a guardian animal. To the fifth-century Japanese, geomancy was significantly more developed than the native practice of divining heat-induced cracks in the bones of deer or shells of tortoises. Geomantic study became known in Japan as the Way of Yin-Yang (*on-yō-dō*) and in the seventh century a branch of the government, called the Yin-Yang Bureau (*on-yō-ryō*), was established to handle matters of divination. Unfortunately, geomancy in Japan rapidly swayed from its rigorous intellectual origins, so that by the Fujiwara epoch it had degraded into a pseudo-religion catering to the superstitions of the ruling class.

Early Japanese gardeners' use of geomancy can be seen in the way they designed the flow of water and positioned specific plants and rocks (which were believed to be imbued with geomantic properties) to create a harmonic state within the garden. The Chinese garden design concept of harmonizing the opposing forces of Yin and Yang by balancing voids and fluids (both Yin) with masses and solids (both Yang) was very likely also applied in the design of Heian-period gardens.[4]

北
NORTH

TORTOISE
WINTER
BLACK
WATER

西 **WEST** — TIGER · AUTUMN · WHITE · METAL · CENTER YELLOW EARTH · WOOD · BLUE · SPRING · DRAGON — **EAST** 東

FIRE
RED
SUMMER
PHOENIX

SOUTH
南

Above: A chart depicting some of the basic geomantic characteristics associated with the five elements.

Right: Pagodas, which are derived from Indian stupas, contain sacred Buddhist relics or sutra.

Buddhism is a philosophy that tries to reveal *dharma*—the true eternal law, or the true nature of life. Buddhism teaches that we are all bound in an endless cycle of suffering, the root cause of which is want and desire. To free ourselves from this cycle of death and rebirth, we must realize dharma and look past the superficial appearance of things to see them as they really are. The historical Buddha, Siddhartha Gautama (known as Shakamuni in Japan), was born a prince sometime in the mid-fifth century B.C. in Bimbini in what is now Nepal. He gave up his life of luxury and through a rigorous process of meditation became enlightened (realized dharma) and went on to teach what he had learned, although he concluded that enlightenment itself could not be taught—it must be experienced. Buddhism spread throughout eastern Asia and developed into myriad forms, as certain aspects of Buddhist doctrine were stressed in favor of others, and combined with local religions, rituals, and ethics. By the second century A.D., Buddhism had entered China and later spread to the Korean peninsula from where it entered Japan.

Buddhism arrived in Japan in the mid-sixth century, introduced by Korean scholars as was Confucian thought earlier. *The Chronicles of Japan* lists the year 552 as the time when emissaries from Korea brought the first gifts of sutras and a gilded bronze statuette of the Buddha, but it is likely Buddhism was already known in Japan.[5] Once established, Buddhism became a vital force shaping social norms and aesthetics. By the Fujiwara epoch, several schools of Buddhism were established in Japan, including Tendai and Shingon.

The builders of the first Japanese gardens incorporated Buddhist symbolism in their gardens in several ways. Prime among these were images of the mountain *Shumisen* (Sanskrit: *Sumeru*) and of the Pure Land of Amida Buddha. Shumisen is the legendary central mountain of the Buddhist cosmology. Towering above its surroundings, Shumisen is surrounded by eight rings of lower mountains with eight seas lying enclosed in succession between them. Man's abode is believed to be on the outermost set of mountains next to the eighth sea. This image of ranks of mountains surrounding a central taller one became one of the central motifs in Japanese gardens depicted by setting one prominent, upright stone and, at times, surrounding it with a cluster of smaller stones. Because of their similarity to the ancient iwa-kura, Shumisen stones must have seemed very familiar to the Japanese when the idea was first introduced from the continent.

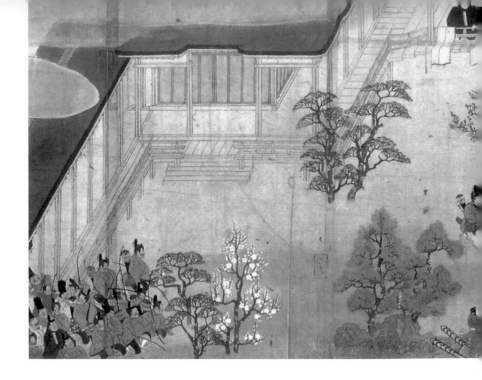

Another Buddhist image used in the garden was that of the Pure Land (*jōdo*), which stems from teachings of the Amida Buddha, well known in Heian times even though they did not become the focus of a distinct, popular sect until the middle ages.[6] Amida Buddha presides over the Pure Land, a heaven where the spirits of enlightened individuals enter at death to be removed from the endless cycle of death and rebirth. This image of the Pure Land influenced many Heian-period garden designers, some of whom built gardens specifically as earthly replications of the Pure Land. The most famous of these gardens is Byodo-in in Uji, south of Kyoto, a country residence of a Fujiwara noble that is now a temple. The central hall of Byodo-in is miraculously still extant, over 900 years after it was built. Heian-period garden designers created the image of the Pure Land image by creating an island in the "sea," in fact a pond, sometimes planted with lotus. The central island was often connected to shore by one or more bridges which implied the potential of attaining the Pure Land. The similarity to the ancient *kami-ike* is immediately evident and is another instance in which a native idea was melded with a new continental one.

POETRY

The Heian court is considered to have placed more importance on poetry than any other society in history—it pervaded all aspects of court life from lovers' communiques to imperial edicts. Knowledge of the existing body of poetry, both Chinese classics and those written in Japan, was *de rigueur* and poetic allusions were used constantly in all forms of discourse of the period. At first, poetry was limited to the Chinese classics which were learned by rote. Later the Japanese began to write their own poems but in a Chinese form. By the time of the Fujiwara epoch the Japanese had developed a phonetic writing system called *kana*, spawning a rich body of poetry based in their native language, which expounded native themes—local heroes and the beauty of the natural world as found in Japan. The pervasive interest in nature is clear from the frequency of nature images in the poetry.

GARDENS

The Chronicles of Japan relates another event in which the Japanese court first comes in contact with the idea of gardens.[7] In the year 612, a man emigrated from the Korean kingdom of Paekche and took the Japanese name of Michiko no Takumi. The locals called him Shikomaro (ugly-maro) because his face and body

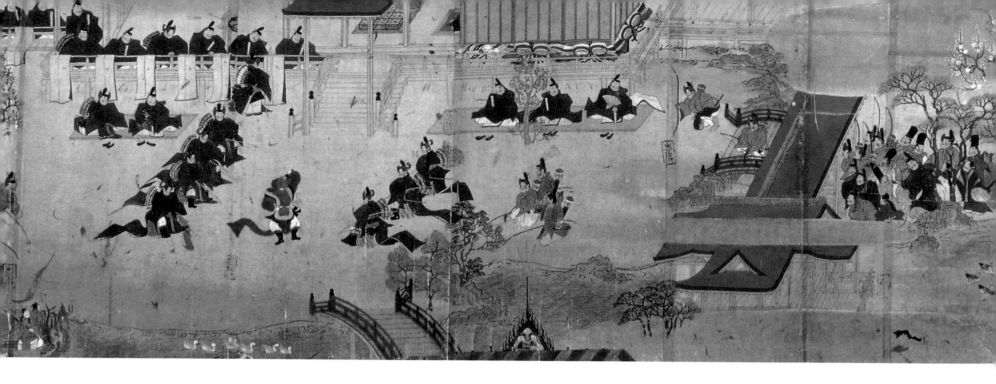

were covered with white blotches caused by ringworm. At this time contact with the more advanced continental culture was actively encouraged but since Michiko no Takumi was disfigured, it seems the local authorities were planning to banish him to an island off the coast. He pleaded for clemency, claiming that he had a certain skill, that of "making hills and mountains" —in other words gardening.[8] Accordingly, he was allowed to stay on and is said to have created the figures of Mount Shumisen and the Bridge of Wu in the Southern Court of the empress.

This tale is instructive in two ways: the first is that it shows the stress put on "mountain" building, and the creation of Buddhist images, as a core principle of gardening at that time; the second is that it reveals that the initial gardens built in Japan were Korean (Chinese) style, built by continental craftsmen for Japanese nobles. The status held by foreign craftsmen and scholars, and the influence their ideas had at this time over the Japanese aristocracy, was a basic component of the early society. Undoubtedly the gardens (as with the architecture, writing, clothes, etc.) were for the most part replicas of those found in contemporary Korea and China. All of the images that were being woven into the garden such as Shumisen, Amida's Pure Land, and various geomantic protocol, were imported from China and Korea. The gardens would have differed from those found on the continent only to the degree that the climate and the local flora were different. However, during the cultural changes of the Heian period, garden design evolved as Japanese nobles began designing their own gardens.

A performance of dance at a Heian-period shinden residence. The shinden is seen at top center, and the tainoya, chūmonro, and izumidono to the left and right. Of note in the garden are: the winding stream, generally sparse plantings, the boat on the pond, and the curved, vermilion bridge that leads to the central island. Placed on the island for this event, is a musician's stage; the flame-like panel is the decoration of a large drum (dadaiko). From nenjū gyōji emaki: mai goran, original c. 1165; this copy seventeenth century. Tanaka Family Collection

THE PHYSICAL SETTING

The rapid introduction of continental culture that followed the consolidation of the imperial line included innovations in architecture and town planning. Rulers abandoned the practice of building large burial mounds for themselves and began constructing Buddhist temples to pray for their souls instead. In addition, the emperor and the leading families of the court changed the architecture of their residences from simple thatched-roof dwellings to large structures roofed with finely-split wooden shakes. The influence of Shintō, with its stress on ritual purification, dictated that each time an emperor died the palace needed to be built anew, in a different place. This may at times have been no more than a few hundred meters away from the original place, but such a move was necessary in order to avoid the pollution caused by death. The first permanent imperial capital, Fujiwara-kyō (*kyō* = capital), was built in 694 south of what is now Nara city. It had a formal, symmetrical plan based on Chinese models, as would all the capitals after that up until, and including, Heian-kyō, founded exactly 100 years later.

The valley that held Heian-kyō (which Kyoto City completely fills today) has low mountain ranges on all sides except the south, forming a protected cove. Beyond this obvious physical benefit the valley also fit certain geomantic conditions for a harmonic abode—some existed naturally and some were created. First among these conditions was the expression in the landscape of the four protective gods (*shijin*)—Black Turtle (*genbu*) in the north, Blue Dragon (*shōryū*) to the east, Crimson Phoenix (*suzaku*) to the south, and White Tiger (*byakko*) to the west. The image of the Black Turtle was divined as a low, rounded mountain (Funaoka-yama), setting the central axis of the city. The southerly Crimson Phoenix was represented by a large pond (Ogura-ike) south of the city, and a line drawn due south from Funaoka-yama to the pond bisected the city plan perfectly. A large river (Kamo-gawa) that ran through the valley diagonally was rerouted so that it bordered the eastern edge of the city, thereby representing the Blue Dragon, and the westerly White Tiger was given form by building a long, straight canal-lined road (Konoshima-ōji) parallel to the city outside its western border.[9] In addition, the northeast corner of the valley, considered to be the devil's gate or *kimon*, from which evil most easily enters, was naturally protected by a prominent mountain, Hiei-zan. Hiei-zan was already home for the temple Hieizan-ji (later Enryaku-ji) which would eventually grow into a massive complex strengthening the shield at the devil's gate.

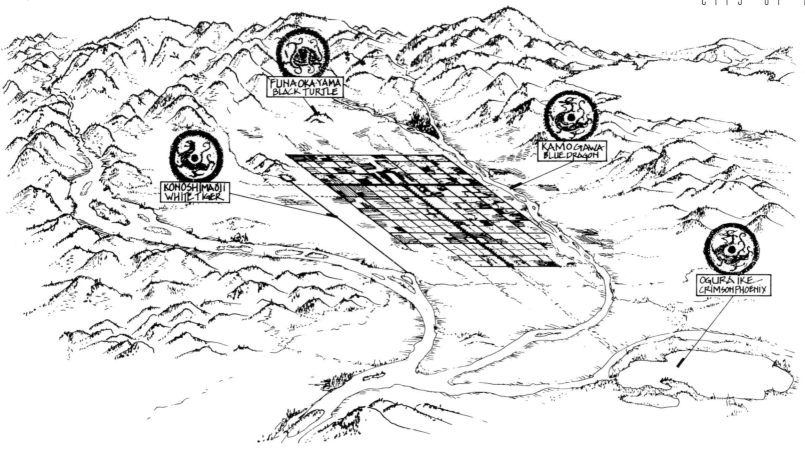

Part of the reason for going to the great expense and energy required to build a new capital was certainly to avoid the aforementioned defilement inherent in an existing capital. In the case of Heian-kyō, the move also had to do with Emperor Kammu's idealist visions for the future of his nation. The Confucian ideals of a just and moral society were highly commendable and there is every reason to believe that this particular emperor sought to see them instituted. Unfortunately, life in the old capital at Nara had grown increasingly incestuous with time, and the intrigues of various parties for control of power became overbearing. Under despotic conditions, with each petty priest and prince out for himself,

Heian-kyō sat nestled in a protective valley, open only to the south. The four cardinal directions each had a protective kami; *and the northeastern "devil's gate"* (kimon) *was defended by Mt. Hiei.*

Some of the illustrations on pages 29 and 31 have been adapted from *Kyoto no rekishi atorasu,* Chūō Kōronsha.

the implementation of a Confucian state based on altruistic leadership was next to impossible. The separation of the court from the immediate influences of Nara's great Buddhist temples was among the prime reasons for the removal of the imperial house from that capital. Heian-kyō would be, in its very form, a physical representation of the values it would promote. Rational in its symmetry, hierarchical in plan, and fairly disposed for all who would live in it. Heian Japan was not a democracy, but all citizens would be allotted their portion according to their status in society.

By Japanese standards the valley that held Heian-kyō was rather large and flat, providing enough space for the grand urban planning schemes of the emperor. Built as a scaled-down version of the T'ang-dynasty capital Chang'an—as were Fujiwara-kyō, Nara-kyō, and Nagaoka-kyō before—Heian was laid out on a grid, 5.2 kilometers north to south by 4.5 kilometers east to west.[10] The city was divided symmetrically east and west by a broad (84 m) central avenue called Suzaku-ōji and the imperial palace was positioned at the northern end of this avenue facing south. This southern orientation is revealed in the fact that the eastern half of the city was called, and still is, Left Capital (Sakyō) while the western half was Right Capital (Ukyō).

The overall grid of Heian-kyō was created by avenues that were 24 to 51 meters wide depending on their importance. Nine were laid out running north-south and eleven east-west, dividing the city into seventy-four large blocks.[11] The imperial palace comprised six of these at the top/center. Lesser streets were built within each block dividing them into four equal parts called *hō*, which in turn were each split into four *chō*. A chō, about 120 by 120 meters (1.4 hectares or 3.5 acres), was the standard lot size for an aristocrat or person of standing although some families of high rank had properties that were two or even four chō in size.

The chō could be further divided into 32 *henushi* (four east-west by eight north-south) which was a standard commoner's lot. Heian-kyō was created entirely for the support of the imperial bureaucracy and therefore, initially, it had no uncontrolled "private" sector. Each sector was assigned a specific purpose—an area for the residences of the aristocracy, for temples, markets, and so forth. Only two temples were officially sanctioned (Tōji and Saiji, East and West Temple, respectively) in accordance with the imperial desire to keep the Buddhist influence at bay. The residences of the aristocrats, where the gardens were built, were mostly in the northern and eastern sections of the city.

HEIAN-KYŌ

1. **EAST TEMPLE,**
   Tōji

2. **WEST TEMPLE,**
   Saiji

3. **EAST MARKET,**
   Higashi no ichi

4. **WEST MARKET,**
   Nishi no ichi

5. **EAST COURT**
   FOR DIPLOMATIC RECEPTION,
   Higashi kōrokan

6. **WEST COURT**
   FOR DIPLOMATIC RECEPTION,
   Nishi kōrokan

7. **IMPERIAL GARDEN,**
   Shinsen en

8. **IMPERIAL COURT**
   AND RESIDENCE,
   Dai dai ri

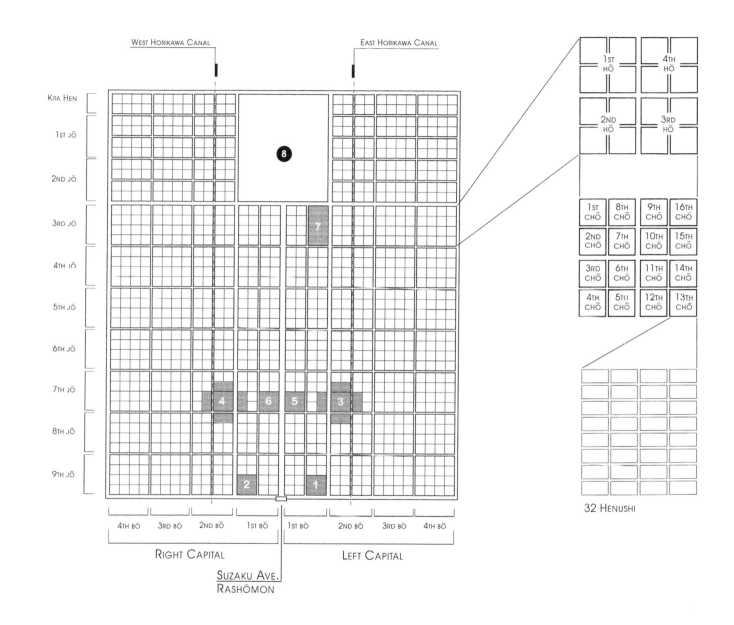

WEST HORIKAWA CANAL

EAST HORIKAWA CANAL

KITA HEN

1ST JŌ

2ND JŌ

3RD JŌ

4TH JŌ

5TH JŌ

6TH JŌ

7TH JŌ

8TH JŌ

9TH JŌ

4TH BŌ | 3RD BŌ | 2ND BŌ | 1ST BŌ | 1ST BŌ | 2ND BŌ | 3RD BŌ | 4TH BŌ

RIGHT CAPITAL   LEFT CAPITAL

SUZAKU AVE.
RASHŌMON

| 1ST HŌ | 4TH HŌ |
| 2ND HŌ | 3RD HŌ |

1ST CHŌ	8TH CHŌ	9TH CHŌ	16TH CHŌ
2ND CHŌ	7TH CHŌ	10TH CHŌ	15TH CHŌ
3RD CHŌ	6TH CHŌ	11TH CHŌ	14TH CHŌ
4TH CHŌ	5TH CHŌ	12TH CHŌ	13TH CHŌ

32 HENUSHI

SHINDEN RESIDENCES

1. WESTERN GATE

2. FISHING PAVILION,
   tsuri dono

3. CORRIDOR WITH INNER GATE,
   chūmonro

4. WEST HALL,
   nishi tainoya

5. MASTER'S HALL,
   shinden

6. SOUTHERN COURT,
   nantei

7. EAST HALL,
   higashi tainoya

8. WINDING STREAM,
   yarimizu, kyokusui

9. CORRIDOR WITH INNER GATE,
   chūmonro

10. EASTERN GATE

11. WELLSPRING PAVILION,
    izumi dono

12. ARCHED BRIDGE,
    soribashi

13. CENTRAL ISLAND,
    nakajima

14. POND

Within the grid of the city, each man built his home. The location, size, and quality were prescribed by one's status but the basic form of the residences of the nobles was similar. A high wall was built around the property—most likely a solid, tapered wall made of rammed earth (*tsuiji-bei*). The main gate into the property was built on the east side, often with a second gate to the west. Central in the property (but not perfectly so) was a large, southern-facing hall called the *shinden* (lit. sleeping hall) which was the residence of the lord of the house. From this hall comes the term *shinden-zukuri,* which refers to this type of architecture in general. In its classic form, the builders bracketed the shinden hall with two smaller halls, *tainoya*, and perhaps others to the rear (the northern portion of the property). These held the residences of various wives and consorts as well as service quarters. From the tainoya, long roofed corridors were built southward into the garden ending in pavilions with names like *tsuridono* (lit. fishing pavilion, but more likely used for musical performances or garden viewing) and *izumidono* (the wellspring pavilion) which was built above or near a spring that fed the garden pond. The entire arrangement of buildings—shinden, tainoya, and the pavilions—was constructed so that they would look out over a large garden. The garden may have covered as much as one third of the whole property making it about one-half hectare (1.2 acres) in size.

The compression of the gardens into the urban frames of the shinden residences influenced the development of the Japanese garden. The Korean gardens from which Japanese gardens were derived were often built in the countryside within the larger context of the natural landscape, the surrounding environment playing a predominant role in the design of the garden. The Heian gardeners, however, attempted to compress the sensory qualities of the natural world in the relatively small space of a shinden property. In order to do so the garden designers devised a more rigorous theory of gardening, which they termed *fuzei*. Fuzei, written with the characters for 'wind' and 'emotion' can be interpreted as an emotional response to nature.[12]

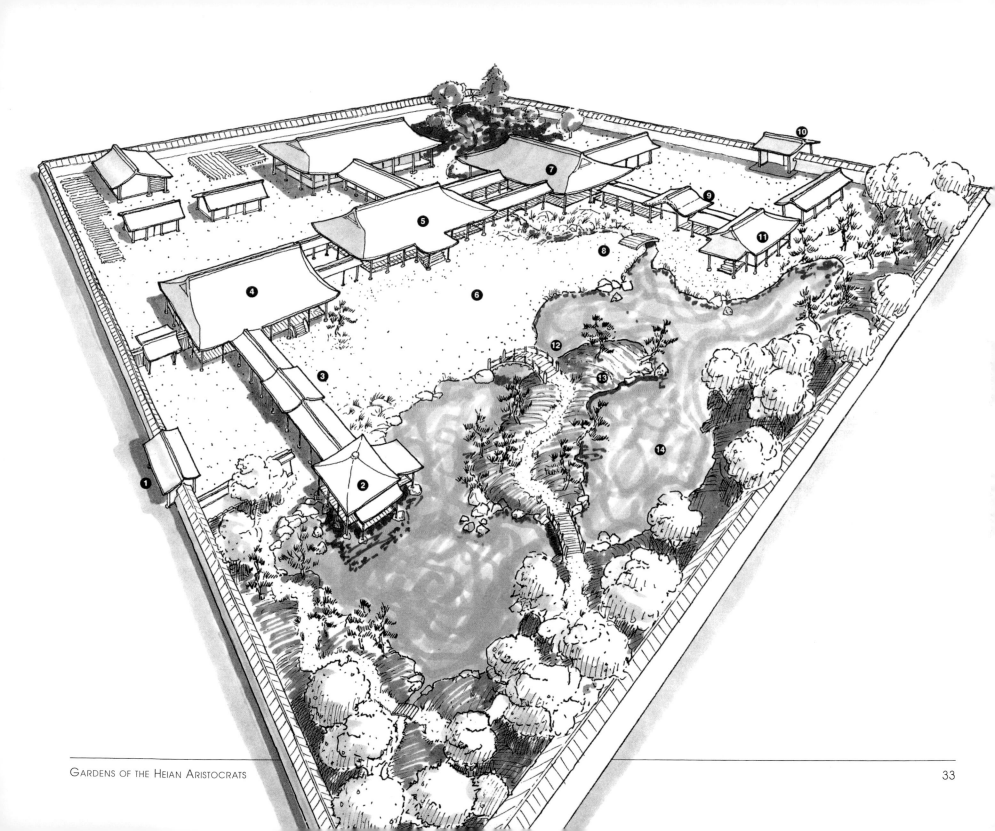

AESTHETICS

MIYABI

The imperial court during the Fujiwara epoch became increasingly detached from the realities of the world beyond Heian-kyō and progressively introverted, creating an aesthetic sub-culture where a well-turned poem could mean an appointment to a higher post and a mismatched color in a multi-layered kimono brought icy stares and ostracism. Despite an oppressive habit for political intrigues, members of the Fujiwara aristocracy initiated a wide range of highly advanced arts, including a creatively inspired garden.[13] *Miyabi*—elegance and refined taste—was the supreme aesthetic principle of the Fujiwara court. In all aspects of the Fujiwara culture—knowledge of literature, musical ability, understanding of court protocol, clothing, and physical deportment—fluid grace and a sensitivity to the uttermost detail were absolutely essential. Miyabi was the overt aesthetic of the court which the aristocrats chose to emulate; but there was a deeper, melancholy aspect to the culture which has become a trademark of Heian times.

MUJŌ

This melancholy stemmed in part from the influence of two fundamental aspects Buddhism: *mappō* and *mujō*. Traditionally it was believed that during the 2,000 years following the death of the historical Buddha, Buddhism would move through three distinct periods: *shōbō* (true law), *zōbō* (imitative law), and *mappō* (end of law)—the last being a time of declining social and religious mores. Although the paintings and literature of the time do not feature it, by the mid-eleventh century the social structure of Heian-kyō was breaking apart. Daylight robbery was common, nobles had their homes burned, and even the emperor was besieged by warrior-priests. Conditions outside the capital were even worse. Since mappō was thought to begin in 1052, this Buddhist prophecy was seemingly confirmed and the Fujiwara epoch was laden with a sense of impending dread.

Mujō, impermanence or transience, is a concept derived from the first of the Three Laws of Buddhism, *shogyō mujō*, "all realms of being are transient," which instructs that all things fade and pass with time. Indian Buddhism may consider this concept on a metaphysical plane, but in Japan mujō was interpreted literally by the Heian courtiers. The evanescence of life, the instability of social positions, the sudden death of loved ones, the inevitable change from youthful beauty to decrepit corpse, the constant passing of the seasons (not to mention mappō, and the end of the ordered world)—all were interpreted with a lingering sense of sorrow that pervaded the arts of the day, expressed in the aesthetic *mujō-kan*.[14]

Another aesthetic born out of this somber climate, which has become emblematic of the Heian period, is called *awaré* (pronounced "ah-wah-reh"). In Heian literature, *awaré* usually appears as a single word, but when referring to awaré as an aesthetic, the phrase used is *mono-no-awaré*—the heightened awareness of things. To a sensitive and cultured person, mono-no-awaré was an imperative quality. Awaré can be described as an intense emotion felt in response to beauty, especially one of a subtle, ephemeral nature or an emotional response to the inherent sadness of life itself. The word is said to derive from the sounds *ah!* and *hare!*, both of which are expressions of surprise. Awaré is an epiphany at the discovery of beauty in the pathos of life. When confronted with such beauty, a person who is sensitive to the aesthetics of awaré will inevitably react emotionally. As emotion builds past the point of bearing, it bursts forth spontaneously as what is called *yojō* (literally an overflow of emotion). Awaré and yojō were typically used in reference to poetry but it is certain that these emotions were not confined to one art but rather pervaded all aspects of court life.

During the Heian period, there was no professional class of gardeners. Although little evidence remains regarding who actually created gardens, people presumably designed their own gardens or asked the advice of other courtiers who showed an affinity for such things. As such, gardens were designed by the same group of people who wrote and reveled in awaré poetry; they certainly applied the same emotions and aesthetics to both. The lingering sadness of awaré and the stately elegance of miyabi, being the primary emotional and aesthetic qualities of Heian culture, were undoubtedly applied to gardening as well as to poetry.

GARDENS OF THE HEIAN ARISTOCRATS

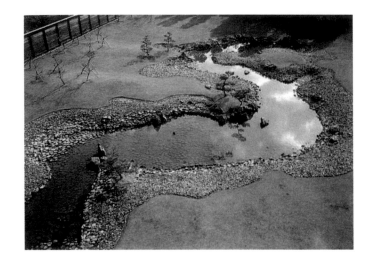

A pre-Heian garden that was excavated in Nara.
Heijō-kyō Sakyō Sanjō Nibō Kyūseki, Nara

What we know of the gardens of the Heian period, since there are no extant examples to study, comes from a variety of sources including remnant gardens (like Mōtsuji in Iwate Prefecture), archeological digs, paintings from the end of the Heian period (though most of these are copies dated from two to five hundred years after the original), and the literature of the time. A compilation of all these sources shows that just to the south of the shinden the designers created a flat area called the *nantei* (southern court). They covered the nantei with sand, partly for aesthetic and spiritual cleanliness but also to facilitate a wide variety of garden events—poetry readings, kickball (*kemari*), archery, and cockfights to name a few. The gardeners punctuated the borders of the expanse of sand, next to the verandas of the shinden and the long corridors, with a few trees and tufts of grasses and flowers. Without using symmetry they were thus able to give the nantei an atmosphere of formality—a proper setting for elegant events. They used water extensively and often built a winding stream (*yarimizu*) along the eastern edge of the nantei that was used to feed the central pond. In the contrasting naturalism of the winding stream and formality of the shinden architecture one can feel the designer's playful juxtaposition of man-made and natural elements which is so characteristic of Japanese garden design.

To the south of the nantei, and wrapping back around the projecting corridors as well, the gardeners built a large, irregularly-shaped pond that may have occupied half of the entire area of the garden. It is possible that some gardeners preferred to extend the winding stream through the whole garden using it in lieu of a pond as a central motif. Within the ponds they built at least one large central island which they connected to shore, north and south, by two or more bridges. In fact one of the words used during the Heian period to mean garden was island (*shima*). These gardens are now termed Pond-touring Gardens (*chisen shūyū teien*) because of the central pond as well as the custom of using the garden for boating rather than strolling.[15] The aristocrats had their boats painted brightly, the bows carved with images of dragons or phoenixes and had gaily attired musicians ride about the pond making for a festive air. The formal clothing worn by the owners of these gardens and their guests at important occasions made it unlikely that they would ride in the boats themselves, certainly impossible for the women in their twelve-layered kimono. At more private times, and in less formal dress, they enjoyed boating as well as writing poetry from this new vantage point. The Heian ponds, though, in contrast to the huge lakes built by the Chinese, were not particularly extensive. A full circuit of a Heian garden pond by boat would not take very much time. In fact, if the bridges that connected the central island to shore did not arch high up over the water it would have been impossible to make a circuit at all. It is very likely that the primary reason for the boats was to create a sumptuous vista to be enjoyed by those who viewed the garden from the buildings nearby.

The Heian designers created gardens that were light and open—playfully including diverse elements of the natural world, including a variety of flowering shrubs, flowers, grasses, and animal life from ducks to crickets.[16] The inclusion of the deciduous and perennial plants they planted meant that their gardens must have changed much more through the seasons than those we see today which are mainly composed of the structural elements of rocks and evergreens. It feels as though, in the formality of the nantei, the designers were striving for miyabi—the courtly aesthetic—and in the evanescence of the plantings they were expressing awaré. Naturally, aspects of both aesthetics are intermingled and one can sense in these gardens how the creators were balancing the needs of their increasingly mannered society with their ancient attraction to the natural world.

Two texts from the Heian period stand out for their clarity in revealing the gardens of the time: *The Book of Gardening* (*Sakuteiki*) and *The Tale of Genji* (*Genji Monogatari*), a depiction of the romantic trials and tribulations of a Heian prince. The insights found in these texts are invaluable, although their forms are rather different—stemming in part from the fact that the former was written by a man and the latter by a woman.

GEOMANCY IN THE GARDEN: THE SAKUTEIKI

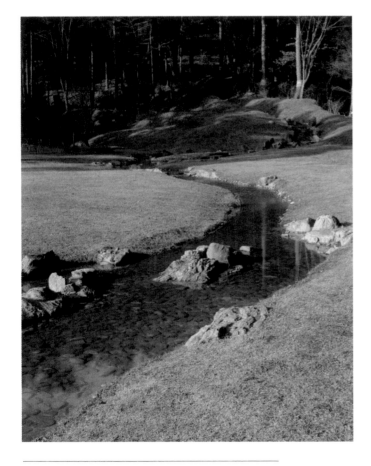

A curved stream that fed a Heian-period pond garden in the far north of Japan. Mōtsū-ji, Iwate

The writing of the *Sakuteiki* is attributed to Tachibana no Toshitsuna, and dates from around the mid- to late-eleventh century, though the earliest extant manuscripts are copies from the twelfth century. Toshitsuna's father was the builder of two of the period's most famous gardens, Kaya-no-in, a grand Kyoto estate, and Byodo-in, in Uji. We can assume, therefore, that Toshitsuna was exposed to the art of garden building by observing his father's work. The *Sakuteiki* gives very straightforward advice on how to build a garden and can be very specific, detailing measurements for the depth of the nantei depending on the rank of the owner, and discussing the proper slope for a stream to create just the right gurgling sound. In comparison to the dreamlike images found in Heian paintings, where objects are lost in veils of mist, it is surprising just how precise the *Sakuteiki* is. The book addresses several aspects of gardening including garden styles and the use of water, rocks, and plants. The specific information on garden construction is basically good gardening technique and is still applicable today.

Geomancy was also given considerable mention in the *Sakuteiki* as a guide for garden design. The text goes to some length to describe taboos according to this way of divination, claiming that a poor arrangement of one's garden can invite the visitation of any number of calamities; conversely, evil can be warded off by creating a garden with the proper positioning of geomantic elements, specifically the conscientious use of water, rocks, and plants. For example, we are told that water should be made to flow from northeast to southwest, which allows the power of the eastern Blue Dragon to wash out evil that may block the way of the western White Tiger. To take another example, there are many taboos regarding stones, especially upright ones. Upright stones, which represent mountain forms according to geomantic thought, have the power to block or affect the flow of *ki* (life energy). The designer is warned that stones are never to be placed on the linear extension of the pillars that support the residence nor should a large upright stone be set in the northeast (devil's gate) as it may allow entry to evil spirits. This second idea—where spirits use rocks as "touchstones" to alight on earth—may stem in part from the ancient iwa-kura and displays the admixture of native beliefs and Chinese geomancy. The *Sakuteiki* goes on to advise the designer in the use of plants at cardinal points in lieu of a usual geomantic form; for instance the requisite stream to the east of a residence could be replaced by nine willows. Employing plants for their restorative powers also hints to ties with ancient animistic ideas. This particular vision of the garden may well be a masculine one for it does not show up in *The Tale of Genji*.

The Tale of Genji, the world's first novel, is a fantastically candid exposé of Heian court life during the Fujiwara epoch. Unlike the *Sakuteiki, The Tale of Genji* is about love, not gardens—but what is so interesting is the degree to which images of nature and gardens appear. Not only does the novel give us glimpses of Heian gardens but it shows the importance they played in the lives of the courtiers. Curiously, buildings are hardly described at all, although there are numerous references to the various screens and blinds that concealed the court women from public view and physically represent the veiled quality of Heian society. A reconstruction of a shinden residence done solely from *The Tale of Genji* would reveal only gardens and the sleeves of princesses peeping out from behind screens.

The pinnacle of Heian culture is literature, and the literature of the time privileged poetry, which informed all aspects of aristocratic society. Skill with the intricacies of poetic nuance could determine one's position at court. So fundamental was the role of poetry in court life that it is impossible to conceive of any of the other arts of the time divorced from poetic influence—so it was with the garden. It is the special quality of poetry to express through metaphor or allusion rather than precise description, thus revealing a deeper essence of the subject than might be approached through prose. The poetry of the Heian period is called *tanka,* and has been described as "self-expression through nature description," a process of creation, initially applied to literary efforts, which would also become the impetus for garden design.[17]

The link between the garden and poetry can be seen in three ways. First, gardens and poems were very likely to have been created for similar reasons—as a means of self-expression using a variety of images drawn from nature. The *Sakuteiki,* as well, encourages designers to draw from nature but, also, to imbue their designs with their own personal spirit or taste—what the *Sakuteiki* describes as *fuzei.* It would seem that from the very beginning Japanese gardeners, rather than recreating nature as found in the real world, were distilling images and arranging these poetic fragments into an amalgam in the garden. In this sense, the Heian gardens were not perceived as total compositions but rather as a collection of poetic images.[18] But images of nature were not always derived first-hand by going out on excursions; many of the images may have been taken from references to nature in the existing body of poetry, of which there were abundant examples.

Here then is the second link between poetry and the gardens—the use of existing, commonly understood poetic images as a basis for garden design. Countless images could

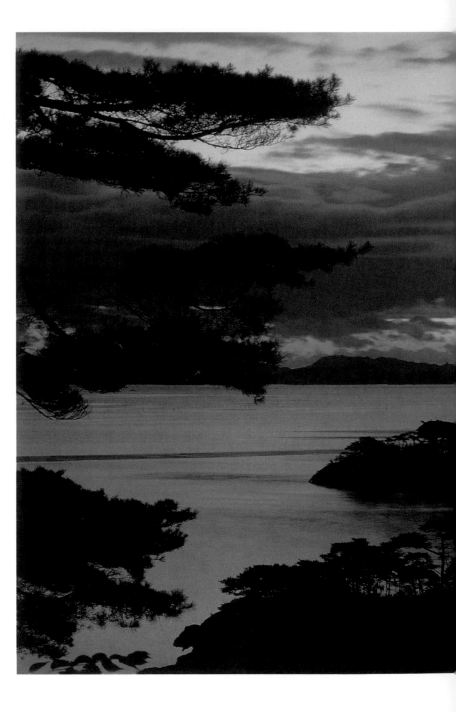

HEIAN POETRY LEXICON[22]

A few of the puns (*kake-kotoba*) associated with Nature and the garden

---

• PLANTS

Bamboo: the segments of bamboo evoke the image of generations.

Cherry blossoms: a metaphor for women.

Flowers: *hana*: used to mean both flower and beautiful.

Forest: in Japanese, *mori*, the word is similar to the verb *moru*, to guard or protect.

Hollyhock: in Japanese, *aoi*, also can be understood as "meeting day" or rendezvous.

Irises: related to patterns and festivals.

Mandarin orange: in Japanese, *tachibana*, which can be understood to mean "wait."

New grass: in Japanese, *wakakusa*. Symbolizes young love or a spouse.

Pine trees: in Japanese the word for pine, *matsu*, is also the pronunciation for the verb "to wait." Pines therefore suggest waiting or yearning for a lover or the resolution of an impossible situation. The pines of Sue-no-Matsuyama are linked to infidelity. Pines were also symbols of longevity or permanence.

Root: as in tree root, in Japanese, *ne*, also meaning to sleep.

Sakikusa: (a plant with three leaves), a pun for *mitsu* (three).

Japanese snowflower: in Japanese, *unohana*. "*U* " implies gloom or sorrow.

Wild carnations: *nadeshiko*, also the name used for young girls.
Another name for the same plant is *tokonatsu*. *Toko* (bed) is linked to *nuru* (sleep).

• ANIMALS

Chirping/singing: as of birds and crickets, both of which were kept or released in the gardens for their song. In Japanese, *naku*, means both to chirp/sing and to cry/weep. Naku is thus linked with sadness.

Crickets: *higurashi*, also means "sunset."

Spiders: connected with lovers—a neglectful one or one approaching.

Thrush: the call of which, *hitoku, hitoku*, can be heard as "someone's coming."

Tree frog: in Japanese, *amagaeru* can also mean "a nun returning."

Wild Goose: evanescence or transience.

• NATURE

Autumn: besides other obvious seasonal connections, the Japanese word for autumn, *aki*, is linked to the verb *aku*, to weary of. The oppressiveness of misfortune and wearying of life are often mentioned.

Falling rain or snow: passage of the years.

Rain clouds: in Japanese, *amagumo*, can be heard as "nun's clothing."

River, shallows: suggests a meeting to happen in the future or the desire for such.

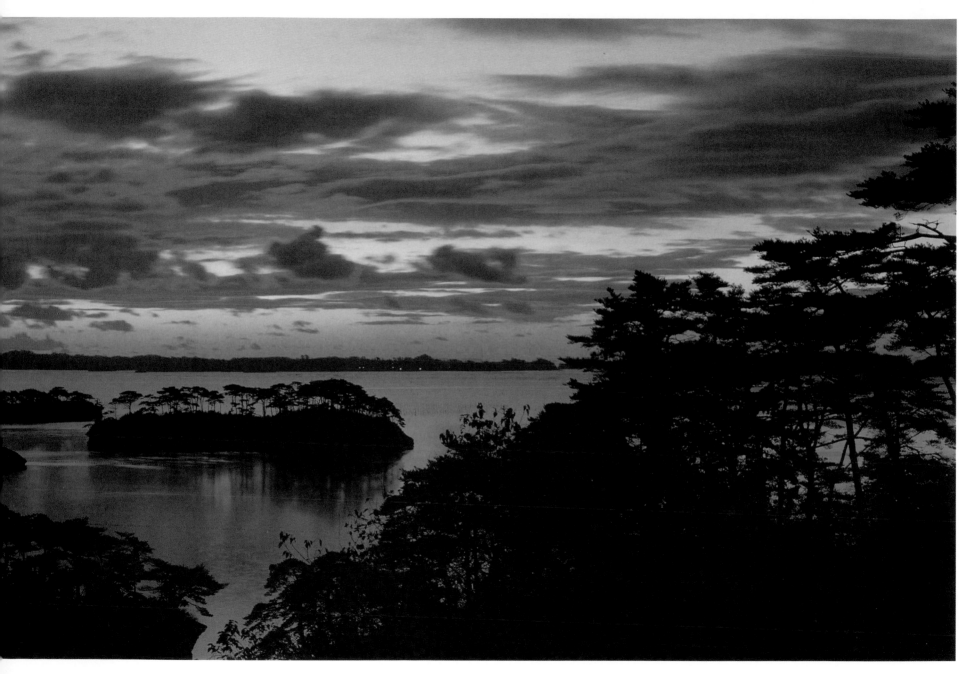

In the Heian period the pine tree was a poetic epithet for waiting—for a lover or for the resolution of an impossible situation.

ARISTOCRATIC PASTIME

By the time of the Heian period (794–1185), garden building had progressed for hundreds of years in Japan—by the end of the period complex texts on gardening, like the *Book of Gardening*, *Sakuteiki*, had been written. A large body of knowledge had developed regarding garden construction and design. Although not yet specifically garden professionals, there were people who were skilled in design. In contrast to the earlier Asuka and Nara periods, the increase in gardening knowledge and skills among the Japanese, combined with an end to official relations with the Chinese government, made the Heian period a time when gardens were designed and built almost entirely by Japanese.

The garden designers of this time were primarily the aristocrats. Some nobles of very high standing are known to have had a hand in overseeing the construction of their own gardens. Fujiwara no Yorimichi designed for himself the resplendent palace Kayano-in, as well as Byodo-in in Uji, the main hall of which remains to this day. It is likely, however, that more often lesser members of the aristocracy who showed an affinity for design helped others with their gardens. Rather than a professional venture, gardening was a pastime that nobles dabbled in, perhaps using their design skills to advance themselves at court.

Some of these gardening advisers were not of an aristocratic family but were priests. En-en Ajiri, for instance, was a priest, painter, and garden designer who is known to have worked with Fujiwara no Yorimichi on the building of Kayano-in. It is thought that he may have been one of the first garden-building priests (*ishi-tate-sō*) who became popular during the later, medieval period. The people who actually built the gardens were most likely to have been serfs (*domin*) who were attached to an aristocrat's estate (*shōen*).

be drawn from the ample body of literature since much of Japanese poetry was given over to nature description. The process was made more sophisticated by the existence of epithets known as "pillow words" (*makura kotoba*), linked images that were so well known and standardized they could be used to refer to each other. A particular form of pillow word that seems to occur on almost every page of *The Tale of Genji* is the pun (*kake kotoba*) that makes use of phonetic similarities between two or more subjects. As written by the Heian men the use of Chinese characters essentially precluded punning. Each word, being identifiable by its character, could not be mistaken for another even if the sound was identical. Heian women, on the other hand, wrote exclusively in *kana*, a phonetic writing system developed to bridge the grammatical gaps between Chinese and Japanese. Kana freed writers from a meaning-specific use of the language and gave them free reign to make plays on words. The most ubiquitous use of this ambiguity is the pine tree—in Japanese, *matsu*—which is also the pronunciation of the verb to wait. Hence the pine tree has become suggestive of waiting, in particular, yearning for a lover or the resolution of an impossible situation. Pines were often planted in the gardens as evidenced by not only the literature and paintings but also by archeological work that has found pine seeds on dig sites. It is hard to imagine pines viewed anywhere by Heian courtiers, including in the garden, without their evoking in the mind of the viewer some of the many poetic images associated with them.

The third connection between poetry and the garden is found in the way the gardens were used. According to the literature of the time, writing poetry in the garden was a common event. Composition could take the form of an idle line written while sitting on the edge of the veranda gazing at the garden or a ritualized event such as the poetry contests that were held regularly. A seasonal turn, the flowering of a plant like the wisteria, or the visit of a guest—anything seemed to be an excuse for a poetry festival. One such poetic event was the Feast by the Winding Stream (*kyokusui-no-en*), a pastime imported from China or Korea. Participants in the feast sit alongside a narrow meandering stream. A cup of *saké* is floated down the stream—a poet picks it up, drains it, and composes a poem on the spot. The use of the garden for poetry writing brings the poetry/garden connection full circle—first, poems are written while viewing nature, then those images are poetically re-created in the garden, and finally the garden is used to write poems, some of which undoubtedly incorporate the now rarefied, original images of nature.

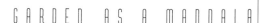
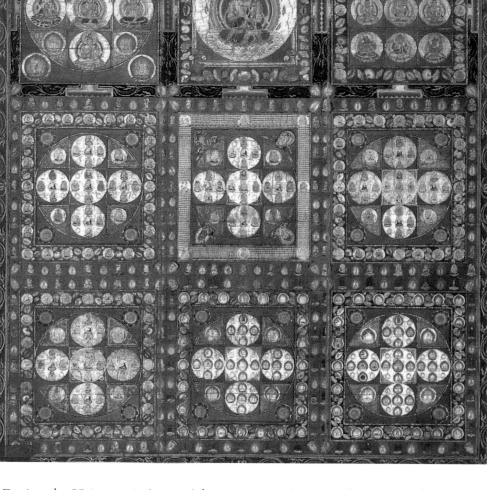

This painted silk mandala, from the late-ninth century, is one of a set of two: the Diamond World Mandala and the Womb World Mandala. Shown here is the Diamond World (kongōkai) depicting the transcendental Buddha, Dainichi Nyorai, in relation to other phenomenal Buddhas which have existed at different times. The layout of the mandala is strikingly similar to the plan of Heian-kyō. Kyōōgokokuji (Tōji), Kyoto

During the Heian period one of the strongest religious influences on the aristocracy was the Shingon sect of Buddhism, an esoteric sect introduced to Japan by the Japanese priest Kūkai in the early-ninth century.[19] Shingon Buddhism is distinguished by the use of complex mystical rites and religious objects such as secret gestures (*mudra*), chants (*mantra*), and religious diagrams (*mandala*).[20] Mandala portray the essential structure of the spiritual universe in a variety of ways: in abstract philosophical terms; in three dimensions, as in sculpture or architecture; or in a two-dimensional form, usually as a complex arrangement of concentric, interlocking geometric shapes. Whereas there are mandala in both Hindu and

Buddhist traditions, the mandala of Heian Japan were Buddhist, depicting various manifestations of the Buddha and their attendants in proper cosmic order.

In India, mandala were created two-dimensionally of sand or earth, as well as in architectural forms. Later, when Buddhism was introduced to China, they were depicted as paintings on silk and it is that form which was brought to Japan by priests like Kūkai. Shingon adherents believe the mandala to be not only representative of religious teachings but, in addition, to be imbued with mystical powers which can be evoked through the use of mudra and mantra. The mandala is seen as a protective entity and the master plans of Shingon temples—the arrangement of Buddhist statues within prayer halls, the layout of the halls themselves, the placement of the pagodas (which house sacred Buddhist relics), and the general environs of the temple as well—were designed as large-scale, three-dimensional mandala. One such example is the mountain retreat built by Kūkai on Mount Koya; another is Tōji, the temple Kūkai administered within the precincts of Heian-kyo. Tōji, which was not built originally as a Shingon temple, had been active for about thirty years when Kūkai took over the administration by imperial edict. He commissioned a second pagoda which was specifically built to house two mandalas that were used as the focus of esoteric ritual and contemplation.[21] It was believed at the time that the temple, with its mandalic shield, would act as protector for the nation as a whole, as reflected in Kūkai's new name for the temple—Temple for the Protection of the Nation (Kyōōgokoku-ji).

The influence of the Shingon sect during the Heian period and the general interest in mystic practices among the aristocracy suggest that the designers of the gardens at this time may have perceived their work, to some degree, as mandalic construction. In strictly religious terms the gardens were not Buddhist mandala, in which a central Buddha figure is surrounded by various manifestations of other Buddhas and Boddhisatvas. Nor was the physical construction of the gardens a precise copy of the symmetrical and geometric Indian/Chinese mandala. It was believed at the time, however, that the design of the gardens could—through the proper arrangement of various geomantic entities such as stones, plants, and water—create a metaphysical condition by which the owner of the garden and his household were protected against ill fortune. It can be said, therefore, that the garden designers perceived the purpose of garden design—specifically, arranging the elements of the garden in accordance with the principles of the spiritual universe in order to encourage good fortune—to be similar to that of the creation of mandala.

THE ART OF EMPTINESS

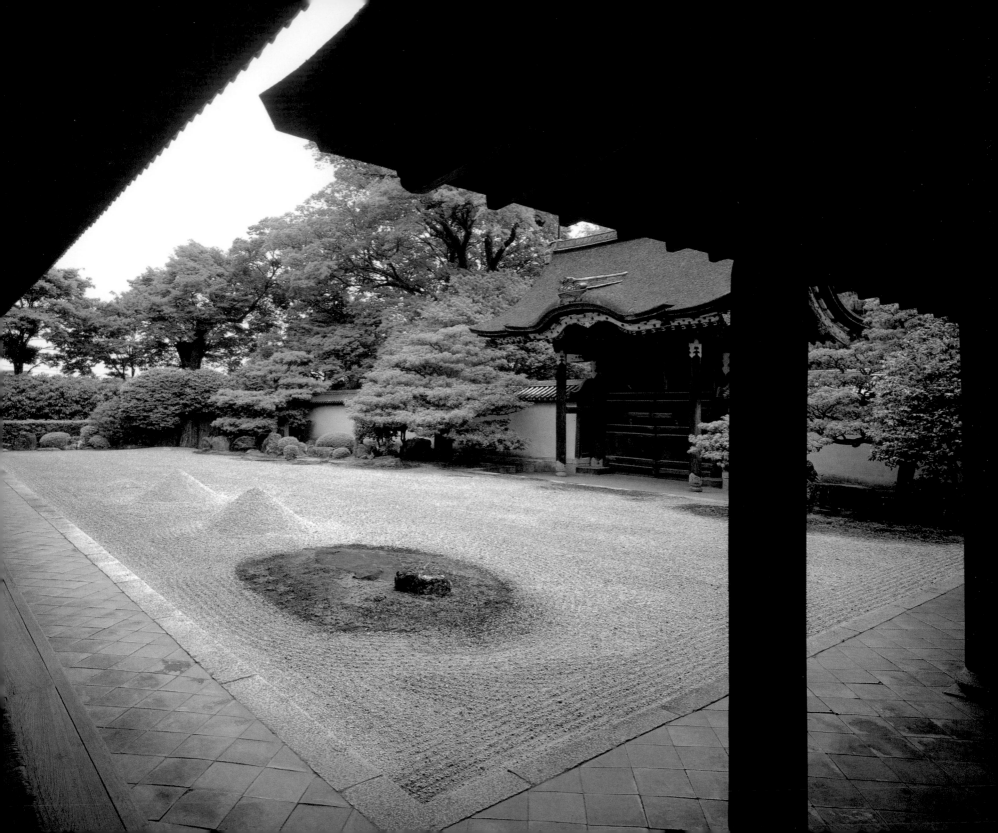

THE GARDENS OF ZEN BUDDHISM

The idealism of Heian-kyō gave way to reality. By the end of the twelfth century the inability of the aristocracy to control their vassals and lands led to a general breakdown in society. The warriors (*bushi*) wrested control from the noble class ushering in the medieval era. In order to understand the medieval gardens it is necessary to look at the development of society in general at that time: First, the changes in the socio-political arena with the establishment of the supremacy of the warrior class which set the masculine tone of the age and encouraged an aesthetic of frugality; second, the development of the cultural environment which was influenced by another great wave of Chinese ideas, in particular Zen Buddhism; finally, the development of a new physical setting as gardens began to be built within the comparatively narrow confines of warrior residences and urban Zen temples.

Left: The southern gate is used for imperial processions once every fifty years. At these times the piles of white sand arc spread out to purify the garden. Daitoku-ji Honbō, Kyoto

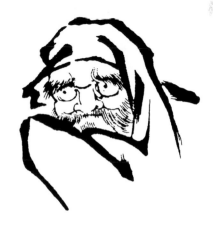

SOCIETY AND POLITICS

The shift of power from the aristocracy to the warrior class actually began in the middle of the Heian period, at the height of the Fujiwara epoch, when many great aristocratic gardens were being built. Through their disinterest in the duties of government the aristocrats let control of their lands slip. One warrior families, the Taira, gradually solidified its position and in 1156 took control of the court in Kyoto (by this time the common name for Heian-kyō), but only briefly. Within three decades the Minamoto—a family of warriors the Taira had defeated to take the city—rebounded and utterly defeated the Taira. This series of battles is carefully detailed in one of the great epics of the time, *The Tale of the Heike* (*Heike monogatari*). Unwilling to get caught up in court intrigues, the Minamoto set up their capital a healthy distance away from Kyoto. They chose to base themselves near their ancestral lands in the east, near present-day Tokyo. This transition of power ushered in the Kamakura period (1185–1333), named after the town that held their new seat of government. Even the name of the new government—*bakufu*, literally: curtain government— suggested its martial origins. *Baku* (a curtain) refers to the custom of delineating an area of a military encampment with a long cloth the height of a man to act as a screened meeting place for the upper echelon.

The imperial court had lost its real power but was maintained as a measure of status. One function allowed the court was the right to consign titles. Among these was the title *seii-tai-shōgun* (barbarian-subduing generalissimo) or *shōgun* for short. This appellation dates from the Nara period when it was assigned to warriors who would ride against the *ezo*, native tribes who lived on the northern periphery of the realm. In Kamakura three ranks of warrior followed the shōgun: *kenin, samurai,* and *zusa.* Kenin were vassals close to the shōgun, samurai were beneath them, and the zusa were foot soldiers. Even as the name bakufu reveals the military origins of the government, so kenin (origin: houseman) and samurai (origin: one who serves) depict the upward mobility of the warrior class during the Kamakura period. Eventually, during the Edo period, the samurai would become the top rank in a rigid class structure and the cult of the warrior would further develop into a formalized chivalry (*bushidō*). In medieval times, however, being a warrior was a way of life drawn from necessity. With the shōgun as the pinnacle of society the warrior class became the new locus of social life and, accordingly, the patrons of culture. While the Heian aristocrats had been devoted to poetry and subtle artistic pastimes, the bushi were versed in the martial arts and betrayed a predisposition for things that displayed a simple strength. The ascetic wooden sculpture of the Kamakura period can be said to be the epitome of their artistic taste.

As the Fujiwara dominated the emperor in the Heian period, the power of the Minamoto shōguns was usurped by their regents, the Hōjō family. The Hōjō controlled the government until the early-fourteenth century when they were betrayed by two of the leading military commanders of the day, bringing the Kamakura shogunate to a sudden end. That a society which held honor and loyalty as central to life should be destroyed by traitorous moves is perhaps indicative of the state of decay that existed by that time. One of the two disloyal generals, Ashikaga Takauji, took control of the imperial court in Kyoto and had himself designated shōgun, establishing his government in Kyoto. Eventually the political seat was established in the Muromachi district of Kyoto, which lends its name to the era. The choice of Kyoto as capital, a cultured city with great commercial activity, was to affect the nature of the shogunate and the development of the arts as well.

The Muromachi period (1333–1568) is seen as a time of great extremes juxtaposing massive social instability against equally intense economic growth and artistic creativity. Much of the country became embroiled in local struggles for power, and the shogunate's centralized power gradually waned to the extent that over the ten years starting in 1467 a struggle for the succession of the shogunate, called the Onin War, reduced much of Kyoto to ashes. In the midst of this havoc, in blatant contrast to the harsh conditions of society in general, the shōgun and the great Zen temples supported artists who produced Noh and Kyōgen theater, linked-verse poetry, and gardens. With regard to the gardens of this time it can be said that their guiding aesthetics were born in austere Kamakura but came to fruition amidst Kyoto's economic vitality.

One influence the social conditions of the medieval era had on garden design stems from the protective, if not escapist, attitude the violence of the times induced. Gardens, in keeping with the nature of society in general, became withdrawn, tightly enclosed, and introverted. The themes incorporated in the gardens began to change as well—shifting from a focus on that which was close at hand to fantasies of foreign lands—specifically from the natural world of the Japanese archipelago to images of Chinese landscapes that expressed themes from the newly favored religion, Zen Buddhism.

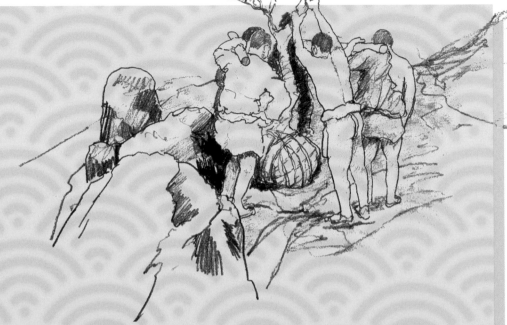

ISHI-TATE-SŌ

The priests who built gardens during the Kamakura period were called "rock-setting / standing priests"—*ishi-tate-sō*—derived from the term *ishi wo tatsu* (to set rocks upright) which was synonymous with garden building, revealing the importance that stones held in the whole scheme of garden design. The name ishi-tate-sō was first used in the late Heian period, applied to priests of Ninna-ji, a temple of the Shingon sect of Buddhism. Two priests of note were Hōin Jōi and Zōen, Sōjō, both of whom appear in the fifteenth-century gardening text *Senzui narabi ni yagyō no zu*.[11] It would seem that at this time many of the ishi-tate-sō were itinerant priests traveling the land and trading their services as garden builders in return for support from wealthy patrons.

By the Muromachi period the term ishi-tate-sō is used mostly in reference to priests from Zen temples, a shift that reflects the increasing popularity of, and therefore the financial sponsorship available for, the Zen sect.

KAWARA-MONO

The ishi-tate-sō were first and foremost religious men. The Muromachi period, however, witnessed the development of a group of semi-professional garden builders developed who were exclusively laymen. These gardeners were called *senzui-kawara-mono*. *Kawa-ra-mono* was a pejorative term given to an underclass who lived by the river (*kawara*) which—because of insects, pestilence, and floods—was considered the worst place to live. From Heian times, kawara-mono were assigned unwanted tasks like butchering, grave digging, and the lowest level of heavy construction work—as such they were often called to perform the menial labor required to build gardens.[12] Over the course of time, the kawara-mono gained a great deal of knowledge regarding plants, rock setting, and other aspects of gardening. As class structure shifted during the medieval years, they were finally able to gain rightful recognition as skilled gardeners. Eventually the appellation *senzui* (mountain + water, i.e., "garden") was added to their collective name.

Two of the men who apparently built the famous rock garden at Ryōanji, Kotaro and Seijiro (their names are carved on the back of one of the rocks), are known to have been senzui-kawara-mono. It is telling of the medieval times—when general social upheaval was breaking down old class structures—that the kawara-mono, who used to be considered "untouchable," were now sought out for their knowledge and skills. At first, only the warrior class associated with the senzui-kawara-mono. Later the aristocracy began to use their skills and by 1430 even a retired emperor is recorded as having availed himself of their services.[13]

CULTURAL DEVELOPMENT

It would be wrong to equate the middle ages of Japan entirely with Zen Buddhism; it was a time when many other sects of Buddhism also flourished—in particular, non-esoteric forms which spread widely among the common people. In fact, considering the impact on the nation as a whole, the popularization of Buddhism during the middle ages has had the most lingering impact. It was the Zen sect, however, whose sentiments appealed to the upper echelon of the new bushi class, which had the greatest effect on the arts of the time.

The history of Zen is said to begin with the Indian sage Bodhidharma (Japanese: Daruma) who took his particular teaching of Buddhism to China in the early sixth century A.D. One thousand years after the era of the historical Buddha, Buddhism had divided into a great number of sects. Many of these sects considered the notion of self-enlightenment to be beyond the powers of mortal men and instead called on the benevolence of those who had already been enlightened (Buddhas or Boddhisatvas) to save their souls for them. Bodhidharma instead focused on the practice of meditation which was the vehicle to enlightenment that Shakamuni, the historical Buddha, had employed. The word for meditation, *dhyana* in India, became *ch'an* in China, where Bodhidharma's original teachings evolved into Ch'an Buddhism. Zen is the Japanese pronunciation of the Chinese word ch'an. Meditation Buddhism had been introduced to Japan during the Heian period but did not find a following among the nobles, who preferred the elaborate ritualism of the esoteric Buddhist sects. By the twelfth century things had changed: Ch'an Buddhism was at its pinnacle of development in China, and Japan had shifted toward a warrior society which was more receptive to the tenets of that sect than the Heian nobles were.

Two priests most commonly associated with the founding of Zen Buddhism in Japan are Eisai and Dōgen. Rinzai, the sect established by Eisai, advanced the theory of "sudden enlightenment" while Dōgen's Sōtō sect followed a path of "gradual enlightenment." In practice they both advocated meditation, which of course is central to Zen, but in Rinzai the master guides the disciple through a process of questions (*kōan*) and answers called *zen mondō*.[1] The disciple mentally focuses on a kōan, the intense pondering of which—during meditation and throughout the day—breaks down dualistic thinking, eventually causing a sudden breakthrough to a higher plane of consciousness. The central exercise of Dōgen's Sōtō sect is *zazen* (or *shikan tanza* = just sitting)—meditation in the seated "lotus" position—in which the legs are folded and the back held straight. Zazen stresses slow, natural breathing and an uncontrolled flow of thoughts and emotions. One seeks the middle way—no fear, no desire—and enlightenment is the epiphany that accompanies an eventual, complete self-realization.

The appeal of Zen Buddhism to the warrior elite of Kamakura can be found in several aspects of the religion.[2] First of all, since the sect was new it lacked the power bases and penchant for political meddling of the old Buddhist organizations. Zen temples did not develop extensive land holdings but were subject to the control of the warrior class whom they relied on for sponsorship. Another aspect of the Zen religion appealing to the warrior elite, especially true of the Rinzai sect, was it's association with cultural ideas and artifacts from China. The Mongol invasion of China, which ended the Sung dynasty, caused many Chinese Ch'an priests to flee to Japan. These priests brought with them knowledge of a variety of intellectual and artistic pursuits, cultural trappings of the Chinese literati which were highly prized by their Japanese contemporaries.

These socio-political explanations not withstanding, the appeal of Zen as a religion to the bushi elite can be found in its self-reliant nature—in Zen one relies on oneself, through personal effort, to attain enlightenment. *Tariki* and *jiriki* illustrate this concept. The practice of other sects to call on the help of a higher being for salvation is considered tariki (external aid/strength) while Zen's use of individual meditation to attain enlightenment is jiriki (self-aid/strength). Clearly, for men who spent a great deal of their lives in self-training, and whose success in the field was dependent on such, the Zen sect's focus on self-enlightenment would appear as a natural extension of their lives.

The inner strength and composure that meditation was capable of bestowing was also appealing. The release from worldly attachments—both fear of pain as well as desire for pleasure—eventually leads to a detachment from oneself, a state of non-self (*munen musō*: no form, no thought). In battle, more than raw physical strength, the ability to clear one's mind, and rid oneself of inhibiting thoughts—even to the extent of forgetting oneself and the fear of death—could easily spell the difference between victory and defeat. A practice that could so empower the warrior was certain to be indulged.

The ideals of Sung-dynasty Chinese literati, Chinese Ch'an Buddhism, and later Zen Buddhism strongly influenced Japanese garden design. Primary among these ideals was the common quest, shared by all three, to see beyond the superficial aspects of the world in order to perceive a greater truth that lies hidden within. This focus on "inner truth"—and the accompanying disdain for superficiality or ornamentation—became the basis for the rarified quality of all the arts related to these groups and is clearly evident in the sparse design of gardens found in the medieval Zen temples.

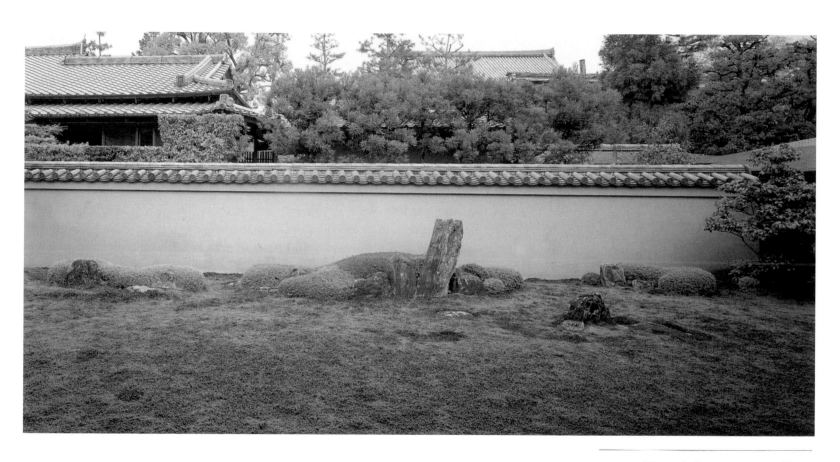

The central stone represents Mount Shumisen; the other stones evoke, in highly abstract form, the image of the eight ranks of mountains and seas which were said to surround the sacred mountain.

Ryōgen-in, Daitoku-ji,
Kyoto

SHOIN ARCHITECTURE

HOSOKAWA RESIDENCE, KYOTO
Redrawn from Rakuchū rakugai zu, *c. 1550*

1. SLIDING DOORS, shōji

2. GARDEN

3. OUTER WALL

4. ENTRY COURT

5. MAIN GATE

6. CARRIAGE APPROACH, kuruma yose

7. SERVICE GATE

8. CUSPED GABLE, kara hafu

9. MAIN HALL

10. TATAMI

THE PHYSICAL SETTING

The large-scale temples and *shinden* residences of the Heian period gave way to a new form of architecture in the middle ages. The residences of the warrior (*buke-yashiki*) began to show a greater division of space through the use of walls and sliding screens that clearly delineated private and public areas. Temples in general became more compressed in size resulting in, among other things, smaller outdoor enclosures in which to build gardens. By the Muromachi period these architectural changes had further developed into a distinctive form of architecture called *shoin-zukuri*. The *shoin*, which gives name to the style, is an alcove in an outer wall, with papered windows and a low, built-in shelf that allows for a well-lit reading and writing area. As a symbol of the intelligentsia, the shoin became an important part of both warrior residences and the *hōjō* of Zen temples.[3]

There are several aspects about the change to the shoin style of architecture that affected the way gardens were designed. One of these changes was a new form of entry. Temples formerly had a roofed gate built in the wall directly south of the main hall (*hondō*) through which people of rank would enter. A path led directly from the gate to the main hall across a formal courtyard. In the case of the shinden residences, the entry was through the middle gate and across the southern court. In both the temples and shinden residences the means of entry precluded the building of a garden directly to the south of the main buildings. The shoin style incorporated a new form of formal entry called a carriage approach (*kuruma-yose*) and later an entry vestibule (*genkan*).[4] These were off to the side of the main hall (or main structure of a residence), usually attached directly to a secondary building. By shifting the entryway away from the outdoor space directly associated with the main buildings, that space was now made available for designers to use in a more artistic way.[5] The relatively small size of the outdoor area—combined with its direct proximity to the main hall—encouraged the design of gardens for contemplation rather than physical entry.

The contemplative nature of the gardens was enhanced by other changes in shoin architecture as well, for instance, the introduction of tatami, reed mats approximately one by two meters in size, that were used to cover the floor from wall to wall. Also, compared to the solid, hinged panels (*shitomi*) of pre-shoin buildings, the new sliding paper doors (*shōji*) of shoin architecture allowed for far greater flexibility in the degree to which the interior and exterior would be partitioned.

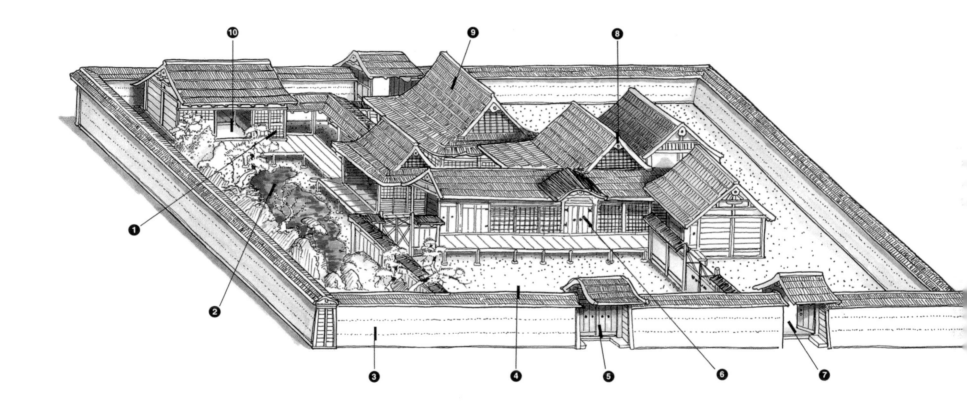

AESTHETICS

YŪGEN

Under the influence of the social shift from an aristocratic society to a society based on the ethics of the warrior, and reinforced by the tenets of Zen Buddhism, the aesthetics of frugality came to the fore. The principle aesthetic of the time was called *yūgen*, written with the characters for "faint/dim" + "dark/mystery," which can be described as meaning "subtle profundity." Chinese in origin, the word originally referred to something too deep to see. In Heian times yūgen was used as an adjective for intangibility to describe poetry that had a profound or mysterious nature. Later, during the Kamakura period, yūgen became an aesthetic term in its own right. Initially applied to poetry, yūgen was the guiding aesthetic of the age, influencing not just literature but theater, painting, and of course the garden. In keeping with Zen Buddhism, yūgen was concerned with the true nature of reality that hides behind the illusory aspects of the world.

There is also a dark aspect to yūgen as implied in the word itself. It is not in the same vein as the sentimental melancholy of the Heian courtiers, but is a richer, more potent emotion. Yūgen represents an aesthetic of a turbulent time and a class of men who have seen a great deal of the harsh and sanguinary side of life. Their experiences, in training and in battle, could not help but leave a mark on the way they perceived life and on their tastes in the arts. The literature shifted from lovers' tales to epics about great battles, poetry began to reveal a dark and moody undertone, and garden design was taken to the limits of austerity.

Another guiding principle of the time was *yohaku-no-bi*, the aesthetic of paucity, literally: the "beauty of extra white." This terse aesthetic can be perceived in the sparse ink paintings of the medieval period with their expanses of unpainted paper as well as in the large empty spaces found in the gardens of that time. Yohaku-no-bi is not, however, an aesthetic reveling in whiteness or promoting the use of white or any such thing—it focuses, instead, on what is *left out* of a design rather than what is put in. The mysteriousness of yūgen is recalled here in that the unascertainable part of a work of art gives it its most pleasing character—perhaps the original "less is more." Although this paucity has meaning simply in the aesthetic beauty it provides, it also represents one of the pillars of Zen thought, which is emptiness (*kū*) or what is often written about as nothingness (*mu*). Zen Buddhism holds that the phenomenal world is an illusion, or nothingness. The realization of this through meditation is fundamental to enlightenment.

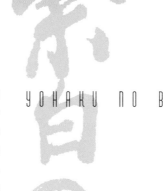

YOHAKU NO BI

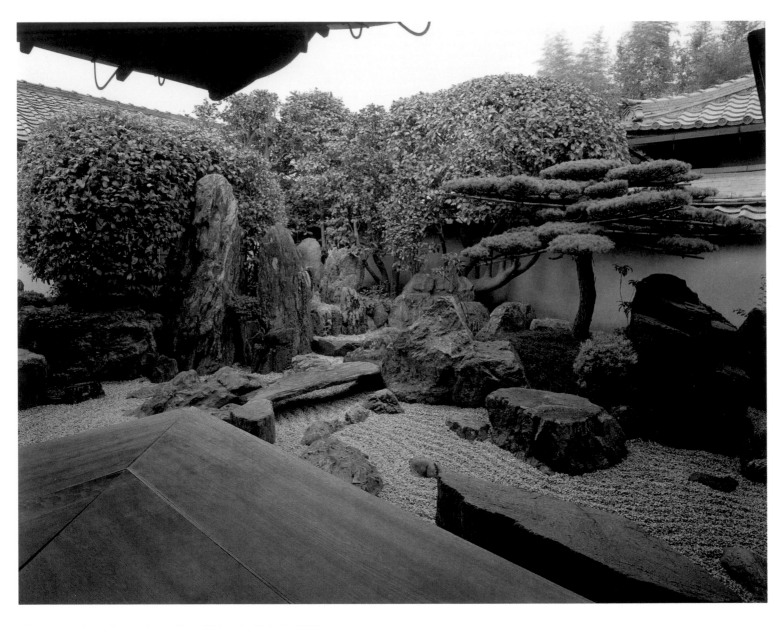

Deep mountains and mysterious valleys. Daisen-in, Daitoku-ji, Kyoto

Gardens of Zen Buddhism

The sand-and-stone gardens that are found in courtyards of Zen temples and some warrior residences are those most often as referred to as "Zen gardens." These are properly called *kare-san-sui*, which literally means dry-mountain-water and alludes to the garden's composition, which includes an abstracted scene of mountains and water (the sea or a river) created without using any real water at all.

Initially, the gardens of the early medieval period began as outgrowths of the large pond gardens of the Heian period. One change in these larger gardens was the shift from boating to walking as the primary way of touring the garden. More significant to the development of courtyard-style kare-san-sui gardens was a change in the use of rocks to depict scenes allegorical of Zen Buddhism. A classic example is the rock arrangement called the "dragon's-gate waterfall" (*ryū-mon-baku*)—a waterfall arrangement, often without running water (*kare-taki*), that represents the following anecdote. In China there was a legendary river with a powerful three-tiered waterfall. If a fish proved strong and determined enough to swim to the top, the fish would be transformed into a dragon.[6] In Japan, this anecdote is seen as allegorical to Zen study and enlightenment through self-training and meditation, although in the original Chinese version, the allegory was to passing the rigorous exams to become a government official. An early example of a dragon's-gate waterfall was built as a part of a larger garden at the temple Tenryu-ji in the Kamakura period, but it was not until the late Muromachi period that the classic kare-san-sui, in which a relatively small courtyard is given over entirely to a sculptural garden, developed as a distinct form.

Although kare-san-sui had existed before the Muromachi period (the word even shows up in the eleventh-century *Sakuteiki*), it was as an element of a larger garden within which one could enter and move around. The new, medieval form was meant exclusively for viewing from the nearby hall and is aptly called a contemplation garden (*kansho-niwa*). The viewer does not physically enter the garden but rather explores it mentally. In this case, what is actually a rather small garden could be found to be limitless, expressing the philosophic idea (included in but not exclusive to Zen) of finding the vast in the small. The first kare-san-sui built intentionally as a contemplation garden may be the famous garden at Ryōanji, which could have been built as early as 1499 when the hōjō was completed.

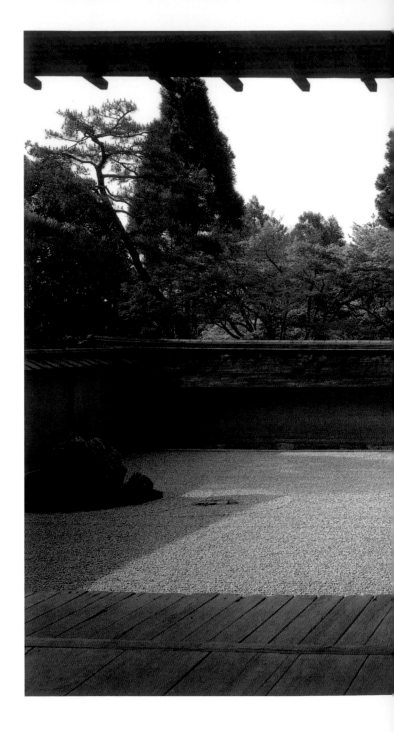

Another choice might be the temple Ryōgen-in, the northern garden of which is said to have been built in 1517, although others which are no longer extant may have existed before. The rather sudden creation of contemplation gardens in the kare-san-sui style is one of the great creative leaps in Japanese gardening history.

The aesthetics of austerity that were formed during the Kamakura period blossomed under the patronage of Zen temples, feudal lords, and wealthy merchants in the Muromachi period. The economic vitality of the era created a society that supported the arts—especially true of Kyoto, which was influenced by the members of the cultured imperial court who resided there. The Zen temples became great centers of learning, compiling treatises on literature and supporting artists within their precincts. The gardens that developed in this cultural environment, with its blend of spiritual and secular activities, came to include aspects of both. On the one hand the gardens reflected the spiritual tenets of Zen Buddhism, and were used in part as tools to aid meditation, but they were also works of art, designed to be seen in a painterly way.

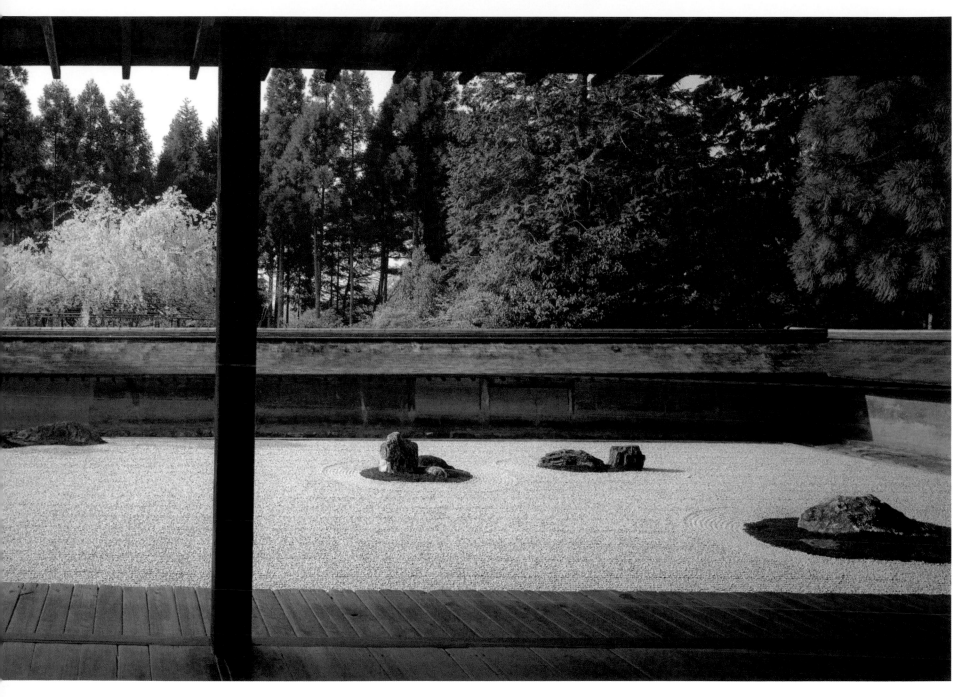

The sculptural, contemplation gardens built in the courtyards of Muromachi Zen temples are one of the great creative leaps in Japanese gardening history. Ryōanji, Kyoto.

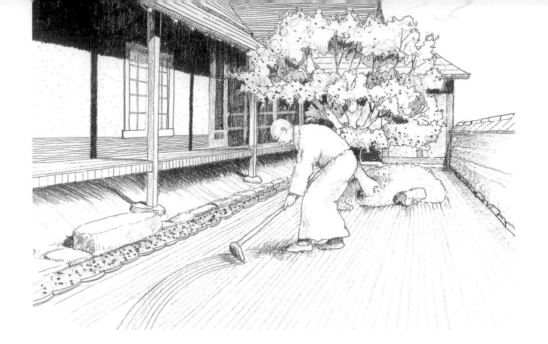

GARDENS FOR MEDITATION

One connection between Zen life and Zen gardens is daily cleansing.

Kare-san-sui gardens are usually thought of as being used for meditation. A line of priests seated in the lotus position in deep repose on the veranda of a temple overlooking a garden is the classic scene. In truth, this rarely happens.[7] Originally, in India, meditation was practiced in a natural setting often in places of natural sensory isolation, such as in a cave or facing a cliff. In China this practice changed so that most meditation took place in *zendō*, dimly-lit meditation halls that eliminate unnecessary external influences. This practice of meditating in a zendō was eventually introduced to Japan. Even to this day, daily communal meditation is practiced in zendō, but privately priests may meditate at any time or place they feel inspired to do so. Sometimes, though not often, this takes place by the garden.

Using the garden as a focal point for zazen can be problematic. For one thing, the wide expanse of white gravel in the gardens is often too bright to be comfortably used for mediation during the day. At night, without the aid of illumination or moonlight, it is too dark to see the garden at all. So the gardens are rarely objects for meditation in the strictest sense, but they do reflect the tenets of Zen in other ways.

The way the gardens were most commonly linked to life in a Zen temple was through their daily maintenance. Cleanliness is basic to Zen life and great energy is put into keeping the temple and the body (which is the temple of the soul) clean. Part of this larger work is the process of getting out into the garden and cleaning it of fallen leaves and uninvited weeds, smoothing the sand and raking the wave pattern back into it. It is a slow, simple process which despite its simplicity requires attention and composure to achieve correctly. This cleaning process is restful, perhaps even meditative, as are other simple chores about the temple such as wiping down the hallways or sweeping the tatami.[8]

In Zen Buddhist practice, although enlightenment is often mentioned as the goal, it can also be said that the process of enlightenment, the way traveled to get there, is equally important. This means being fully alive at each moment and realizing the Buddha nature—the inner true reality—of everything one comes in contact with. All things have Buddha nature and all activities can express it, so one may find enlightenment through zazen meditation but enlightenment may also be realized through the drinking of tea, flower arranging, shooting an arrow, or gardening. Each of these practices, in which a martial or secular art is seen as a means to inner peace or a higher plane of consciousness, is called a *dō* ("a way"), a term that developed during the Edo period. For example, there is *sadō*, "the Way of Tea"; *kadō,* "the Way of the Flower"; *kyūdō,* "the Way of the Bow," and so on. There is no formal "Way of Gardening" but it may be said to have existed in the Zen temples as, of all things, garden maintenance.

Another connection between Zen Buddhism and the gardens is their allegorical nature. The garden designers imbued their work with images that are reflective of Zen precepts. Because of this, the gardens can be used as allegorical models to aid in the teaching of Zen Buddhism, for instance, the story assigned to the garden at the Daisen-in temple. Beginning at the northeast corner of the hōjō, where white sand weaves its way through upright boulders, a scene of a river head gushing out of a mountain ravine was constructed. This image of "deep mountains and mysterious valleys" (*shinzan-yūkoku*) has similarities to the dragon's gate waterfall and is clearly meant to express the concept of a *source* (of life, of truth, etc.) to be found in wild nature. The river head flows on to a broader river, in which its breadth and complexity represent the trials and tribulations of life. Here also we find the tortoise and crane islands, images of longevity and permanence derived from the ancient tales of Hōrai. This river then flows to the southern side of the hōjō (the two are connected conceptually, though not physically) where a broad expanse of raked sand represents the vast ocean and the everlasting peace of paradise.[9]

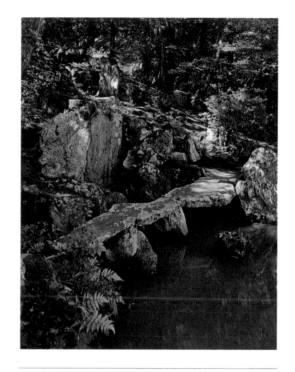

A dragon's gate waterfall: carp become dragons, men become Buddhas.
Tenryū-ji, Kyoto

THE GARDEN AS PAINTING

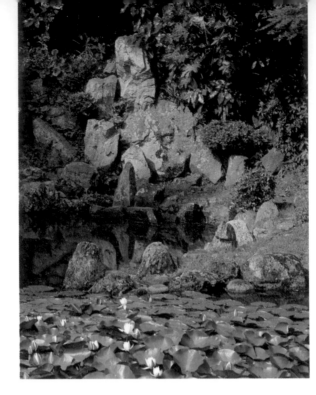

This rock arrangement, attributed to Sesshū, displays the same angular dynamism as his inkwork.
Manpuku-ji, Shimane

Even though various aspects of the garden are linked to the religious teachings of Zen Buddhism, the garden was first and foremost a work of religious art.[10] The strongest influence in the art world at the time were the ink-wash paintings of the Southern Sung dynasty in China (1127–1215), a period that predates the Muromachi period (1333–1568) by two hundred years. Nevertheless, Sung paintings were the primary models for the painters of medieval Japan.

Many of the Chinese paintings were landscapes (*san-sui-ga*) often depicting the hermitage of a recluse scholar within the vastness of the natural world, images which greatly appealed to the Japanese priests. The sparsity of the paintings was in accord with the tastes of the day, as well as with the predilection for things that reveal an inner truth. In time, with developments of papers and ink, the Japanese artists began practicing the same painting techniques, and during the Muromachi period the Zen temples of Kyoto were great sponsors of these artists. It is interesting to note that although many of the paintings were of landscapes, they were rarely of Japanese landscapes. Famous Chinese landscapes found in Sung paintings, or described in poetry, were painted by Japanese artists who had never left their native soil. These were not, therefore, "landscape paintings" in the strict sense of paintings created while actually viewing a landscape but rather paintings that use landscape imagery as a metaphor for religious images or a vehicle for personal expression, somewhat reminiscent of Heian poetry.

Ink-wash paintings were re-created in the garden in several ways, one of which is the overall balance. Garden designers turned the large areas left empty on the painted page into expanses of white sand. These voids, both the unpainted "mists" in the paintings and the fine white gravel of the garden, are called *ma* and express the aesthetic yohaku-no-bi. The designer's use of stones in the garden also mimics the ink paintings in several ways: by layering the garden stones against one another to create a sense of depth; by setting stones in a sea of white sand that takes the place of the unpainted paper; or even by evoking the angular dynamism of brush strokes through the careful selection and placement of stones. In addition, the tonal quality the designers used in the gardens evokes that of the paintings. Through the use of dark stones, white sand, and deep-green plants, the designer practically reduces the whole scene to a monochromatic scale. This simplicity of palate is a trademark of the garden designers of the Muromachi period.

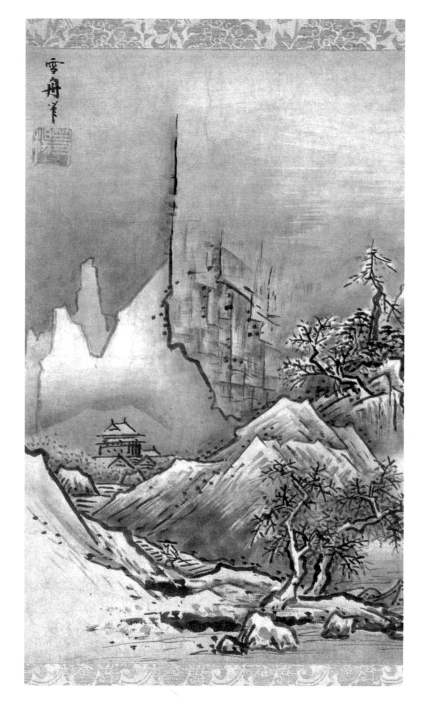

Winter Landscape, Sesshū Tōyō.
Tokyo National Museum

GARDENS AND BONSAI

There is another possible explanation for the sudden appearance of this new, bold style of gardening. Among the many cultural artifacts introduced from China during the Kamakura period was the art of *bonsai*, literally "tray planting." *Kasuga gongen kenki e-maki*, a painting from the early-fourteenth century, shows a scene with a bonsai set on a table in the garden just next to the veranda. By the time kare-san-sui developed in Zen temples, bonsai was an established pastime in Japan. The principle of bonsai is basically the same as that of the garden: personal aesthetics expressed through nature imagery. The inherent paucity of materials required by the compression of a landscape scene onto a tray, as well as design techniques used in making bonsai—such as asymmetric and triangular balance—all have similar expression in the garden. Most bonsai are created with dwarfed plants, but there is also a style called *bonseki* (tray stones) in which rocks are also added, or used alone, to create a natural scene. The striking similarity between bonsai, bonseki, and the kare-san-sui of Zen temples, in both design and material, suggests that tray landscapes may have been the primary inspiration for the creation of those gardens.

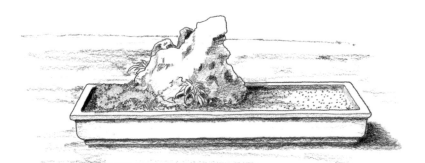

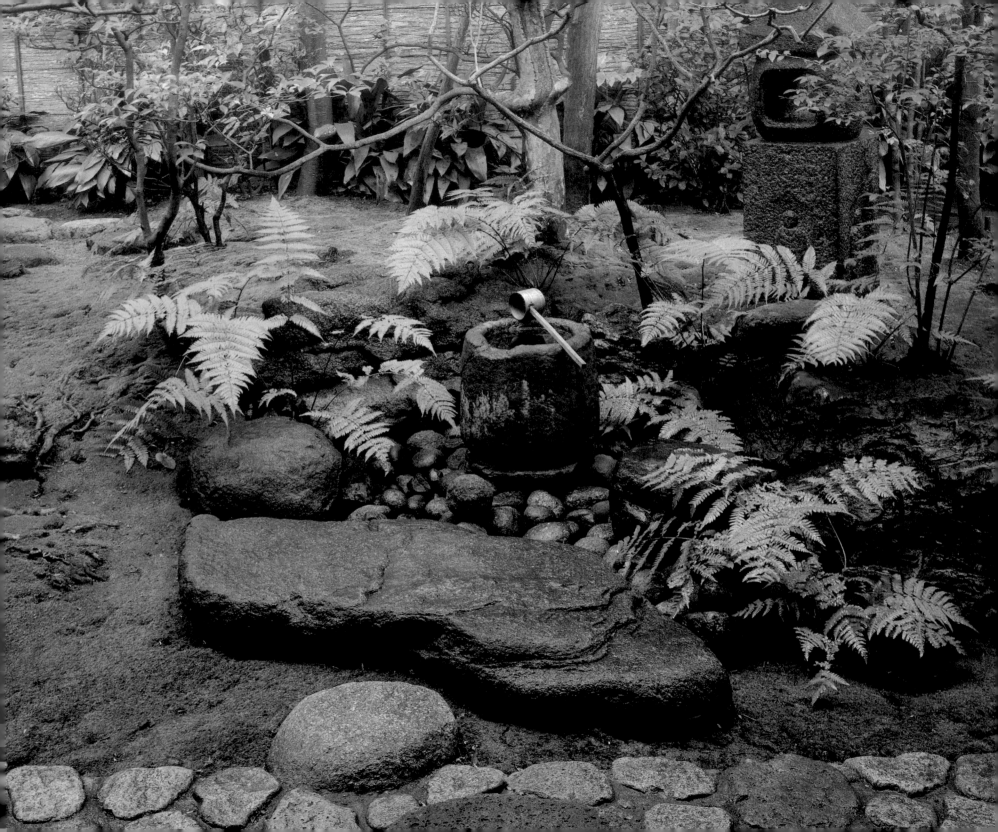

THE TEA GARDEN

The final years of Japan's medieval period were fraught with contrasts. Violent uprisings at all levels lay waste much of the country; yet this time also inspired profound developments in the arts. The opposing aesthetics of opulence and restraint existed side by side in late medieval Japan and nowhere are these differences seen more clearly than in the two contrasting forms of architecture that flourished during the time—the castle and the teahouse. Associated with the teahouse is an understated, naturalistic garden.

Among the general developments that gave rise to the tea garden was, socially, an increasing desire on the part of the warrior class to emulate the aesthetic life of the aristocrats and at the same time a greater intermingling between classes especially the warriors, priests, and wealthy merchants. The primary cultural influence on garden designers was the development of the rustic tea ceremony (*wabi-cha*), an aesthetic current that ran contrary to the predominant trend among the warrior class toward overt luxury. The physical setting was the confined quarters associated with the *sōan*, a simple grass-roofed hut that became the apotheosis for the architecture of the day.

Left: At the water laver (tsukubai) guests ritually cleanse their hands and mouth, symbolically purifying their spirit as well. Matsuo-ke, Aichi

SOCIETY AND POLITICS

The socio-political environment that fostered the development of the tea garden was complex. It included the gradual shift in character of the ruling warrior class to incorporate the refined court life of the imperial aristocracy, the rapid growth in wealth, and accordingly social stature, of the merchant class, as well as the increased economic importance of trade missions to China. During the brief thirty years sandwiched between the Muromachi and Edo periods—known as the Azuchi-Momoyama period (1568–1600)—three shōguns, one after the other, succeeded in unifying the nation under one rule and initiated two and a half centuries of relative peace. Named after the location of the grandiose castles of the first two of these rulers—Oda Nobunaga and Toyotomi Hideyoshi—the Azuchi-Momoyama period is a transitional one marking the change from medieval to modern society.

The move from Kamakura to Kyoto in the Muromachi period was sparked by, among other things, a desire on the part of the shōgun to be close to the economic and cultural activity there. Subsequent shōguns and their vassals grew increasingly expert in all the fine arts that their predecessors in Kamakura had initially shunned, amassing immense collections of artwork and maintaining a staff whose work was solely to catalogue the objects and advise on aesthetic affairs.[1] The blending of the Zen-influenced tastes of the warrior class with the vestigial *miyabi* of the imperial court was the basis for the development of many arts including tea. The shōguns, however, were not the only ones to support the arts.

The merchant class also became ardent sponsors of the arts during the Muromachi period. At the end of the Heian period, peasant craftsman—who were formally obligated to a landowner—now found themselves free to work for various clients. In Kyoto and the surrounding region these newly freed craftsmen began to form guilds, called *za*, that monopolized certain crafts; at the same time markets, which were sporadic until then, became regular affairs. This explosion in production provided an opportunity for the growth of a new class of citizen: the merchants, who made a business out of the purchase and resale of all goods. Many merchants amassed great wealth, in fact becoming much more wealthy in some cases than the warriors who were not directly involved in trade.

Aspiring to cultured society, *nouveau riche* merchants not only dealt in the trade of art objects, they themselves became active collectors, and within a few generations became a class of cultured art *aficionados*. When relations with China were reopened the merchants positioned themselves to take advantage of the new trade.

In the first years of the fifteenth century Japan officially entered into a tributary relationship with the Ming dynasty and sent gifts that the Chinese fancied: swords, fans, gilded screens, and raw copper. The Chinese emperor in return would lade them with copper coinage, silks, and ceramics. The missions from Japan always received more than they gave, as was proper in a tributary relationship, and with the addition of private trade on the side, the missions proved extremely profitable for those who sponsored them. First among the sponsors was the shogunate, later to be joined by military lords called *daimyō* (literally: big name) and, eventually, merchants from Hakata (Kyushu) and Sakai (near Osaka). Aside from profits, the trade missions succeeded in introducing great quantities of Chinese art into Muromachi society. The culture of tea finds its beginnings in gatherings held to exhibit these new artworks.

Another quality of the Muromachi and Momoyama periods that nurtured the tea culture was the cosmopolitan nature of the society. This stemmed in part from the introduction of foreign ideas, first from the Chinese trade missions and then from Europe. The Europeans came on the heels of the termination of the tributary trade to China in the mid-sixteenth century, beginning with Christian missionaries from Portugal in 1543. Another factor encouraging cosmopolitanism was the mixing of social classes within Japan—nowhere more evident than in the network created between the warrior class, Zen temples, and merchants to accomplish their trade missions. In order to enter Chinese ports, boats needed an official tally (permit) that would be examined upon arrival by Chinese officials. The shōgun, and later the daimyō, were a necessary part of the trade because only they possessed these tallies. Zen Buddhist priests were involved in the trade since the tributary nature of the missions required many diplomatic documents which they were most capable of writing. Priests also accompanied missions, lending a religious air to the procedure. Merchants were needed partly for their business acumen but also because they could help to underwrite the venture.

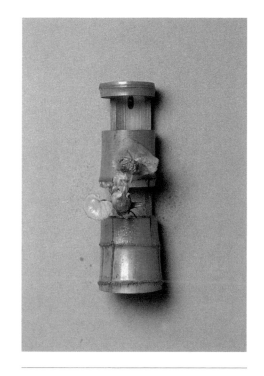

The aesthetic of understatement, wabi, *influenced all aspects of the tea ceremony— from flower arrangements to the garden.*
Flower: fuki-no-tō *Vase: Double-cut bamboo by Fukensai, Edo period*
From *Ro no Chabana,* Tankosha Co. Ltd.

CULTURAL DEVELOPMENT

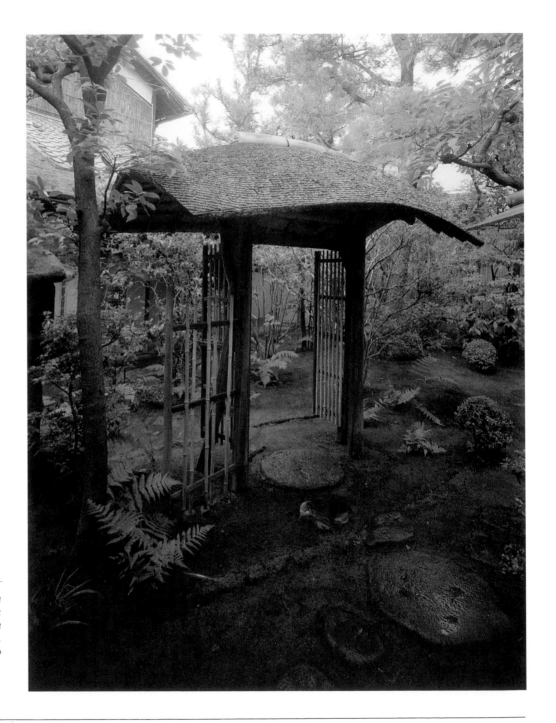

The inner and outer roji *are divided by a middle gate. Its function as a barrier is nil; instead it is symbolic of a passage into a state of deeper consciousness.*
Kankyū-an, Kyoto

The Muromachi and Momoyama eras mark a time when art was used extensively as a symbol of power and prestige in the political world. The shōgun and his vassals were notorious for their lavish use of ornamentation in their residences and castles. This extravagance is especially evident in the paintings that adorn the sliding doors, walls, and even ceilings of the architecture of the day. The overt sumptuousness of these decorative arts inspired a backlash movement by arbiters of taste from the Zen temples as well as the merchant class which, eventually, gave rise to the rustic tea ceremony known as *wabi-cha*.

Wabi-cha is not a tea "ceremony" per se, although it can be said that its staid, precise format seems ceremonial to Western eyes; in Japanese it is alternately called *cha-no-yu* (hot water for tea), *sadō* or *chadō* (the way of tea). Traditionally, tea as a beverage dates back to Bodhidharma, the Indian sage who not only brought Zen teaching from India to China but tea drinking as well. Tea was widely appreciated for its stimulating properties, as well as for various medicinal purposes, and a ritual developed in T'ang China centering on the drinking of tea. Tea was introduced to Japan by the Nara period—along with the other aspects of continental culture—and was used as a beverage from that time on. In the early Kamakura period the Zen pioneer priest Eisai brought with him seeds of the tea plant from China, the offspring of which came to be known in Japan as "true" tea (*honcha*).

Beginning at the end of the Muromachi period and continuing through the Momoyama period, the tea ceremony evolved into the artistic form we now know. At first tea drinking as a cultural event was entirely festive; activities included contests to discern different types of tea (*tōcha*), and the consumption of copious quantities of *saké*. These gatherings were also a pretext to show off newly acquired artwork and ceramics from China. Zen priest Murata Shuko and the wealthy Sakai merchants Takeno Joo, Sen no Rikyū, and his grandson Sen no Sotan are the tea masters most often credited with guiding the tea culture away from lavish, overt displays of wealth to a more ascetic form. In succession each tea master contributed his philosophy and taste to the rustic tea culture, called wabi-cha. Whereas once tea gatherings had been held in large halls of formal *shoin* architecture, wabi-cha was held in a simple thatch-roofed hut called a *sōan*. Expensive tea utensils imported from China, which used to be the center of attention, were replaced by simpler ones. In particular the fine porcelains were rejected in favor of common ceramic bowls, initially those found among local farmers or on trips to Korea, and then later pieces made in Japan especially for the "tea society." The mood of the tea gathering (*cha-kai, cha-ji*) itself shifted from one of excess and display to that of reserve and humility, and the tea garden was created to complement these changing priorities.

THE PHYSICAL SETTING

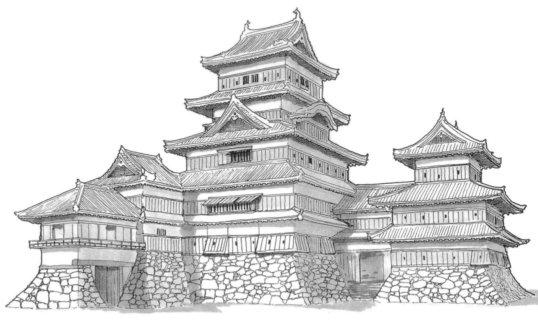

Built in 1597, this castle is one of the few remaining from the medieval period.
Matsumoto Castle, Nagano

Castle construction began amid the repeated wars of the early Kamakura period.[2] The first castles were simple, stone or wood redoubts built at the very top of a hill overlooking a local warlord or chieftain's domain. These castles were exclusively military fortifications—they were used only in times of war and had no residential or bureaucratic facilities within them. In time they grew more elaborate, and by the Muromachi period, castles were used as much as architectural symbols of power as they were for defense. Warlords began to build their castles next to their residences, further down the mountains, or even on flat land, often at crossroads, using them as toll posts along routes of commerce.

The two castles that give name to the Azuchi-Momoyama period—and symbolize the era's opulence—were Nobunaga's Azuchi Castle (in what is now Shiga Prefecture) and Hideyoshi's Jurakudai (in Momoyama, south of Kyoto). Neither of these is extant but contemporary literature and paintings suggest that they were extravagant, sprawling structures. The posts and beams were painted black and vermilion, the roof tiles were gilded, and the walls and ceilings were covered with sumptuous paintings. In direct contrast to the palatial aesthetics of these castles was the simplicity of the sōan.

SUKIYA • SŌAN

Tea gardens show up in a great variety of settings reflecting the wide variety of classes that were involved in fostering the growth of tea culture. Incorporated into the existing residences of the military class and merchants, and into Zen temples, the tea garden has no standard setting but there are certain similarities that shaped its basic physical form.

Size would be foremost among these factors. Tea gardens were mostly built within Kyoto, or merchant towns like Sakai, and were often retrofitted into an existing plan. The teahouse and garden were designed to fit into a remaining open corner of the property. Designing a tea garden was inherently, therefore, an act of compression.

Under the influence of wabi-cha, the tea masters created a new form of architecture, moving away from the formal shoin style to one called *sukiya*, which was based on the sōan, incorporating natural elements in a less restricted overall plan. The tea masters continued to use some of the characteristic elements of shoin architecture—the alcove and shelves for displaying artwork (*tokonoma* and *chigai-dana* respectively) and the built-in desk for writing (*shoin*)—but they were freer with their placement within a room. The designers replaced other aspects of shoin architecture—decorative wall coverings, squared posts and beams, and coffered ceilings—or intermingled them with elements that were more natural and less ornate. They finished the walls with plain earth, used simple tree trunks in their natural state as posts and beams, and made the ceilings out of plain slats of wood.

Although the designers had purposefully included "natural" elements, sukiya could not be called rough. The owners were people of wealth and position, and although they were enamored of the beauty found in natural materials, they desired an elegant architecture. The earth they used for plastering was only the finest, most refined colored clay-and-sand mixes; the posts and beams they selected were natural, but not just any log would do, only carefully chosen pieces whose shape or color expressed a subtle beauty. Even the plain slats of wood used for the ceiling were cut from knotless lumber with a straight grain—a rare commodity.[3]

The introduction of these building materials resulted in a stronger relationship between the architecture and the garden, not simply in the openness of the style, but also in aesthetic and sensory terms. The designers of the buildings no longer employed entirely man-made forms but included elements whose beauty stemmed from their natural state. Since this was the same natural beauty—the line, color, and tone—that would be found in the garden, the architecture was aesthetically linked to the garden. The garden, in turn, is an artistic work that expresses the *spirit* of nature. Architecture linked to the garden; the garden linked to nature. In this way the garden acts as an interface between architecture and the natural world.

◆ THE DESIGNERS

TEA MASTERS

During the Azuchi-Momoyama period a backlash movement against the opulence of the contemporary political and social leaders led to the development of a new cultural activity: the rustic tea ceremony, known as *wabi-cha*. The designers of the gardens associated with wabi-cha were masters in the ways of the tea ceremony (*cha-no-yusha*), who took careful pains in the design of the tiny gardens they created as entryways to their teahouses. Among these men were feudal lords, Buddhist priests, and wealthy merchants.

Cha-no-yusha were not professional gardeners; rather they were skilled in all aspects of the wabi-cha culture: cuisine, calligraphy, flower arrangement, and architectural and garden design. A central figure of the tea world at that time, Sen no Rikyū, was purported to have advocated "life as art," through which all aspects of one's daily life are imbued with the aesthetic sensibilities of wabi-cha. Momoyama tea masters took as much personal concern with the design and care of the garden as they did with the other aspects of their refined, introverted tea world.

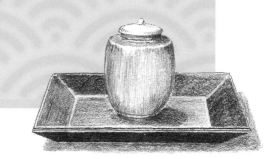

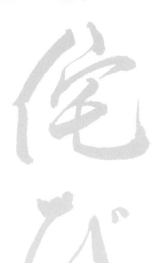

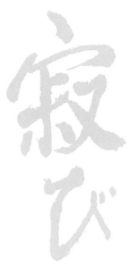

AESTHETICS

WABI-SABI

The aesthetic term *wabi* is usually translated as subdued taste and is often used in tandem with the term *sabi,* which has similar meanings. A look at the etymology gives insight into the meaning of these words. Wabi is derived from *wabishii* (wretched, lonesome) and *wabiru* (to grieve, worry); sabi stems from *sabishii* (lonely, desolate) and *sabiru* (to mellow). Both words came to describe the kind of beauty that tea masters found in the simplicity of common materials when used in a refined way. The gloss of a bamboo tea scoop touched over and over in the same place; the minute fissures that network the surface of coarsely glazed pottery; the unobtrusive quality of a garden that is created out of years of tidying more than initial design. One way to use the terms wabi and sabi (there are as many definitions as tea masters) is to say that sabi is the patina or aura that honest materials acquire with age if well cared for; wabi on the other hand is the aesthetic that appreciates things that have or express sabi.

SUKI • SAKUI

The appreciation of simplicity and rusticity inherent in wabi-sabi may be the dominant aesthetic of the tea garden but it is not the only one. Others, like *suki* and *sakui,* were also influential. Suki meant connoisseurship and sakui meant personal creativity or creative flair. All aspects of wabi-cha—from the selection of tea utensils and artwork to the construction of the teahouse and garden—were an expression of the taste of the tea masters, who called themselves *sukisha,* connoisseurs. Some masters considered artistic expression as the central aspect of a tea gathering, while others deemed it secondary to practicality and natural efficiency; but independent of how artistry was stressed the tea masters considered themselves artists, with the tea gathering as their instrument of expression.

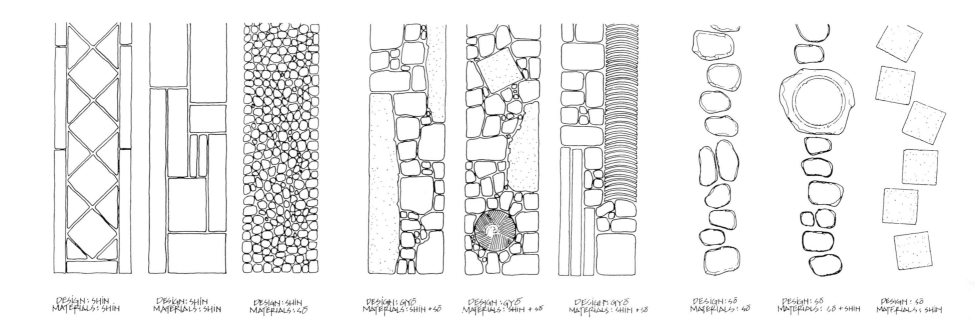

DESIGN: SHIN
MATERIALS: SHIN

DESIGN: SHIN
MATERIALS: SHIN

DESIGN: SHIN
MATERIALS: SŌ

DESIGN: GYŌ
MATERIALS: SHIN + SŌ

DESIGN: GYŌ
MATERIALS: SHIN + SŌ

DESIGN: GYŌ
MATERIALS: SHIN + SŌ

DESIGN: SŌ
MATERIALS: SŌ

DESIGN: SŌ
MATERIALS: SŌ + SHIN

DESIGN: SŌ
MATERIALS: SHIN

Another set of terms that were related to many arts including that of gardening was the ranking system of *shin-gyō-sō* which is sometimes described as formal, semiformal, and informal but has other implications as well. The terms are derived from *kai-gyō-sō*, terminology for three forms of calligraphy: formal block characters, informal rounded characters, and the cursive style, respectively. *Shin* is used in reference to things that are highly controlled or shaped by man, and thus a path made entirely of cut granite, a formal post and beam gate of squared, planed wood, and a white plastered wall are all shin. Shin does not imply opulence, but rather cleanliness and sparseness. *Sō*, on the other hand, is an expression of naturalness; materials are used in their original state. A stepping-stone path of river rocks, a lattice gate of woven bamboo, and a fence made of bundles of twigs are all sō. *Gyō* can be considered an admixture of shin and sō accomplished in such a way as to play one off the other.[4]

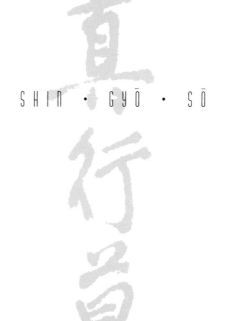

SHIN · GYŌ · SŌ

THE TEA GARDEN

The tea garden is more properly called a *roji*, which traditionally means alleyway or path, but was assigned new characters by tea masters with the more poetic connotation of "dewy ground," an apt image to capture the feeling of Kyoto's cool, mossy tea gardens. The roji is designed to act as a pathway to the tea house, although most tea rooms were also made accessible from the main buildings by way of a corridor.

The plantings of the roji were designed to be as naturalistic as possible. Whereas the designers of the gardens within the castles sought to create the nostalgic mood of a mountain hamlet (*yamazato*)—perhaps through the use of such flowering, agricultural plants as the peach or loquat (*biwa*)—the designers of the tea gardens sought the quiet atmosphere of the deep mountains (*shinzan-no-tei*). This was achieved by using a mix of evergreen trees and shrubs, with only a few deciduous plants, collectively called "miscellaneous trees" (*zōki*), which were selected for their unobtrusive quality. Designers shunned perennial or annual flowers and rarely used flowering trees or shrubs, if at all.[5] Often the ground of the roji was carpeted with moss, but it must be remembered that moss is part and parcel of the natural ecology in Kyoto and not necessarily the choice of the designer. Normally, if soil is left bare and partially shaded, within six months it will be covered with moss.

Some of the stereotypical elements of "Japanese gardens," like stepping stones (*tobi-ishi*) and stone lanterns (*ishidōrō*), were first used by creative tea masters in the late-sixteenth century. Even though stepping stones had existed prior to the tea garden as a way to cross muddy ground, their selection and placement was brought to an artistic level in the roji. Stone lanterns had been only used along approaches to, or within the grounds of, temples and shrines. The tea masters began col-

1. OUTER GATE,
   soto-mon OR roji-mon

2. TOILET,
   setchin

3. WAITING BENCH,
   koshikake machiai

4. MIDDLE GATE,
   chū-mon

5. DUST PIT,
   chiri-ana

6. LAVER,
   tsukubai

7. WELL,
   ido

8. THATCH-ROOFED TEAHOUSE,
   sōan

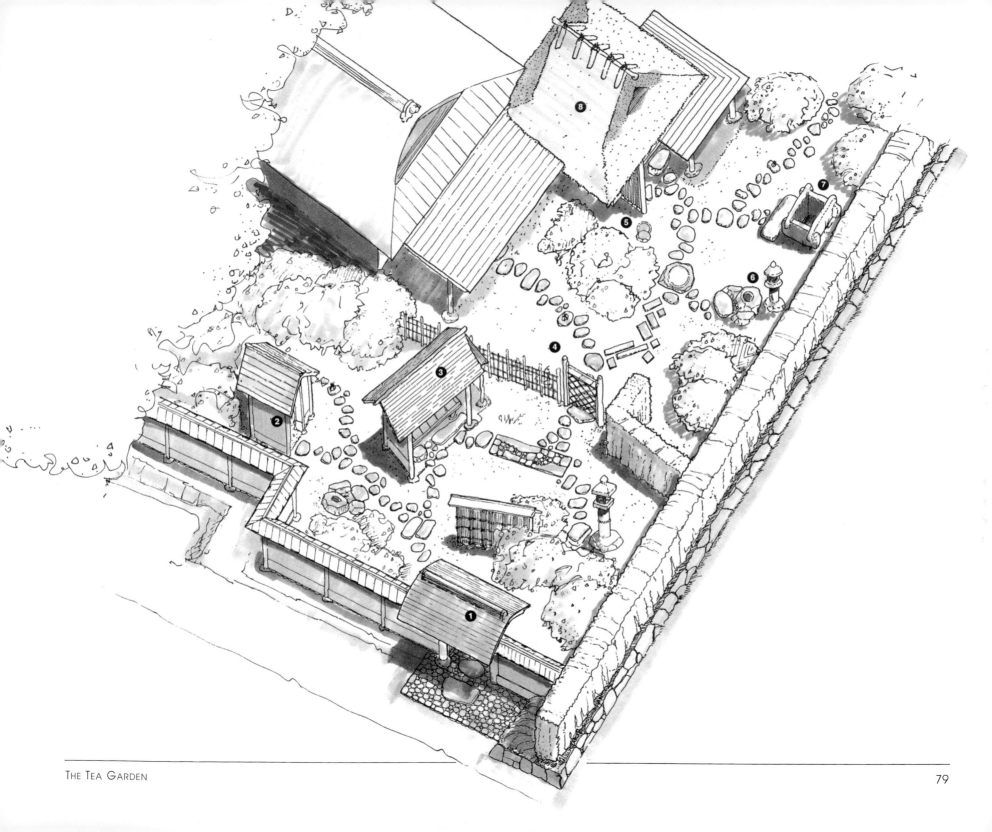

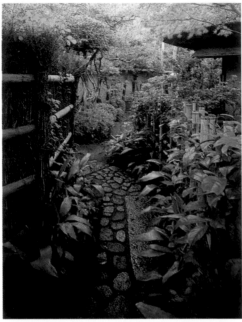

Left: The roji *compresses the sensory experience of a walk from town to a hermit's hut in the short distance from entry to tearoom.*
Shōkadō, Yahata

Below: A waiting bench in the tea garden allows guests to commune with the many ephemeral sensations in the garden before entering the tearoom.
Urasenke, Kyoto

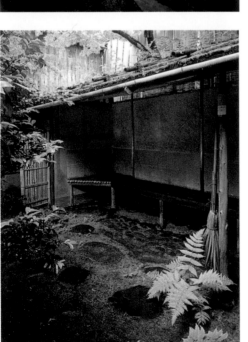

lecting old, weathered stone lanterns to add atmosphere to the roji and later designed lanterns that would express their own personal style. The designer's reuse of old, discarded objects (*mitate-mono*) is a trademark of the tea world. *Mitate* is usually translated as "select or appraise" (*mono* means "thing"), but it can be said to mean "seeing anew," implying that these old and forgotten things are given new life in the roji by discovering a new use for them or observing a beauty in them that was not noticed before. Turning lanterns into sculptural elements that add mood to the roji is one example, as is the reworking of stone stupas and old granite bridge piers to create *chōzubachi*, the water lavers placed before the teahouse. The designers also took slabs of cut stone, formally used in temple walkways or as architectural foundations, and incorporated them into artistic patterns in the paths of the roji.

By definition, the roji was not a garden, but simply an entrance path that led to the tea house. The idea that the roji was created as a passage rather than a garden meant for viewing is aptly summarized in a quotation attributed to Sen no Rikyū in which he refers to the proportions to be used when designing a roji: "passage six parts; landscape four."[6] The roji was a carefully designed environment, a corridor whose true purpose was to prompt the mental and spiritual repose requisite to the tea gathering. To walk the length of a roji is the spiritual complement of a journey from town to the deep recesses of a mountain where stands a hermit's hut. The designers of the tea garden compressed that emotional and sensory experience into the short distance between the street and the teahouse—expressed, for instance, in the subdued and naturalistic plantings. In addition to the general serenity, they designed into the roji a series of thresholds, some of which are physical barriers and some more abstract. At each of these thresholds the guest is encouraged to release worldly cares and progressively enter a "tea state of mind."

The first of these thresholds is the outer gate (*soto-mon* or *roji-mon*) that separates the roji from the outside world. Passing this gate, which may face onto the street or a part of a larger garden, one enters the outer roji (*soto-roji*). The last guest to enter closes and locks the gate—the outer world has been left behind. Divided into two parts, the outer roji is usually more sparsely planted, lighter and airier than the inner roji.[7] Within the outer roji is a covered bench (*koshi-kake machiai*) where guests sit and wait to be signaled forward by their host although there is no practical reason to make the guest wait. The preparations for a cha-kai start at dawn—regardless of the time of the gathering—when the water drawn from the well will be the freshest.[8] The garden and teahouse are cleaned and all is prepared well in advance so that the host will also have time to compose him- or herself. The point of making the guests wait is to give them time to relax, settle their thoughts, and commune with the garden. Seasons are reflected in the roji: leaves turning color in the autumn or a haze of new spring buds. There is the delicate scent of moist moss, the sound of wind or a summer cicada, or the warm autumn sun felt on the skin. The time waiting in the roji gives one a chance to attune to these ephemeral sensations.

The host appears and bows are exchanged (*mukae-tsuke*). The guests move forward, slowly one by one along a path leading to a small gate called the middle gate (*chū-mon*), which is the next threshold. The middle gate marks the division between the outer and inner roji. The middle gate may be roofed with hinged doors or it may be a mere suggestion of a gate such as a panel of woven bamboo that is held up by a stick to let people crouch under and pass.[9] The middle gates are never strong barriers and are rarely flanked by fencing. Since it is possible to go around the fence to the left or right, the gate has lost its sense of being a physical barrier. The only meaning left to it is as a marker—a symbol of a threshold—and passage through it is symbolic of entering a deeper state of consciousness.

Having passed the middle gate the guests find within the inner roji a water laver called *tsukubai*, which is used to rinse one's hands and mouth in an act of purification before entering the teahouse.[10] The influence of Catholic missionaries during the Momoyama period has led to the belief that the tsukubai may have been derivative of the Christian baptismal font, but it is equally as connected to the ancient Shintō absorption with defilement and purification and the Zen emphasis on cleanliness. In any event, water is uni-

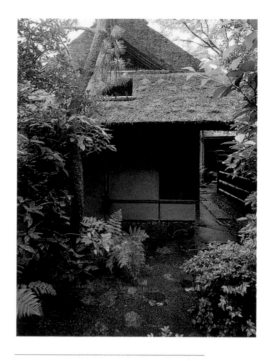

A sōan, *the simple grass-roofed hut that is the apotheosis of tea architecture.*
Urasenke, Kyoto

versally equated with purity. The proper term for the laver itself is *chōzubachi* (hand-washing bowl), while the tsukubai refers to the entire arrangement of stones that includes the hollow stone to the rear that holds the water, and, other stones at the sides and front, each with a particular purpose. These stones include the *yuoke-ishi* where a bowl of warm water would be set in winter, the *teshoku-ishi* where one can set down a hand-held lantern carried into the roji at night, and the *mae-ishi* on which one stands to use the tsukubai.

Following the tsukubai, the next threshold in the roji is the dust pit (*chiriana*), a small hole in the ground often lined with roof tiles or stones to keep it from collapsing. Originally the chiriana was a functional feature of gardens used to temporarily dispose of garden debris such as fallen leaves. In the roji the chiriana is used in a ritualized way and assumes a number of symbolic meanings. For example, just before the cha-kai, an evergreen branch is cut and set in the hole, and two large chopstick-like twig pickers are laid on top. This is a visual image of cleanliness, implying that the host has prepared properly and all is ready. Moreover, the chiriana is interpreted as a place for the "dust of the mind." If there are any troubles or concerns with worldly affairs left in one's heart or mind then they need to be left in the chiriana for they have no place in the tea room.

The final threshold is the small crawl-through entry (*nijiri-guchi*) to the teahouse. A square opening set low in the wall, it forces the guest to duck and bow when entering the tearoom. A practical side is that samurai were forced by the physical nature of the entrance, as well as by custom, to remove their swords before entering. There is a rack just outside the entry where swords can be placed. Another, more important meaning was the humility inherent in the act of bowing before entering. This ritually reinforced the ideal that all who enter the tearoom are equals, a radical frame of mind for a hierarchical society and one that only had partial success in becoming reality.

The evergreen boughs in the dust pit indicate the host's careful preparations.
Kankyū-an, Kyoto

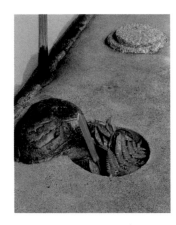

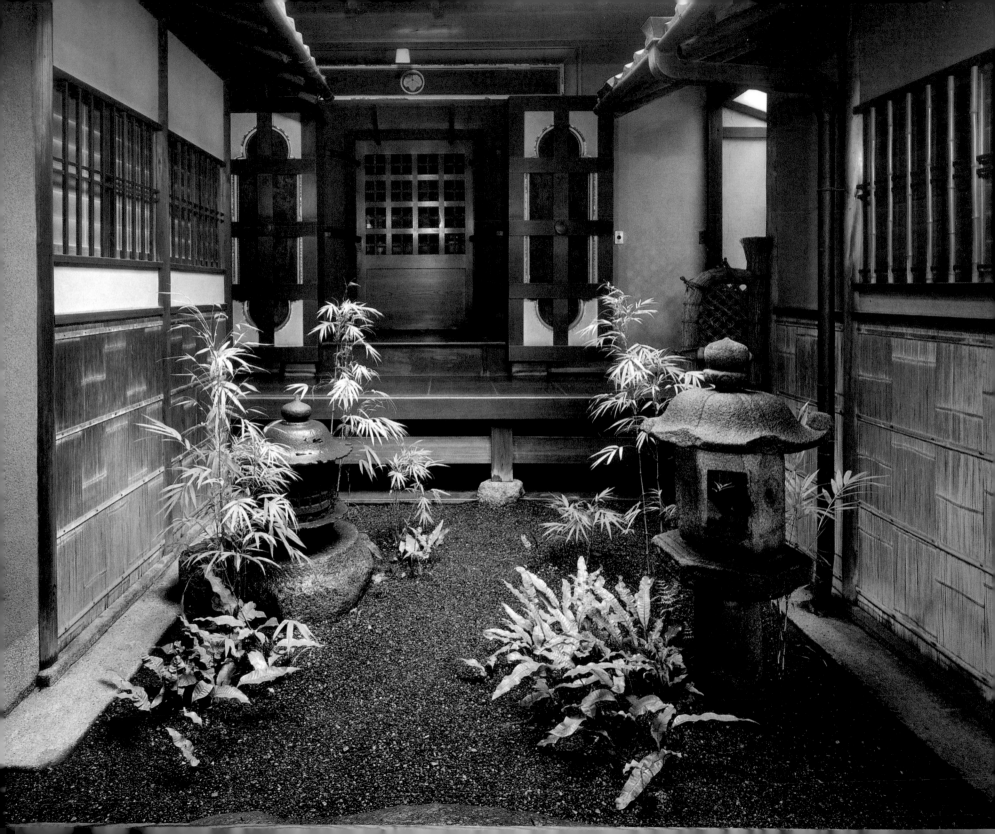

TSUBO GARDENS

In China, it is said, certain Buddhist priests meditated by entering a large ceramic vessel and found all the world within. The idea that the cosmos is contained in a grain of sand, or a single thought, is beautifully expressed in the *tsubo-niwa*, the tiny gardens enclosed within the town houses of the urban merchants from the early Edo period onward. Like the development of other gardens, the design of the *tsubo* gardens evolved from a series of changes in society in general—the dramatic rise in social status of the *chōnin* (townspeople: i.e., merchants and craftsmen), the popular culture based on their tastes, and a new physical setting within the narrow confines of their urban residences (*machiya*).

Left: The small space in front of a storehouse designed as a tsubo garden.
Private residence, Kyoto

SOCIETY AND POLITICS

By the Muromachi period a new class shift was afoot—a general increase in affluence and community spirit among chōnin, in particular the rise of a wealthy merchant class. The development of regular markets gave the chōnin a measure of independence. In Kyoto, resident townsmen formed groups called *machi-shū* that attempted to regulate the affairs of their district (*machi*).[1]

The Momoyama period witnessed massive war campaigns of three successive shōguns who sought to bring the nation under their control. The last of these, Tokugawa Hideyoshi, was successful in establishing his seat of government in Edo (present-day Tokyo). This period is marked by the elaborate political and social structures created to regulate each and every aspect of society, from basic class structure to the style of one's clothes. Foremost among these regulations was the division of society into four official classes (*shi-no-ko-sho*): samurai, farmer, craftsman, and merchant, from top to bottom.[2] In order to maintain stability, a separation of the classes was strictly enforced. Samurai were not allowed to farm, effectively divorcing them from the land that they had once controlled (*heinō-bunri*). Farmers, in turn, were stripped of their swords, becoming militarily impotent. Yet another of the checks and balances built into the system was the social inversion of farmers and merchants. Farmers, traditionally at the lower end of society, were placed next in importance to the samurai, while the merchants were consigned to the bottom even though their financial resources and cultural acumen often rivaled or exceeded that of the samurai.

While Edo was the seat of government, the provinces were divided up among the *daimyō,* retainers loyal to the *shōgun*. Each daimyō was required to build a castle which, although mostly cosmetic, had a dramatic effect on society. Lower-ranking samurai, cut off from their lands, gradually made their way to these new castles seeking employment. These assembled samurai in turn required all manner of goods and services and soon the castles were surrounded by bustling towns (*jōka machi*) populated by chōnin. The Edo period marks the rapid growth of these towns and the ensuing emergence of the chōnin as exponents of a dynamic popular culture.

Cultural Development

The popular culture of the chōnin, which had its seeds in Muromachi times, flowered in the Edo period, first in Osaka and then later in Edo. The fruits of this new creativity are among today's most commonly-known Japanese arts: Kabuki theater, woodblock prints, and haiku poetry, to mention a few. While the samurai were given to the more staid studies of the classics or martial arts, the merchants reveled in the commercial vitality of the towns, giving rise to a rich bourgeois culture. The appeal of the merchant's world was so great that it was not uncommon for samurai to shed their swords in order to mingle in the gay quarters of town. As regards the garden, the most important effect of this popular era was not a specific form of poetry or painting but the simple fact that the chōnin were becoming conscious of themselves as purveyors and sponsors of culture. They expressed their individuality to the fullest within the limited world that the shogunate constructed for them to live in. This often meant cultivating a carefully controlled public face and carrying on as one wished within one's private world, as can be seen with startling clarity in the clothing (kimono) that originates from this time. While the outer cloth is a somber mixture of colors, a peek inside reveals lavishly vibrant colors, and sometimes gorgeous paintings of landscapes, people, animals, or abstract designs.

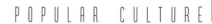

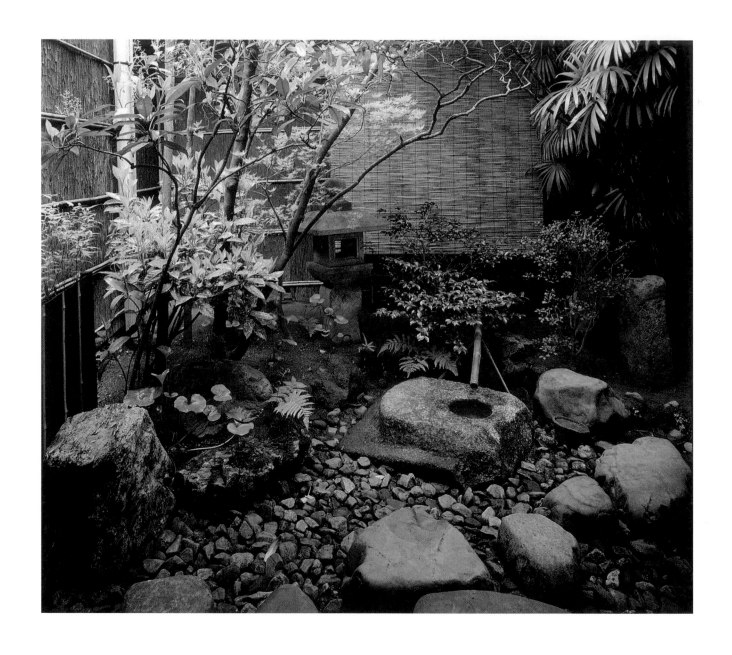

Left: The stepping stones and water laver are elements derived from the tea garden.
Kawamichiya Inn, Kyoto

Right: Only the most essential elements remain: lantern, water, and evergreen plant.
Tawaraya Inn, Kyoto

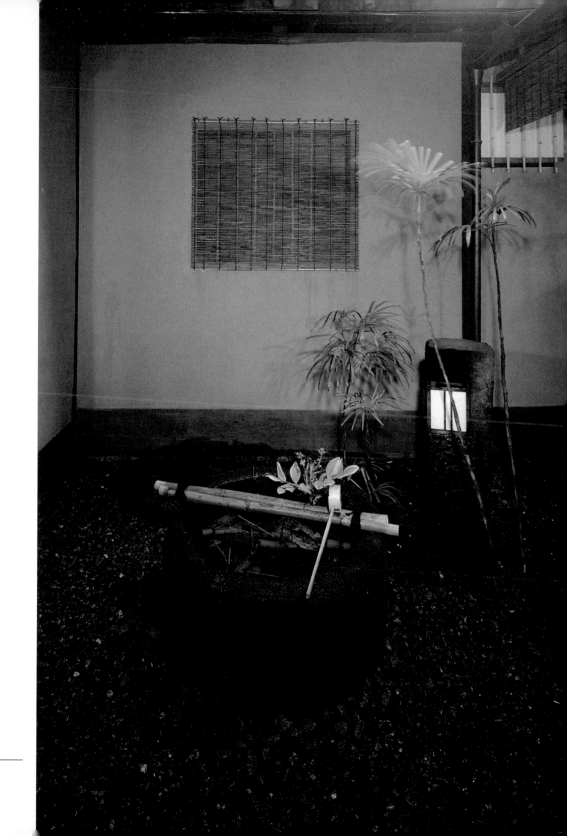

THE PHYSICAL SETTING

1. MAIN ENTRY

2. ENTRANCE HALL, *mise niwa*

3. FORMAL PRIVATE ENTRY, *naka tsubo*

4. FORMAL ENTRY ROOM, *genkan*

5. PRIVATE ENTRY, *naka no ma*

6. PASSAGEWAY & KITCHEN,
hashiri niwa, tōri niwa

7. SERVICE KITCHEN, *daidokoro*

8. TOILETS, *benjo*

9. BATH, *furo*

10. STOREHOUSE, *kura, dozō*

11. REAR GARDEN, *senzai, nakaniwa*

12. DISPLAY ALCOVE, *tokonoma*

13. GUESTROOM, *zashiki*

14. DISPLAY SHELVES, *chigaidana*

15. SITTING ROOM, *tsugi no ma*

16. GARDEN, *tsubo niwa*

17. SHOP, *mise no ma*

The tsubo garden was influenced more than any other garden by architecture and the city plan. In the case of Kyoto, the city was initially laid out as a grid with the smallest of the blocks being a *chō*. The chō was further divided four times north to south and eight east to west to form 32 lots called *henushi*. By the end of the Heian period, though, much of the original idealistic plan of the city had changed to accommodate the more practical aspects of day-to-day life and so it was with the layout of the chō. Of the 32 henushi, the outer ones that lined the street proved the most viable since a building could be used as a storefront directly accessible to people passing by. The center of the chō devolved into an unbuilt area that was used for communal wells, vegetable plots, and toilets—a convenient if unsanitary combination.[3]

Until the Edo period, the houses of commoners were crude: simple woven mats for walls and a board or grass roof held down against the wind by a crisscross of bamboo poles weighted at the intersections by rocks. Beginning in the Edo period with advances in construction techniques—and financial resources newly available to the chōnin—a new form of residence was born called *machiya*, or town house. The merchants built a particular form of machiya which incorporated both shop and residence called *omoteya-zukuri* (street-front construction). The *omoteya* style consisted of a one- or two-story structure beside the street, with one or two more units going back on a long thin lot. Taxes levied on frontage (the width of the building facing the street) were, in part, the cause of this deep and narrow architectural design. In its classic form, the front building was for business, and the buildings in the back were for an extended family. Between these separate buildings, small spaces were left open for light and air. Eventually these tiny spaces would be turned into gardens, in the style of the tea garden. The houses of the merchants expressed the same social duality as the kimono—façades were generally simple but they contained hidden "treasures" within.

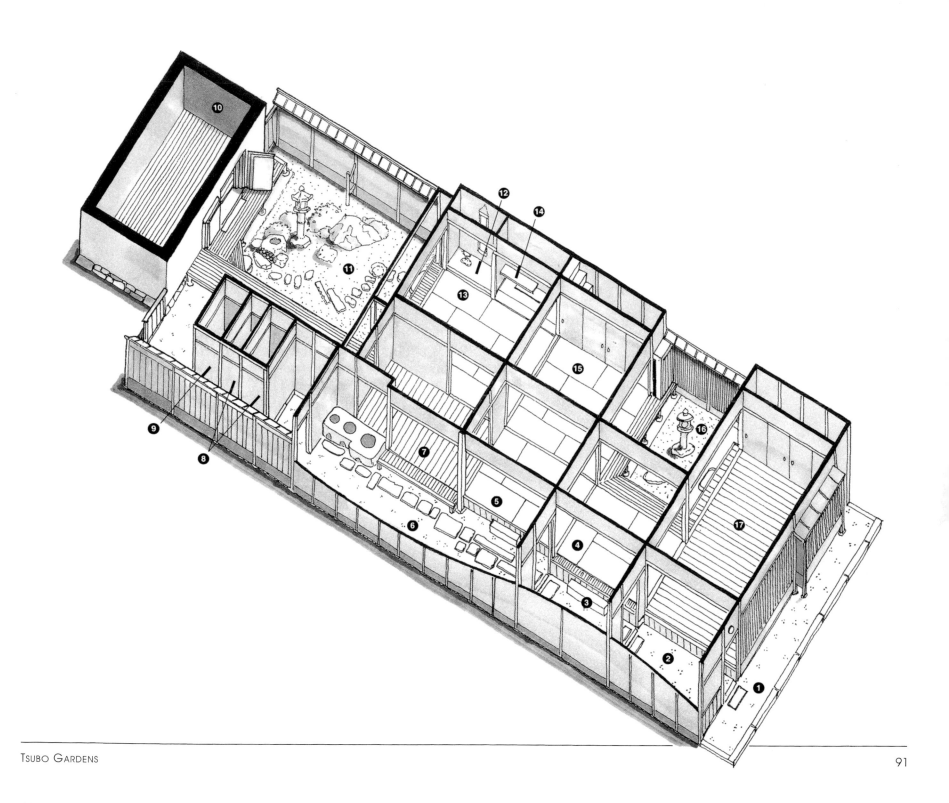

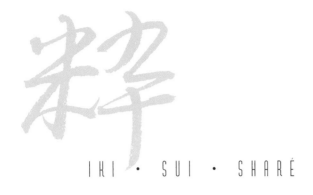

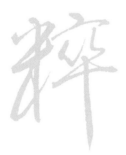

IKI • SUI • SHARÉ

AESTHETICS

The Edo period became an age of extroverted aesthetics—the sensual took precedence over the spiritual. *Iki, sui, sharé, tsū, shibumi, asobi,* and *tanoshimi* are all representative terms of the time. These were the words the chōnin used to describe their own world.

Iki and sui are similar in meaning, the former being a term from Edo and the latter from Osaka. Chōnin culture during the Edo period was strongest at first in the Osaka region, as it was physically distant from Edo and, consequently, more relaxed in its control of the nonsamurai classes. By the mid-Edo period, however, Edo became the center of popular as well as political culture. Indicative of Edo chōnin culture in general, iki and sui were initially amorous terms. One who knew the ways of the world, life's pleasures, and how to enjoy them to the fullest was said to possess sui and was dubbed a *sui-sama*.[4] Sui was applied to both men and women, revealing the degree to which women were now involved in cultured life, in contrast to the restrictive medieval bushi society. Women were not necessarily trend-setters but they were the center of adoration and amorous attention. Sui eventually developed into a term that might be translated as "worldly." Iki had similar roots, with an aura of coquettishness, liveliness, or style, in a word, "chic." *Sharé*, which means fashionable, was applied to those who affected a certain style in their personal appearance and in the way they conducted their lives in general.

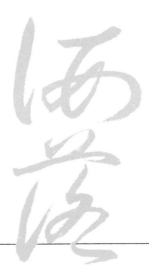

Tsū means connoisseurship and is used in conjunction with a person who is active in the pursuit of the aesthetic ideals of sui or iki, thus the term *tsū-jin* (a person with tsū). The terms iki, sui, sharé, and tsū reveal the flamboyant nature of the Edo-period chōnin who focused on worldly pleasures and insisted on proving themselves aesthetically refined. Edo society may have refused the chōnin entry into the samurai or noble classes, but the tsū-jin would outshine them with sheer dandyism. An alternate meaning of tsū—professionalism—reveals another aspect of Edo-period culture: trade specialization. The Edo period witnessed the development and institutionalization of many specialized trades, including professional gardeners, the *ueki-ya.*

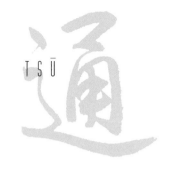

TSŪ

Shibumi is an aesthetic term that grew out of the word *shibui* meaning astringent. Originally, in classical literature shibumi was not a positive adjective but shifted connotations during the middle ages as society developed a taste for simple and unornamented beauty. The Edo-period chōnin brought the word into common usage but, while shibumi expressed a similar aesthetic as *wabi-sabi*, it lacked the specific spiritual qualities that they were imbued with. Shibumi described unpretentious artwork, ceramics with a subdued beauty, or even the skills of an actor with just the right understated touch to his performance. Shibumi is still used today, as are many of the terms from this period, which reveals the "modern" quality of the Edo period. The wholesale introduction of Western thought during the Meiji period (1868–1912) is usually said to be the beginning of Japan's modern era—which is true in terms of society or politics—but, as these terms show, modern notions of aesthetics have a longer history. Shibumi, for instance, remains a key characteristic sought after by architects attempting to create "modern" Japanese buildings.

SHIBUMI

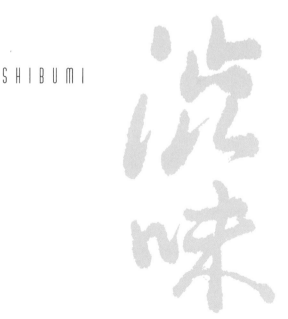

THE TSUBO GARDENS

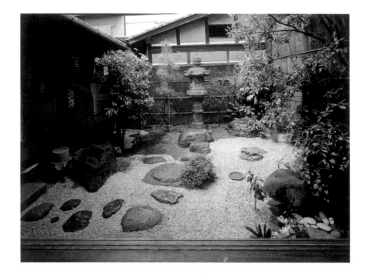

A large tsubo garden, also known as senzai, *at the rear of a town house.*
Private residence, Kyoto

Although associated with the gardens of Edo-period merchants, tsubo gardens actually date back to the shinden palaces of the Heian period. At that time small courtyards were enclosed between the various wings and outer rooms of sprawling palaces and were known as tsubo, often named after a single or dominant plant that was used in each one. The Wisteria court (*Fuji-tsubo*) and Paulownia court (*Kiri-tsubo*) from *The Tale of Genji* are good examples. In *The Tale of Genji*, princesses who reside next to those courts take their name from the courts, thus Fuji-tsubo and Kiri-tsubo also refer to people in that book. What is most outstanding is the private nature of these spaces. During the Heian period, whether among the lowliest farmers or the highest courtiers, privacy as we know it today was unheard of—the nature of the society and the architecture precluded privacy. Within the larger realm of the shinden palace, a place of official business as well as residence, the most private places were the small confines of the back rooms and tsubo gardens. The overriding character of tsubo gardens therefore, more than a specific design form or style, was the privacy they were associated with.

Tsubo gardens can also be found in Zen temples and the residences of the medieval bushi, but it is in the town houses of the Edo-period chōnin, and the restaurants and inns that catered to them that they evolved into the form we know today. The physical structure of the machiya formed the frame within which the tsubo gardens were built. This meant that gardens could not be large and for the most part were meant as contemplation gardens, to be enjoyed from nearby rooms but not actually entered. Whereas most business was transacted in the front section of the machiya, closest to the street entrance, important clients would be brought back to the sitting room for entertainment. Clients, however, would only go so far—the quarters further to the rear of the house were strictly for family. The deep and narrow machiya can be said to have been layered in zones according to social use. The proximity of the tsubo gardens with the rooms in the house caused by the physical nature of the machiya meant that they were closely associated with the life of the household, either as a backdrop for important business deals and social life, or for the private pleasure of the owner.

Culturally, the greatest influence on the design of the tsubo gardens was the tea garden. The tea world was synonymous with high culture in the Edo period, and though few sought an austere tea life—"life as art," as Sen no Rikyū is said to have proposed it—a

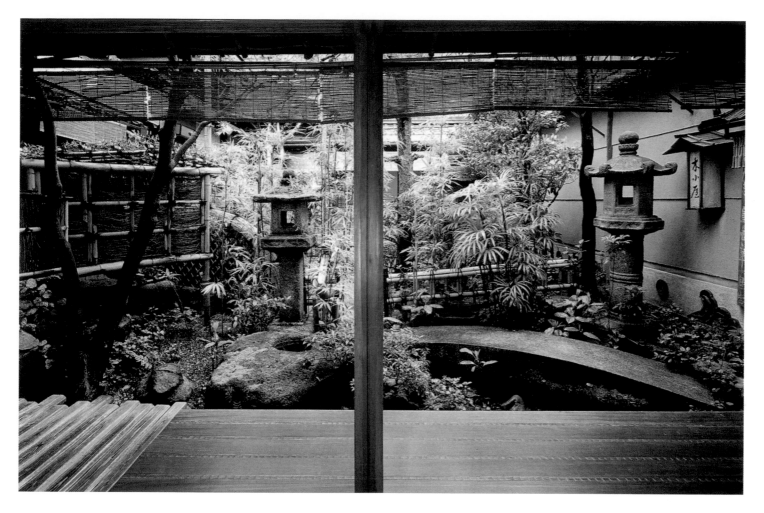

knowledge of tea and possession of tea objects (including a tea room and garden) were as essential for the chōnin as poetry skills were for the Heian courtier. Because of this, most tsubo gardens developed in a "tea" style, they had lanterns, water lavers, and even stepping stones, whether they actually led to a teahouse or not. Influenced by the physical constraints of the space, the designers created gardens that were rarefied versions of tea gardens. Some of the most striking examples contain only the most essential elements—a shallow water basin, a stone candleholder, or a small clump of bamboo.

The layering of elements lends depth to the garden. Toriiwarō Inn, Kyoto

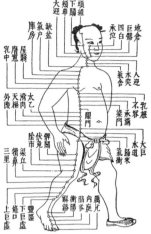

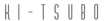

The word tsubo itself suggests a new interpretation of the gardens. The character usually used to write tsubo (坪) refers to a measurement of area—about 3.3 square meters, the size of two tatami mats. Tsubo is the standard measurement for houses or property (except for large agricultural lots that use a bigger unit). Some tsubo gardens are actually one tsubo in size, a few are even smaller, but the majority are several tsubo in size.

Another way to write tsubo is with the character that means a ceramic vessel (壺), like the ones the Chinese mystics used for meditation. This character adds new dimension to the gardens: not simply as *small*, but as three-dimensional spaces—volumes enclosed by the walls of the building with an earthen floor and a lip formed by the projecting wooden eaves. Within this "vessel" the garden is contained like a jewel in a box.

Both of these readings of tsubo are still commonly used. Architects tend to write the first character on their plans and the second character shows up more often in literary descriptions of the garden. Yet there is a third way to write tsubo(経穴)which introduces a metaphysical interpretation. Most Asian countries influenced by Chinese thought regard life as imbued with *ki* (Chinese: *chi*), a "life energy" that pervades all things. The movement of ki through the human body has been studied for centuries and drawn onto charts as a series of lines resembling the nervous system—along these lines of flow are special points that can be utilized to reinvigorate the flow of ki. In Japanese these points are also called tsubo. Finger-pressure massage (*shiatsu*), acupuncture (*hari*), and moxa (*okyū*) are all techniques that utilize body tsubo to affect ki; either opening a blockage or rebalancing a disrupted flow.

A building is like a body: the daily life of the occupants is the flow of ki within. Even as there are tsubo in the body, they exist in a building as well. In the Japanese house the *tokonoma* (appreciating artwork), the *genkan* (entry and greeting guests), and the garden (sensory pleasure) are centers of ki; places of refreshment. By this interpretation the tsubo garden is seen as a vessel for ki. The homeowner introduces ki through the daily care of the garden and, in return, receives ki from the garden in the form of rejuvenating pleasure.

Above: A chart of ki *pathways in the body.*

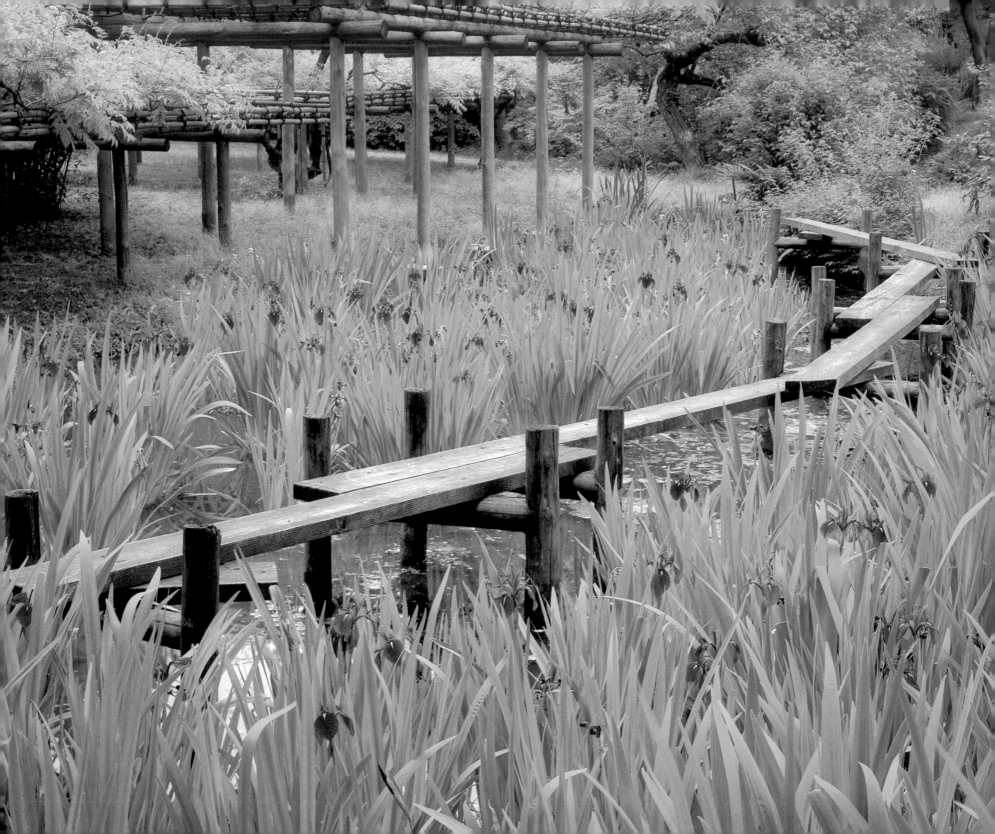

E D O   S T R O L L   G A R D E N S

The art of gardening had existed in Japan for over a thousand years by the time the Edo-period *daimyō* (military lords) began building large, richly landscaped parks called stroll gardens. Acutely aware of their own culture, both past and present, they purposefully set out to collect all manner of cultural images and assemble them in their gardens. The institutionalization of the daimyō system, by which the central government in Edo controlled the provinces throughout Japan, was the social change that led to the development of the stroll gardens. Culturally, the stroll gardens were influenced primarily by the tea ceremony, but also by an interesting blend of intellectual sophistication and spirited playfulness—the former derived from the daimyō's classical, Confucian-based education and the latter a result of the pervasive effects of the chōnin's dynamic culture. Physically, the form of these gardens was most influenced by the broad, open spaces in which they were built.

*Left: Plank bridges (*yatsuhashi*) create a romantic, pastoral scene. This large garden contains mountain, river valley, field, and ocean scenes; the bridge is part of the field scene.*
Koishikawa Kōrakuen,
Tokyo

Below: Two stones, perhaps of Korean origin, representing Yin, left, and Yang.
Ritsurin Kōen,
Kagawa

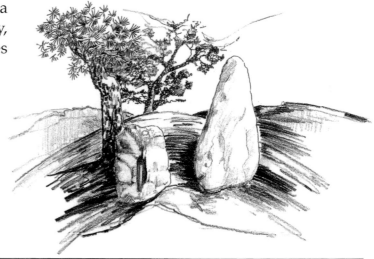

Society and Politics

The Edo period was marked by urbanization and a growth in importance of the *chōnin*, yet another, equally important development was the daimyō system which was central to the strength of the Tokugawa shogunate. Tokugawa Ieyasu was the first shōgun in a line that would last for nearly 270 years. His two successors were extremely effective in instituting a socio-political system that would allow for that extended period of control. The government of the time was known as *baku-han*, in which *baku* refers to the central government (*bakafu*) and *han* to the provinces. The overlords of the provinces were the daimyō, who were granted the right to rule their lands by the grace of the shōgun.[1] During the first years of the shogunate there was much debate over who would remain daimyō and which province they would oversee. Eventually, the number of daimyō stabilized at around 250.

The means of controlling such numerous potential opponents was accomplished through a complex series of laws that carefully balanced rewards with restrictions. The central law among these was *sankin kōtai*, or alternate attendance, which required each daimyō to maintain, along with his estates and castle in the provinces, residences in Edo at which his presence was required.[2] He was allowed to return to his home province at periodic intervals but his family stayed behind, effectively as hostages. The requirement of double residences, aside from providing a polite way to keep "captives" within Edo, succeeded in diverting excess energy and money that a daimyō might otherwise feed into insurrection. The whole system finally had the effect of creating a very stable, if restrictive, society. This social stability allowed for the construction of large gardens by providing a time of peace during which gardens could be given serious attention, free from wanton destruction. A succession of family owners cared for and extended gardens inherited from ancestors, propagating a nonviolent rivalry at work behind the gardens. The daimyō, unable to expand their own position or shake off the yoke of the shogunate by force, contended with one another through material possessions and cultural expressions.

Social developments of the time influenced the function of the gardens. The daimyō was a political leader, a bureaucrat in charge of his province; his residence doubled as his political seat from which he conducted the business of state. When there were visits from the shōgun or a noble prince who was on his way to or from the capital, the daimyō estates provided a place to rest. The gardens were used to entertain guests as well as to

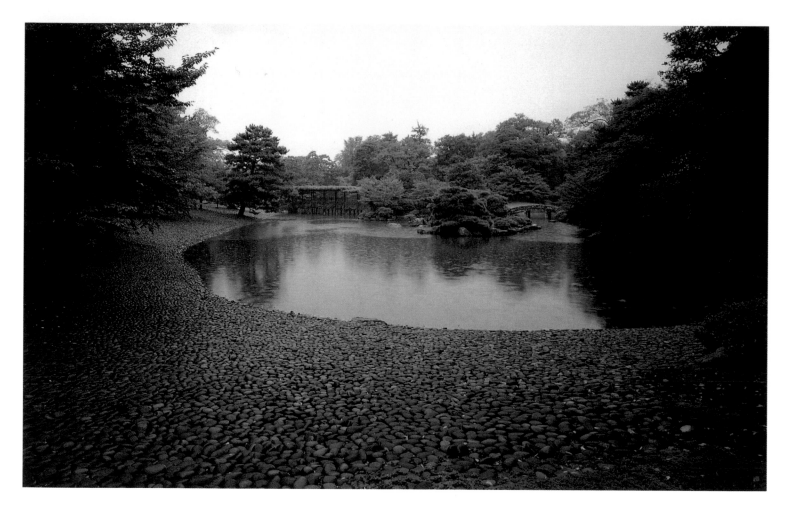

impress them with the wealth and station of the daimyō. In all, the strongest overriding quality of the Edo stroll gardens was their social function—as entertainment parks.

It should be noted, however, that the daimyō were not the only ones who had large estates with stroll gardens; quite a few gardens were constructed by members of the imperial family. The allotment of lands to the imperial family amounted to only one half of one percent of the national total, but there were other stipends to support them. Shugakuin Rikyū, Katsura Rikyū, and the Sentō Gosho in Kyoto and Hama Rikyū in Tokyo are some of the best examples of aristocratic stroll gardens.

Some of the most refined gardens of the Edo period were built by aristocrats. This beach scene was made of small rounded stones, all of which are almost identical in size, shape and color.
Sentō Gosho,
Kyoto

PROFESSIONAL GARDENERS

In the strictly hierarchical society of the Edo period, the provincial governors (*daimyō*) held the highest station. Over a period of many generations, the daimyō designed and built large stroll gardens on their country estates as well as on the properties they were required to maintain within Edo (present-day Tokyo). At the same time, urban merchants (who, despite their wealth, were ranked at the bottom of the social hierarchy) were creating tiny courtyard gardens (*tsubo niwa*) within the narrow confines of their town houses. Both stroll gardens and tsubo gardens were designed with the tea gardens as a model.

Although the daimyō and the merchants undoubtedly took a personal interest in the gardens on their properties, with regard to the designers of gardens during the Edo period, of more lasting importance was the development of a class of professional gardeners (*ueki-ya*).[8] In contrast to the *ishitate-sō* (who were priests first) or the *kawara-mono* (who performed a variety of labor), the ueki-ya were a group of lay-people who did garden work exclusively as a means of earning a living. The ueki-ya served both the daimyō and the merchants, and it is difficult to know to what degree the design of the gardens from the Edo period should be credited to the owners of the gardens or the ueki-ya who built them.

The Edo period also witnessed a division by specialization within the gardening trade: those who grew plants for sale (or specialized in collecting them from the wild), those who built gardens, and so on.[9] The term ueki-ya is still in use today, implying that the Edo period was the beginning of the practice of garden design and construction as it exists today.

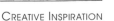

Cultural Development

In comparison with the chōnin who at this time were forming a new and vital culture, the samurai were steeping themselves in the classics. The shogunate, having organized the nation into a unified state for the first time, aimed to keep it that way, and Confucianism, with its focus on a stable society through hierarchy and status quo, was the perfect ideology. Martial arts were, of course, part of the regimen of samurai life but increasingly the samurai's role as warrior was becoming unnecessary and, since having a restless body of well-armed and highly trained men was dangerous, their actual military capability was encouraged less and less by the central government. Despite class separation in Edo society the samurai gradually mixed with the chōnin, especially the merchants. The samurai, enamored of the merchants' extravagant life-style (and often in debt to them as well), often found themselves in mixed company. The cultural world of the Edo daimyō came to exemplify a mix of both worlds, and the resulting blend of classicism and proletariat flair was to form the basis for the design of the stroll gardens.

Another cultural phenomenon during the Edo period which influenced garden design was the increasing interest in pilgrimages. There were restrictions on travel initiated by the central government in order to physically buffer their own position in Edo, including a series of barriers and requisite passports. One way to obtain a travel visa was to join an organized pilgrimage which offered an opportunity for as much sightseeing as praying. The stories of the sights that pilgrims had seen during a pilgrimage became as well known as any local landscape. These stories were reinforced by another cultural attribute of the Edo period: the extensive use of the woodblock print. Although woodblock printing had been used since before the Heian period, Edo craftsmen instigated a revolution in terms of technique, design, and subject matter. The strong interest in travel (restrictions invariably adding to the appeal) explains the popularity of publications regarding famous places to be seen throughout Japan, including scenes of Kyoto, Tokyo, and the long, perilous Tokaido road that connected the two.

THE PHYSICAL SETTING

An important factor that shaped the stroll gardens was the size of the properties they were built on, many being the provincial estates of daimyō who had extensive holdings. The gardens of the Heian-period shinden residences may have covered about 4,500 square meters—one third of an average lot of one *chō*. In comparison, the Edo stroll gardens were often 50,000 to 100,000 square meters or larger. Even the estates within the city of Edo itself were far less constricted than their predecessors in Kyoto. This spaciousness, whether in the provinces or in Edo, allowed the designers to construct sprawling gardens that previously had been rarely achieved in Japan.

The designs were not so grandiose at first, but over the course of time, with successive additions by descendants, the gardens took on immense proportions. As they extended the gardens, the designers often incorporated outlying areas within the overall plan of the garden. This added two interesting dimensions to the garden as surrounding farmland and religious sites were incorporated into the garden itself. Farmland was sometimes left as such and cultivated not only for the produce it would yield but also specifically for the pastoral vista (*nōson fukei*) it would provide. Plum plantations, for example, were a favorite among the daimyō, and the builder of Katsura Rikyū, an aristocratic estate outside of Kyoto, apparently built one teahouse (no longer extant) that was called the "little teahouse in the melon patch."

The inclusion of religious sites added a new, social dimension to the garden. The Japanese countryside was peppered with ancient shrines and local deities which were regularly prayed to and furnished with offerings such as flowers, incense, or water. In particular there were many statues of Jizo, a popular *bodhisattva*, commonly found along pathways and roads and associated with the safety of travelers and the protection of children. When the deities became part of a daimyō's estate they were cut off from the local people who cared for them. As a result, certain days were set aside when the local people (usually only men over eighteen) would be allowed to enter the daimyō's garden to make offerings and prayers. Often these groups would be allowed to stay on and enjoy the garden, or some parts of it at least. In this way, the garden became partially open to commoners, although to say they were "publicly accessible" would be inaccurate.[3]

KOISHIKAWA KŌRAKUEN, TOKYO
Redrawn from guidebook map dated 1923

1. In (YIN) STONE
2. LOTUS POND
3. YŌ (YANG) STONE
4. CHINESE-STYLE GATE
5. HŌRAI ISLAND
6. BOAT DOCK
7. PINE MEADOW
8. TEAHOUSE
9. PADDIES
10. ARBOR
11. YATSUHASHI, IRIS & WISTERIA
12. PLUM ORCHARD
13. PAGODA
14. ENGETSU-KYŌ
15. TEAHOUSES
16. TSŪTENBASHI
17. KANNON
18. LITTLE LU-SHAN
19. OI RIVER
20. FOLDING-SCREEN ROCK
21. TOGETSU-KYŌ
22. DIKE FROM THE WESTERN LAKE

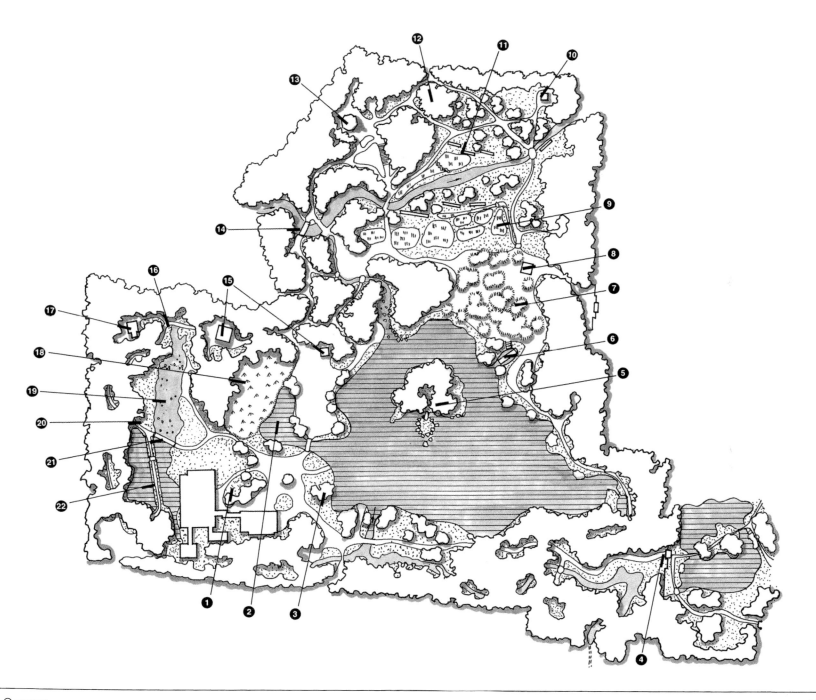

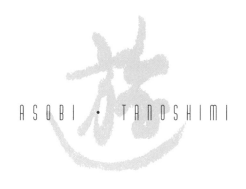

ASOBI・TANOSHIMI

AESTHETICS

Two terms used in relation to the daimyō gardens are *asobi* (play or playfulness) and *tanoshimi* (fun). That asobi and tanoshimi were used by the daimyō at all is interesting; initially these were expressions of the chōnin. The gardens of the earlier medieval period were not used for such common pleasures or referred to in such terms. In contrast, cultural life for the Edo-period daimyō was a peculiar mix, blending classic Sino-Japanese ideas with the more dynamic qualities of chōnin culture. The stroll gardens were used for entertainment—cherry-blossom viewing, playing by the water's edge, and strolls in the woods—pastimes originally associated with chōnin life.[4]

In addition to asobi and tanoshimi, other words used to describe the stroll garden , such as *utsukushii* (beautiful), *kirei* (pretty), *kimochi ga yoi* (feels nice) are ones that are in common usage today and illustrates the closeness between modern aesthetics and those of the Edo period. Utsukushii, for instance, as used in the *Man'yōshū*, meant something like "lovable."[5] By the Edo period this word evolved into "beautiful," the same meaning it has today, revealing that the sensibilities of the people in the Edo period, as opposed to those of the ancient periods, were not so different from our own.

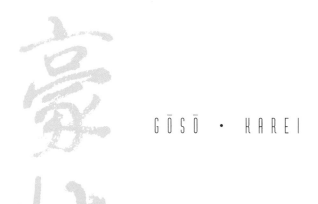

GŌSŌ・KAREI

Two other terms used by the daimyō to describe the garden, *gōsō* (splendor, grandeur) and *karei* (magnificent, gorgeous), betray two cultural concerns of the daimyō: an interest in sumptuousness and luxuriousness that overrode the undercurrent of subdued tea aesthetics; and, since both words are the Sino-Japanese form, they also reveal the affection of the daimyō for things Chinese.

In general, the Edo stroll gardens stressed aesthetics rather than religious matters. Religious practices were carefully controlled under Edo regulations; consequently, it was not a time of vigorous religious growth. Even though Buddhism and Shintō persisted in the hearts of the Japanese people, they were not creative forces in the arts.

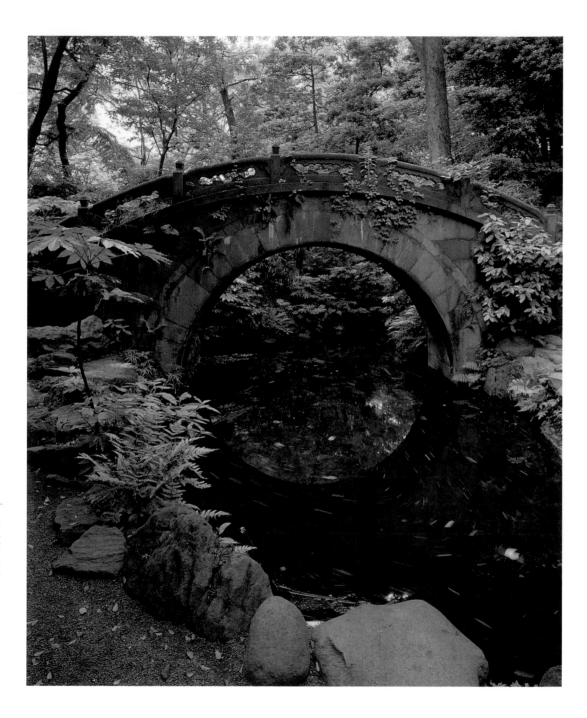

This curved bridge, named Engetsu-kyō,
Bridge of the Round Moon,
is a typical Chinese motif.
Koishikawa Kōrakuen,
Tokyo

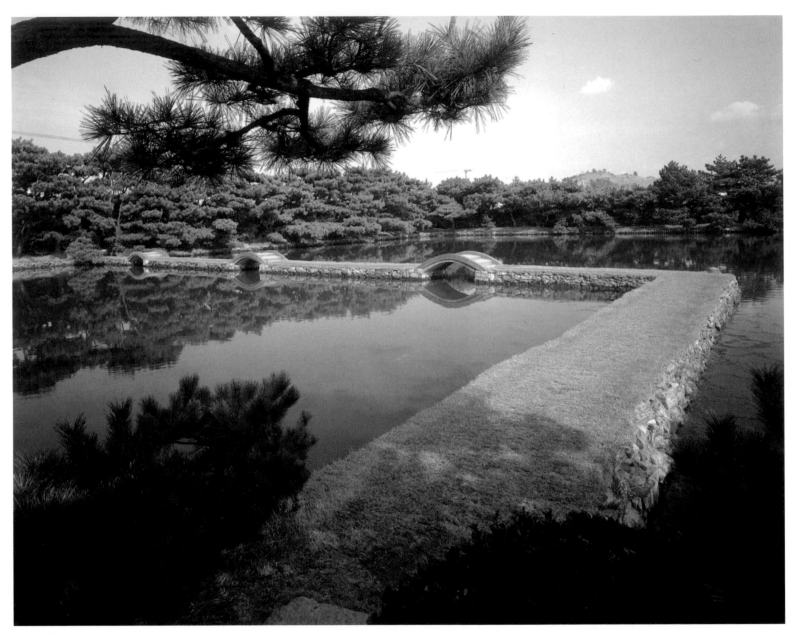

The dike that runs through the Western Lake in Hangzhou, China, well known in Edo times through paintings and literature, is re-created here in miniature. Yōsui-en, Wakayama

THE STROLL GARDENS

The combination of large land holdings allowing for spacious estates, the leisured life of the daimyō and nobles, the general stability of the era, and the interest in travel, created the basis for the stroll gardens of the Edo period. Most of the gardens began as small tea gardens, a requisite feature of a cultured well-to-do household. Over time one teahouse became two, and so on, until an entire collection of teahouses had been strung together in a large parklike setting.

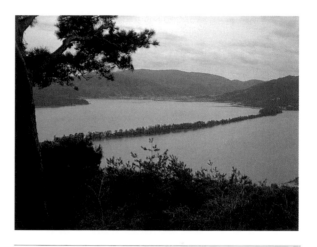

Ama-no-hashidate, the "bridge to heaven," on the Japan Sea coast.

These large gardens are usually called "stroll gardens" because they are meant to be walked around, rather than viewed from a veranda or while on a boat. In the Edo period these gardens were simply called *yashiki*, a general term for a luxurious home, both house and garden together. The modern Japanese term for the garden style, *kaiyūshiki teien* or excursion-style garden, hints at the designer's intent—to provide guest with a large, beautifully landscaped park within which to take an excursion. Designers accordingly built any number of scenes into the garden, collected as it were from the vast repository of common cultural imagery. Famous scenic places from Japan and China were favorite models, as were poetic allusions, usually taken from the Heian-period classics. Designers "collected" these images as if they were sculptures to be set out in the garden, and then blended them into a comprehensive whole. The views were carefully controlled so that while strolling about the gardens along a meandering path, one went from one scene to the next as if moving through the layered backdrops of a stage set. In turn, each scene is revealed and then concealed to be appreciated again much later from a different vantage point. The following examples will give some idea of the variety of images that were collected.

JAPANESE LANDSCAPE SCENES

Mount Fuji is a classic example of a famous Japanese scene, and Fuji-style (volcanic-shaped) mountains play an integral part in many gardens. The best surviving example is in Kumamoto, at Suizen-ji, where clipped grass swells up in a vast pointed mound. Mount Fuji was the subject of many woodblock prints including the famous *Thirty-six Views of Mount Fuji* by Utagawa Hiroshige. Although Mount Fuji would be well known to a daimyō from western Japan and his entourage—who would have passed it while traveling back and forth to the capital—even local vassals might have known the image from the available woodblock prints. Another famous image of the Japanese landscape, known

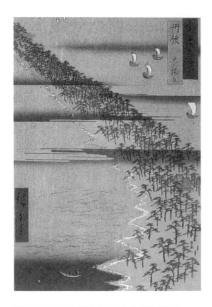

*Woodblock prints popularized
famous scenes from around Japan.
Above,* Ama-no-hashidate
by Utagawa Hiroshige.
Hiraki Museum, Yokohama

best from literature, is that of the Eight Bridges, *yatsuhashi*, a scenic spot where a river branched into eight channels as mentioned in *The Tales of Ise*, a tenth-century anthology of poems.[6] This larger scene is reconstructed in the garden as a bridge made of eight thick planks of wood.

SCENES OF KYOTO

The hillsides of Arashiyama, covered with maples and cherries that cascade down to the Oi River, was a popular image as was Togetsu-kyō, the long wooden bridge that crosses the Oi River near Arashiyama. Images of Arashiyama were used in several gardens including Koishikawa Kōrakuen, where we also find a recreated scene of Tsūten-bashi, a bridge that crosses a deep gorge lined with maples at the temple Tōfuku-ji in southern Kyoto.

SCENES FROM CHINA

The dike that runs through the Western Lake in Hangzhou, China, appears to be a favorite image and shows up in Koishikawa Kōrakuen and Shiba Rikyū in Tokyo, as well as in Yosui-en in Wakayama and Shukkeien in Hiroshima.[7] Engetsu-kyō and Koko-kyō, both curved, Chinese-style bridges, are to be found at Koishikawa Kōrakuen and Shukkei-en, respectively. Little Mount Lu, a Buddhist pilgimage site and one of the famous scenic mountains of China, is found at Koishikawa Kōrakuen in the form of a small hill covered with grass bamboo (*sasa*).

YIN - YANG

Images of Yin and Yang (in Japanese *in* and *yō*), the negative and positive forces of Chinese geomancy, were usually represented with two stones—a "female" with an appropriate natural fold or crevasse as part of its shape and a long, upright "male." In Edo-period gardens it is doubtful that these were actually believed to possess supernatural powers, geomancy having lost much of its influence on society by the Edo period. Instead, they were used as sculptural artifacts.

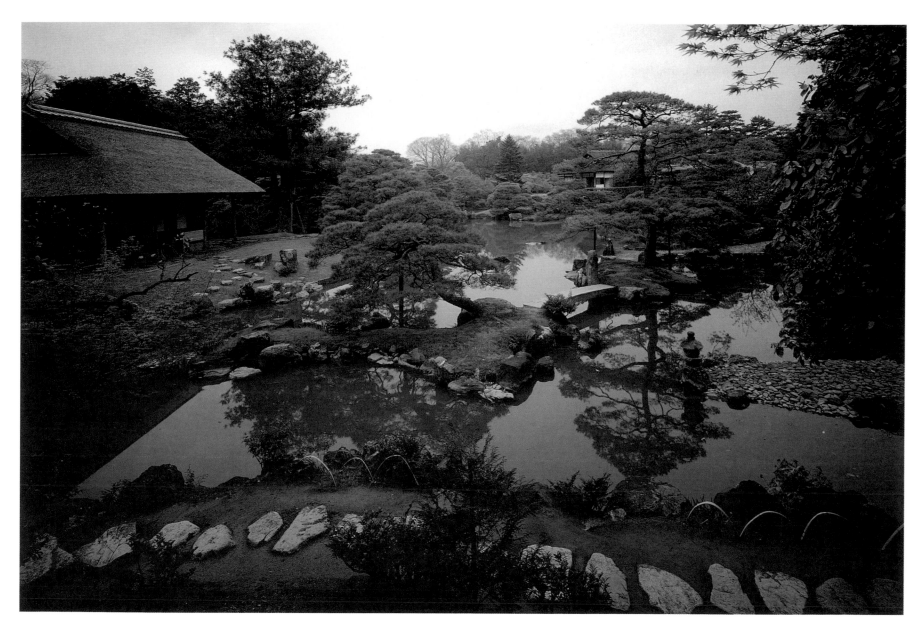

Ama-no-hashidate re-created as the spit of land in the foreground. Katsura Detached Palace, Kyoto

STEREOTYPICAL STONE IMAGERY

Many of the images that were created in the ancient and medieval gardens with stones, such as the mystical mountains Hōrai and Shumisen or the triad groupings that represent a Buddhist trinity, are also found in Edo stroll gardens. It is not likely these had any strong religious significance to the owners of, or visitors to, the gardens, but rather were simply among the various artifacts being collected by the garden owner.

POETRY

Images from well-known poems were a common theme for stroll gardens. Rikugi-en in Tokyo had as the basis for its design 88 scenes from famous *waka* (Japanese poetry). Only a handful of the original scenes remain extant in the garden but the tastes of the original owner are revealed in his choice of poetry as a central design theme. Still, there is a difference in quality between the way poetry was connected to Heian gardens and its role in the Edo stroll gardens, which seem to include poetic scenes with more artifice or deliberateness, like paintings hung at a museum.

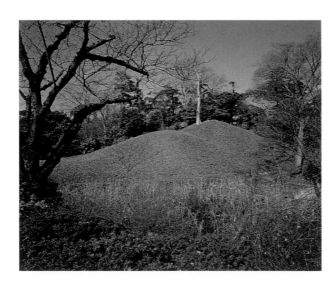

Mount Lu, a Buddhist pilgrimage site in China, represented as a hill covered with grass bamboo.
Koishikawa Kōrakuen, Tokyo

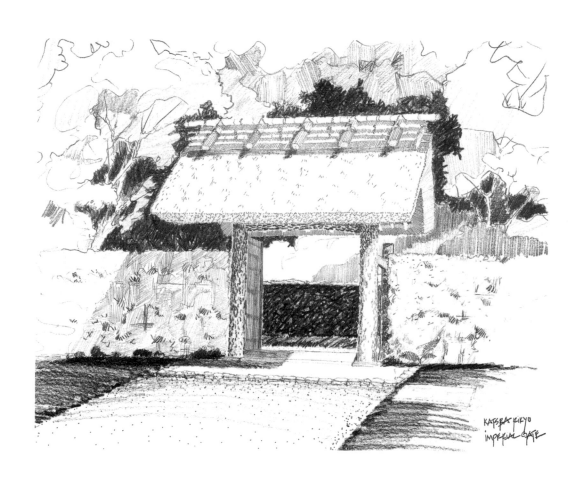

KATSRA KIKYO
IMPERIAL GATE

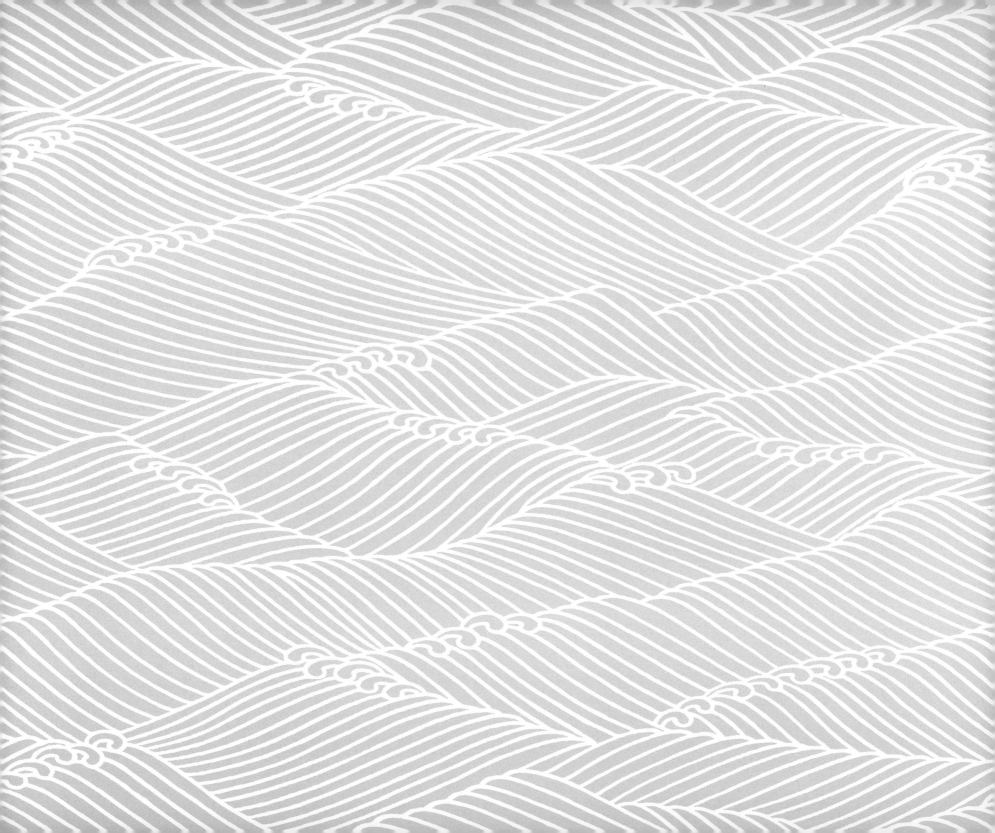

DESIGN

Gardening in Japan has always been a form of artistic expression using nature imagery as a vehicle. Very much like painting or sculpture, gardening is a means of giving physical, sensory form to emotional or spiritual matters. Although gardening is not purely an intellectual pursuit, highly developed theories of the art have nevertheless been detailed in treatises dating back as far as the eleventh century. Garden design, as is true of all the other Japanese arts, is not taught directly; instead, skills are "acquired" over the course of time spent working as an apprentice to a master, primarily by example rather than oral instruction. The process of learning by assimilation may well have existed before the influence of Zen Buddhism but it was certainly reinforced by the Zen sect's inherent distrust of the spoken word and emphasis on "direct transmission" of ideas through action.

Garden design can be broken down into three components: design principles, design techniques, and design elements. Design principles are the guiding ideas by which a garden is constructed—the fundamental spirit the designer hopes to express. Design techniques are the methods by which principles are given form in the garden, and the elements are the physical parts that are used. Another way to express this concept would be that the design principles address the question why design a garden; the techniques, how to design a garden; and the elements, what to design a garden with?

This elementary analysis gives a rational handhold with which to grasp the meaning of design but it must be remembered that it is only a way of understanding—not the design process itself. Design principles and techniques are not foregrounded or used to systematically build gardens; instead, during the course of an apprenticeship, the student is exposed to all three aspects of design. The student indirectly absorbs these lessons and, when they are finally digested, utilizes them unconsciously to build a garden.

Of the three components of design—principles, techniques, and elements—it is the elements that are the most superficial or, let us say, the most "exposed." Because of this exposure, the elements—moss and twisted pines, rocks and white sand, stone lanterns and stepping stones—are the best known and most often associated with the Japanese garden. These stereotypical elements are not, in fact, requisite for making a garden in the Japanese way.

When trying to re-create a garden in an alien cultural or physical climate, importation of the elements alone will only succeed in making a garden "Japanesque," what might be called Japanese style (wa-fu); whereas, with a clearer understanding of Japanese design principles and techniques, one can create a garden with a truer Japanese spirit (wa-shin).[1] Without traditional elements a garden might not even look Japanese at first glance but can still have the harmony and subdued beauty that is most attractive in Japanese gardens. This is not to say that to include traditional elements is wrong, but simply of lesser importance, and avoidable altogether if one so chooses.

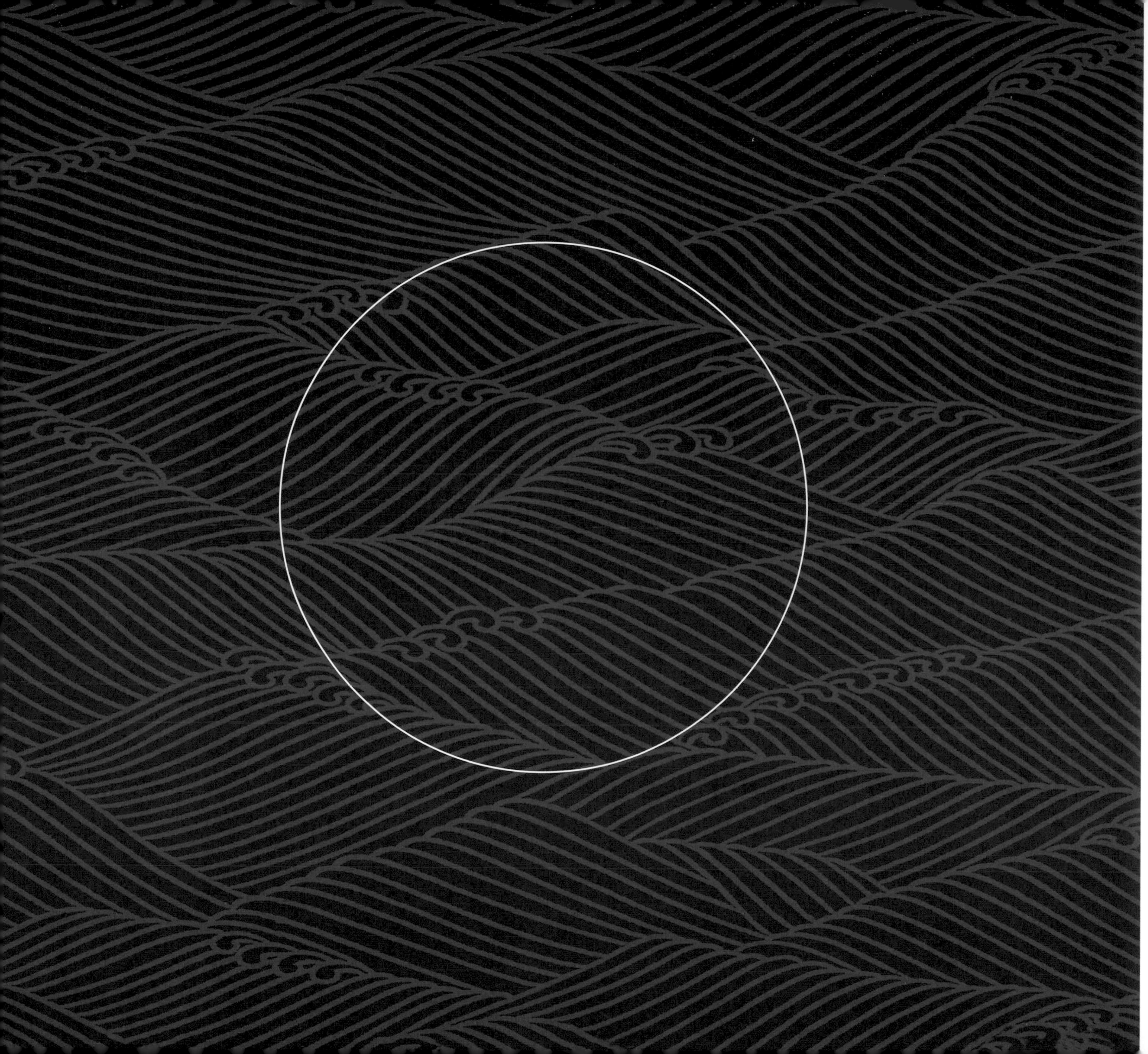

Design Principles

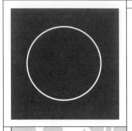

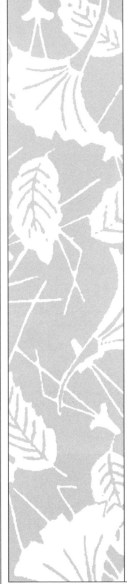

WHY GARDEN? A FUNDAMENTAL QUESTION YET ONE THAT IS HARDLY EVER ADDRESSED. MOST GARDEN DESIGNERS SIMPLY WORK WITHIN THE FRAMEWORK GIVEN BY THEIR SOCIETY. THEIR WORK IS MOSTLY A REPRODUCTION OF ACCEPTED STYLES OR PERHAPS A CLEVER ADJUSTMENT OF VARIOUS DESIGN TECHNIQUES OR ELEMENTS TO CREATE "NEW" FORMS. THE PRINCIPLES OF GARDENING, HAVING LONG SINCE BEEN INCORPORATED INTO A TRADITION, ARE RARELY RECONSIDERED—ESPECIALLY THE FUNDAMENTAL IDEA OF WHAT IS TRYING TO BE EXPRESSED IN A GARDEN. THIS IS THE STORY OF ANY CULTURE: A CREATIVE PERSON BRINGS TO LIFE SOMETHING NEW TO BE FOLLOWED BY THOSE WHO ARE MORE INCLINED TO IMITATE THAN INITIATE. THE FOLLOWERS IN TURN PRIMP AND POLISH, CODIFY, AND INSTITUTIONALIZE THE ORIGINAL IDEA. WITHOUT SUCH A FOLLOWING, NEW IDEAS WOULD DISAPPEAR WITH THEIR CREATORS AND NEVER BECOME TRADITIONAL. LOOKING AT A FOREIGN CULTURE AS A SOURCE OF INSPIRATION, HOWEVER, ONE FINDS THAT THE TRADITIONS OF THAT SOCIETY ARE NOT GIVEN; ADDRESSING THE FUNDAMENTAL PRINCIPLES OF DESIGN IS NOT ONLY APPROPRIATE, IT IS ESSENTIAL.

The gardens of Japan are works of art that use nature as a material of creation. The first and foremost design principle, therefore, is to learn from nature. On the other hand, a complementary principle would be, do not copy nature—interpret it. Both of these principles are as old as gardening is in Japan and can even be found included in the overall principles of gardening detailed in the *Sakuteiki*:

Recall the vistas of various famous places, select what attracts you and add your own interpretation. It is best to use this as a theme to design the whole of the garden while adding just the right amount of changes.[1]

While Japanese garden designers derive inspiration from nature, the gardens they create are not "natural" or wild. Nature in the garden is reinterpreted, rarefied, and abstracted so that what is created is not nature per se, but an idealized vision of nature or the essence of nature—its rhythms and forms. Recreating nature in toto is not the goal of a garden designer; that would be acceptable for a botanical garden or biosphere where the study of natural ecosystems is the focus. The garden is a work of art through which the gardener attempts to create beauty or express emotional or spiritual values.

The designer's intention in studying nature is not imitation but rather appreciation of the lessons that nature holds about life, the cosmos, and man's place in the whole scheme of things. For example, the way water moves through a landscape illustrates the "paths of least resistance"; the shape of windswept pines speaks of perseverance; bamboo and grasses that bend with the wind reveal the power of resilience; and the evanescence of life is seen in the endless cycle of changing seasons. The organic complexity of even the simplest thing—the delicate branching pattern of a mountain azalea or the sculptural construction of a lotus flower—reminds us that there "is more in heaven and earth than is dreamt of in our philosophy."

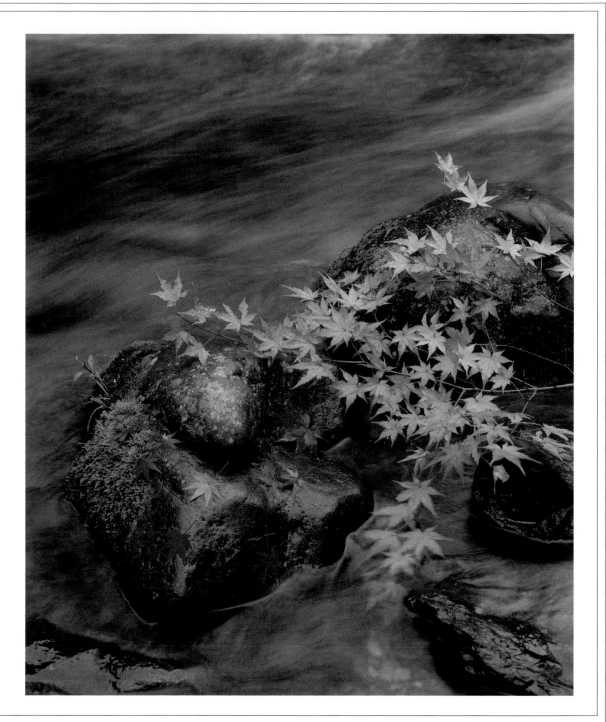

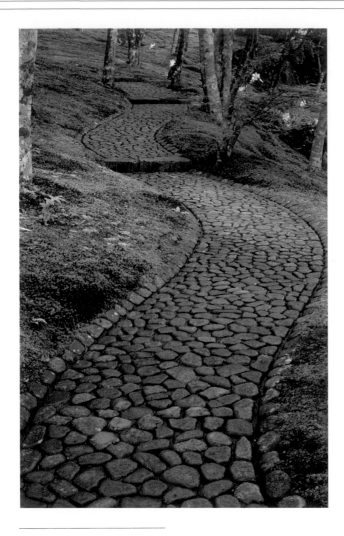

A precise pathway cutting through a soft bed of moss: the juxtaposition of man's hand on nature
Hakone Museum, Shizuoka

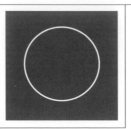

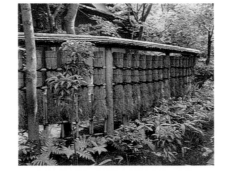

Fences combine natural materials, in this case bamboo twigs, in a clearly man-made form.
Kibune, Kyoto

WILDNESS AND CONTROL

The innumerable themes in Japanese garden design, like those in the poems of Japan, are represented in images of wild nature. Where poets use words, nature images in the gardens are expressed through the controlling hand of the gardener. Striking a harmonic balance between wildness and control of that wildness, between the beauty of nature and that of man-made things, becomes a fundamental concern of the gardener.

Since nature in Japan can rage with untold fury—typhoons, floods, earthquakes, and tidal waves—living with nature means controlling it. Japanese gardens reflect this control but they also display the pacifying influence of Buddhism, which sees man as an integral part of nature, and of the native Shintō religion whose gods inhabit nature. The dichotomy of awe and respect on the one hand, and the need to control nature on the other, fuses within the garden to create a single harmonic aesthetic. This effect is most easily seen in the treatment of plantings whose forms are stylized derivations of natural images—windswept pines, craggy old plums—which are created and maintained very deliberately by the gardener. Japanese gardens are particularly dependent on control, which is why they require so much intensive maintenance.

The juxtaposition of man's hand on nature is also evident in the design of garden elements, for instance, fences. Fencing material will often be used in its natural state, or in a way that draws upon and enhances a natural characteristic, but in the end the fence remains a clearly man-made object. Another example is water lavers (*chōzubachi*) which were first used in tea gardens and are now ubiquitous throughout Japanese gardens. A large natural stone, a river rock or boulder from the seashore that has a sculptural form and a delightfully touchable "skin," will have a basin carved in its top that is precise and clean, the interjection of man's hand on a natural object.[2] Precise pathways cutting through a soft bed of moss, weeping cherries seen through the grid of umbrella trellises, an earthen wall amid a stand of grand old cypress trees—the list is endless.

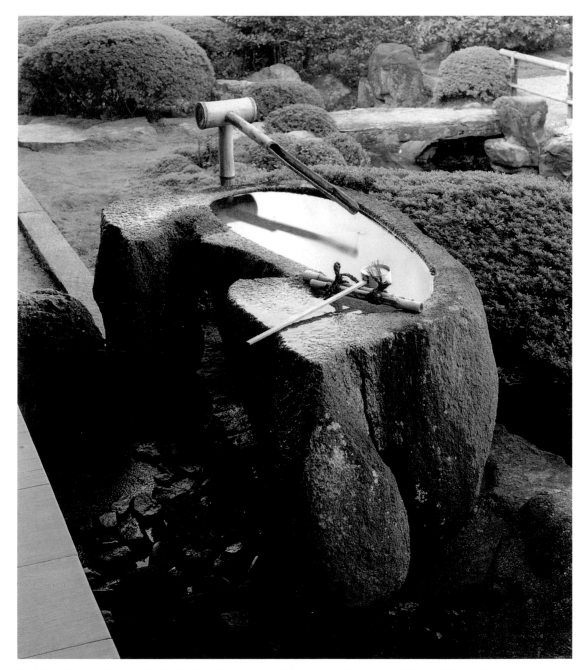

Man's hand impressed on a natural object: a crisp basin carved into a naturally sculptural stone.   Jōju-in, Kyoto

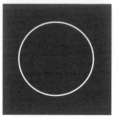

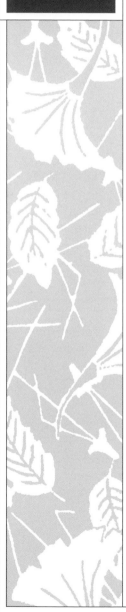

THE SEASONS

Arguably there are two kinds of gardens in the world: those built in harsh climates to provide physical relief, and those built in relatively temperate zones which accentuate and revel in local surroundings. Japanese gardens are most emphatically of the latter variety. The Japanese archipelago is a diverse ecological environment. The Japanese pride themselves on having four distinct seasons, *shiki*, which many (untraveled) Japanese consider unique to Japan. The truth, of course, is that there are many places around the world with four seasons and many places within Japan—to the north and south—without. In fact, only the central region from Kyoto to Tokyo has the quintessential four seasons which smoothly blend into one another so that practically each month has its own distinct feeling. The incorporation of the seasons in all their abundance and subtlety into garden design is a primary consideration, but it could be said more properly that keen attention to the intricacies of the natural world is the dominant consideration of gardening in the Japanese way, no matter how many seasons.

There is an adage that the only permanent thing in our world is change itself. The acceptance of change as intrinsic to the nature of existence in "this world" was expressed in the Heian aesthetic *mujōkan*—a reveling in the ephemeral—and has since become a principle influencing many of Japan's arts. The change of the seasons is an apt vehicle for visualizing this concept and it has long since become a standard motif in poetry, painting, and of course gardening.

The exquisite light green of new leaves, almost transparent and luminescent in the sunlight, is a sign of spring as is the scent of the sweet daphne and the great blush of color the cherries bring. Cherries have become synonymous with Japan—they are the quintessential flower for the Japanese as seen in the expression *hana-mi*, literally, "flower watching," which usually refers to cherries. Another spring classic is the brilliant yellow kerria, which the Heian courtiers found particularly beautiful, attested to in their poems of its pendulous branches reflected in a pond or stream.

The first inklings of summer come with

the blooming of the wisteria, iris, and azaleas, and then as the season progresses, the brilliant blue bellflower (one of the few flowers that the Japanese love en masse), the sweetly fragrant gardenia, the lotus with its Buddhist connotations and the fringed pink whose light and frilly flowers are linked with the image of freshness and childhood.[3] In Heian poetry, willows, whose light branches sway with the slightest breeze and convey a sense of coolness, were a sign of summer. Summer itself is marked more than anything by intense sunlight and ponderous heat; it is the cool shade under the deep canopy of tall trees with the mesmerizing whir of the cicadas that recalls summer most.

Autumn rivals spring as the favorite season in Japan. Like spring, autumn is comfortable, but unlike that rival season, autumn has a beauty that is tinged with the sadness of passing rather than the glow of new life—giving rise to deeper sentiments. If cherries evoke spring, the maple, whose deep red hues are intense enough to color the paper doors of a nearby house, is the symbol of autumn.[4] In fact, seeing the garden indirectly through the shadow of leaves on paper is one of the rarefied aesthetics of the Japanese house. But the maple alone does not stand for autumn—bush clover was a favorite in ancient times, its scattering blooms an effective image of the tenuousness of life, as were grasses drying to pale hues.[5] The osmanthus gives a sweet, ethereal fragrance to the season before littering the ground with circles of fallen gold petals, and the daytime fuss of the cicada gives way to the peaceful concert of twilight crickets.

Chrysanthemums anticipate winter. According to *The Tale of Genji*, chrysanthemums were most attractive when viewed tinged with snow. The winter tree must be the pine. Snow, of course, is a central image for winter—snow on pines, snow on bamboo, even snow on a deciduous tree like a plum, the tufts of which are called the first flowers of the year (*hatsu-hana*). The winter scent is the witch hazel, a pleasant surprise to chilled olfactory senses.

The return to spring is completed by plants that flower at the edge of winter and continue into spring—camellia, magnolia, and most of all the plum whose gentle blooms exude a compelling sweetness that draws one closer to discover their delicate petals. The plum is an aesthetic tour de force—its scent, form, and blossom all evoking rich emotions. The plum serves as a link between winter and spring—a quality most visible in paintings. From one hoary blackened branch, a vivid symbol of agedness, springs a multitude of delicate blossoms, the picture of youth. Simultaneously, age and youth, eternity and the moment.

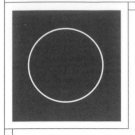

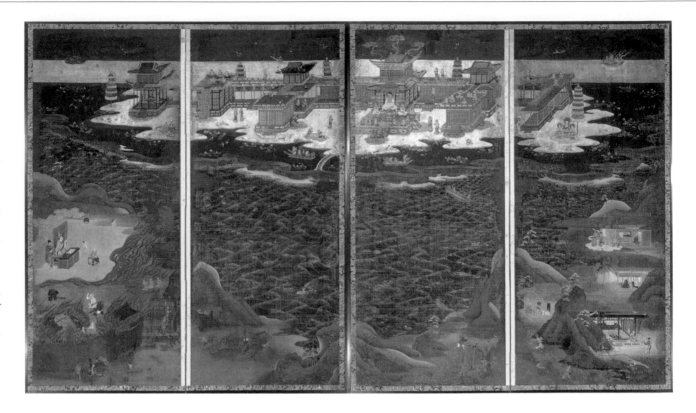

UTOPIA

Most garden design throughout the world has been devoted to the creation of the idyllic—paradise on earth or a utopian vision of man's relationship with nature. Japanese garden design is no exception. Throughout history, under the influence of various philosophies, garden designers have strived to create environments that surpass nature itself by enhancing nature's pleasant qualities while eliminating the distasteful ones.

The first gardens built in Japan—from the early-sixth or seventh century through the Heian period—were specifically created as symbols of everlasting paradise (*tokoyo-shisō*). The design of these paradise gardens was primarily derived from tales of the paradisical Pure Land of Amida Buddha, but it also included other religious images: for instance, Shumisen, the central mountain of the Buddhist cosmology; Hōrai, the islands of the Immortals; and, most likely, various images from Japan's ancient animistic religion as well. Utopian images designed into the gardens of medieval Zen temples were derived from Chinese models, such as the concept of finding the fundamental meaning of life in the splendor of wild nature as practiced by recluse Chinese philosophers. The designers of the tea gardens, the tsubo gardens, and the large stroll gardens, each in its own way, strived to create environments that, according to the social biases of their times, would be perceived as ideal.

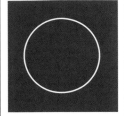

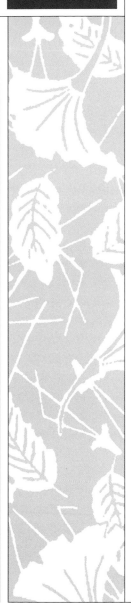

PERSONAL EXPRESSION IN TRADITION

The *Sakuteiki* expounds the following principle:

Keep close to heart the works of past masters and, giving due respect to the opinions of the client, imbue the garden with your own taste.[6]

Giving respect to the client's wishes is a priority for all garden designers; being attentive to the "works of past masters" means incorporating tradition. Japanese artists have characteristically built upon previous styles rather than replaced them —"succession rather than superposition."[7] The importance placed on hierarchy and lineage, strongly reinforced if not initiated by Confucian thought, runs deep in society as a whole. When a garden is designed without a guiding cultural spirit it can be relegated to the status of aesthetic play and may fail to convey any significant meaning to the viewer.

Ninety percent of all "designs" are "givens": aspects that are determined by the nature of the materials, the site, and climate—just to mention a few of the predominant constraints. "Given" aspects of design must simply be obeyed; water does not flow uphill, rocks fall over if not set well, and plants die when planted in the wrong place. These prerequisite factors have become incorporated into a body of knowledge that designers now call tradition. Any design must obey these factors or invite failure. Incorporating tradition does not, however, mean visionless replication of past forms. The proper sense of incorporating traditions was expressed succinctly by the seventeenth-century poet, Matsuo Basho:

Do not seek to emulate the old masters.
Seek what they sought.[8]

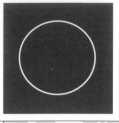

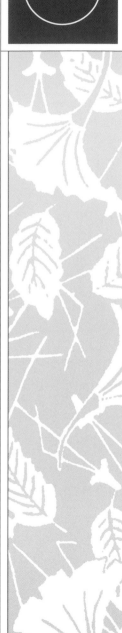

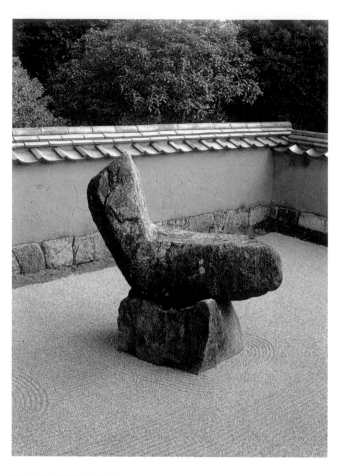

Created for lunar rituals, this garden displays
the hand of a strongly individualistic designer.
Katsura Residence,
Yamaguchi

This quotation of Basho leads us to another aspect of this design principle: the need for personal expression. Art not only reflects social and cultural values, but can also be a vehicle for individual expression. Personal style in gardening can encompass a wide variety of manifestations—indeed, as many manifestations as there are garden designers. For instance, comments on man's relationship to nature, our place in the cosmos, humor or satire—any emotion or spiritual feeling can be represented in the garden. The *Sakuteiki* stresses this point. In the opening lines of the text designers are urged, in addition to studying nature and the works of past masters, to "devise their own taste"—*waga fuzei wo megurashite*. One's taste is an endlessly evolving issue; there is no proper form or limit to the things that can be expressed within the confines of the garden.

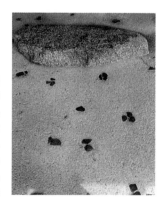

Earthen paving
embedded with an
artful pattern of one,
two, or three pebbles:
hifumi-tataki.
Shūgaku-in
Detached Palace,
Kyoto

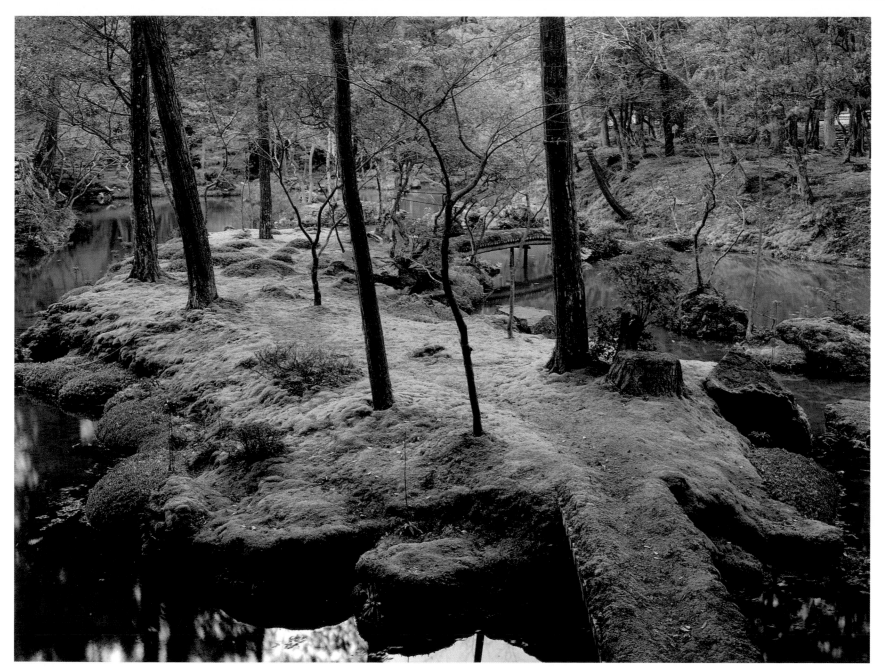

The beauty of the Japanese garden often derives from years of attentive care rather than from the brilliance of the initial design or construction. Saihōji, Kyoto

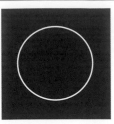

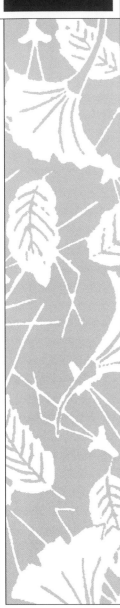

MAINTENANCE

At first glance, simple garden maintenance would not appear to qualify as a design principle. Gardens are usually seen as developing in three stages—design, construction, and maintenance—so design and maintenance would appear to be independent activities. In reality, if the degree of maintenance the client is able or willing to undertake is not considered from the beginning, the design will fail to some degree, so maintenance must be thought about at the outset as a basic consideration of the garden. In addition, a great deal of the elegance and dignity of the Japanese garden is not the result of the designer's brilliance nor the garden builder's skill, but is developed over the course of time by the caring hand that nurtures it. This patina evolves from years of care, like the wooden floors of temples, polished smooth from daily wiping.

One of the fundamental purposes of the garden is to provide a place in which it is possible to be at one with nature, its rhythms, and changing beauties. Caring for the garden is not a chore, but the very point of having the garden in the first place. If we look historically at the Japanese garden, or more specifically at the owners of gardens, we find that this relationship with the garden was rare. Until very recently, society was structured so that people of rank (and garden owners were almost always people of high rank) were "above" certain activities. Working with soil has long been considered unclean in Japan, hence garden work was unsuitable for upper classes. The gardens of Zen temples might seem an exception to this social rule, in that maintenance is part of the daily ritual of the monks who have left behind attachments to society such as rank.

The ideal of the owner caring for the garden is indeed true with regard to the tea garden. Contemporary texts extol the necessity for the host to prepare the garden before guests arrive.[9] Although the heavy work of maintenance would be left to a professional gardener, tea masters are impelled to involve themselves with the care of the garden and in doing so come in touch with the change of the seasons, which is central to the aesthetics of tea.

Design Techniques

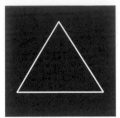

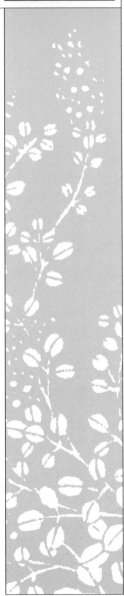

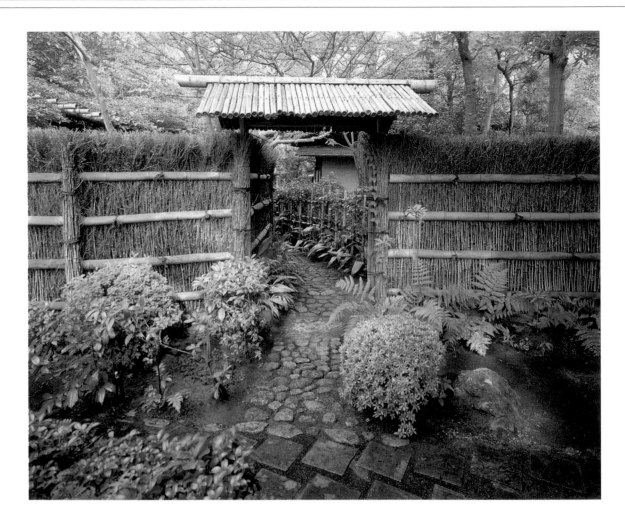

*Enclosure necessitates entries:
the outer gate to a tea garden.*
Shōkadō, Kyoto

How to design a Japanese garden lies mostly within an understanding of design techniques: how to frame a garden, or how to compose and balance the design. Through the skillful use of these techniques a designer can create a garden that feels Japanese with a wide variety of materials, both traditional and contemporary.

ENCLOSURE AND ENTRY

Japanese gardens are often considered visual objects but it is their characteristic spatial development that is fundamental to making them feel Japanese. Designers create spaces in gardens through *enclosure*—which necessitates *entries*—both of which are, in general, highly accentuated in Japan.[1] The concepts of threshold and passage are inextricably woven into the overall fabric of Japanese spatial design because they are also fundamental to the structure of Japanese society in general. Physical entries reflect and reinforce deeply ingrained social patterns. The Japanese are often considered a group-oriented people, who tend to define themselves by the groups they are members of—family, business, school, club. Entering a group, becoming a member, is an act of great social importance. These social patterns are echoed in the landscape in the form of physical enclosures and entries.

Most Japanese gardens are clearly enclosed. At times this is simply due to the compressed nature of an urban site, but more often the enclosure is used as a frame. The designer uses this frame to control how the garden will be viewed and to what degree the surroundings will be incorporated into it. If not for the enclosure, the garden would be juxtaposed against its surroundings and the subtle scale relationships within it would break down. The enclosure allows for the garden to be viewed as an independent work of art—for instance, the *kare-san-sui* of the Zen temples which are viewed like framed paintings.

Enclosure necessitates entries; it is quite common for the garden designer to introduce gates that connect the garden to the outside world as well as gates within the garden which divide it into a series of layered spaces. A good example of these divisions is seen in the stroll gardens of the Edo-period daimyō estates, within which are designed a series of changing scenic views that are revealed in succession as one moves along the garden path. Occasionally, scenes are divided by physical, wooden gates—more likely the transition is marked by a grove of trees the stroller passes through, a bend or rise in the path, or some other ephemeral "gate." Another example of the use of entry in the garden, on a drastically smaller scale, is in the tea garden—not only a physical entry, but a form of spiritual entry as well.

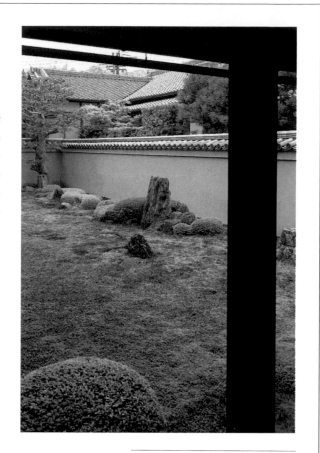

If not for the enclosure, the garden would be juxtaposed against its surroundings and the subtle scale of relationships within it would break down.
Ryōgen-in, Daitoku-ji, Kyoto

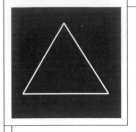

KANJI	PRONUNCIATION	LITERAL MEANING	DEFINITION
間	ma		space, time
間	aida		interval (of space or time)
間	ken		linear, one-dimensional space; the length of a tatami mat, and the standard module for architecture.
間	ma		planar, two-dimensional space; in hiro-ma, a large room for events.
空間	kukan	empty + ma	three-dimensional space
時間	jikan	time + ma	time
人間	ningen	person + ma	people

VOID AND ACCENT

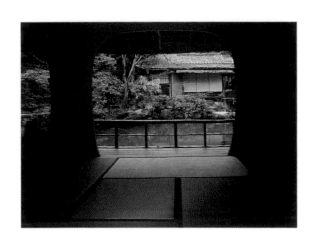

Ma is the result of events or objects that "frame out" a void and cause it to be.
Hakusasonsō, Kyoto

Right: Empty space can be used to represent the concept of mu, *nothingness, a central posit of Zen Buddhism.*
Tokai-an, Myōshin-ji, Kyoto

Another important design technique related to spatial development within gardens is the design of expressive spatial voids called *ma,* a tiny word that has complex meanings as various as space and time. Since the character for ma has several readings—*ma, aida, ken, kan,* and *gen*—the word requires a little study to properly understand. A look at the chart above will help clarify the many nuances associated with this word.

The term ma is defined as a space or void—physical, social, or related to time, or a combination of all these. Ma is the result of events or objects that "frame-out" a void and cause it *to be.* Ma is, in addition, not simply the result of these bracketing elements but the focal point itself. The punctuation of movement in Japanese dance or Noh theater, the moments of silence in Japanese music, the social distance held between host and guest during a tea ceremony, and the emptiness left in an ink painting are all discussed in terms of ma.

Garden designers create ma in a variety of ways: as a physical space experienced when moving through the garden; a visual space in a contemplation garden that is only entered with the mind; or a time /space—a pause that is created in movement through the garden to enhance one's appreciation of it. In religious terms ma is used to represent the concept of *mu,* nothingness, a central posit of Zen Buddhism. Aesthetically, designers use ma to establish *yohaku-no-bi,* the beauty of paucity that was so important to the arts of the middle ages.

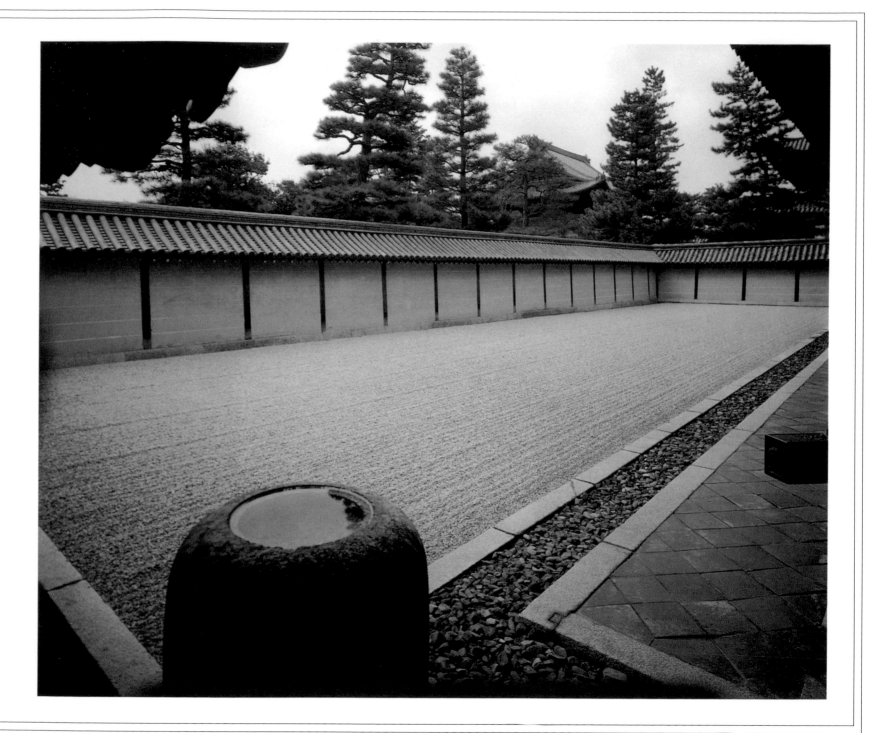

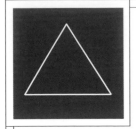

BALANCE

Balance is, along with ma, one of the most important design techniques that will lend a Japanese feeling to a garden. Balance in Japanese garden design can be described as being asymmetric, off-centered, and based on triads.

ASYMMETRY

Balance as it is used in the Japanese garden is derived from natural forms rather than man-made constructions. The Japanese are well aware of symmetry, of course; all of the early plans for temples or even cities derived from classic Chinese models were symmetrical. Symmetrical design never took hold in Japan, however, and plans for temples or cities that were initially symmetrical rapidly transformed into more haphazard, organic forms. Gardens, however, were never designed symmetrically; for many Japanese, who consider the gardens at Versaille typical of Western design, asymmetry is the essential design difference between East and West.

In the case of a contemplation garden in which the view is framed by an opening in the architecture, the garden is designed so that it will not be balanced symmetrically. Instead, the designer presents the viewer with a pleasing arrangement of forms of which no single one is absolutely dominant. Even though there is usually a hierarchy of forms, the eye is not meant to stop at the zenith but instead is always drawn back to a source to begin meandering again.

Right: The view is framed by an opening in the architecture; the garden is designed so that it will be balanced asymmetrically.
Enman-in, Shiga

Below: Even if paths are made straight, the axis of the path will be designed so that the line of sight of a person walking the path dead-ends in a wall or a hedge.
Urasenke, Konnichi-an, Kyoto

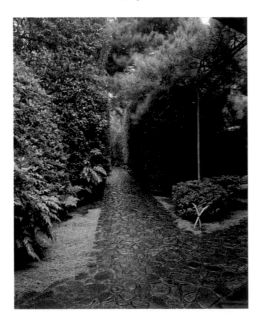

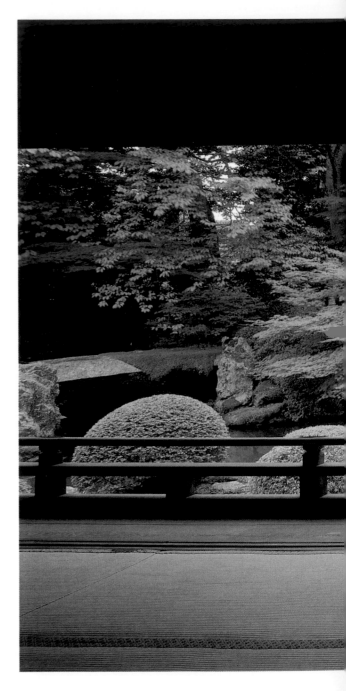

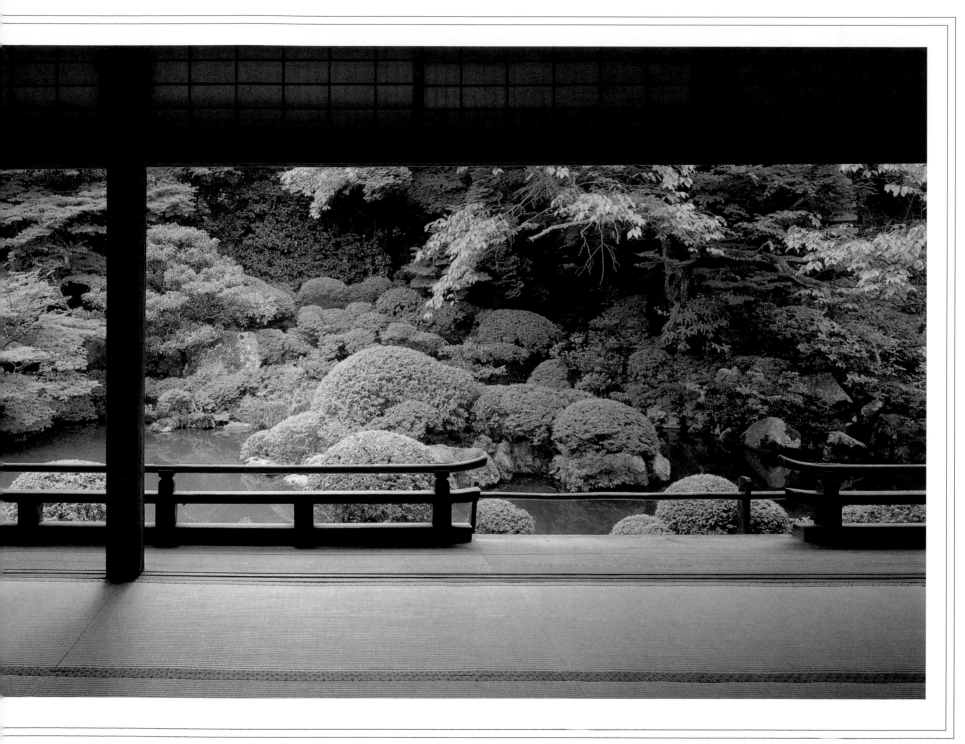

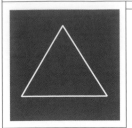

OFF-CENTEREDNESS

Japanese garden designers normally avoid creating a single, dominant focal point in the garden, especially one that lies in the exact center of a design. Centering rarely features in any Japanese design, be it gardens, graphics, flower arrangement, or food presentation—it is considered undynamic and overbearing.[2] In the garden, for instance, straight paths are used sparingly, thus avoiding a centered, axial relationship. Even if paths are made straight, however, the axis of the path will be designed so that the line of sight of a person walking the path dead-ends in a wall or hedge, or includes an askew view of some element of the garden like a gate or teahouse.

TRIADS

Without symmetry or central focal points, the Japanese garden designer achieves visual stability through the use of triads or triangular shapes. Triangles are also a fundamental design technique of flower arranging, bonsai, and the overall arrangement of artwork in the *tokonoma*—the display alcove in tearooms.[3] The most obvi-

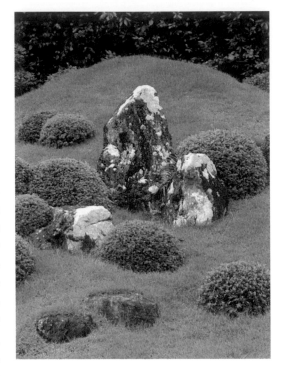

ous example of the use of triads in the garden is the way the designer arranges rocks in groups, and the way those groups relate to one another. In front elevation or plan view, garden rocks are set in a triangle and when multiple groupings exist in one garden a series of complex triangular relationships can be drawn between all of them. Triangular rock groupings may also be used to symbolically represent a Buddhist triad (*sanzon-seki-gumi*), with the largest central stone depicting Shaka or Amida Nyorai (two of the many Buddhas), while the two smaller, flanking stones represent their attendants (*bosatsu*).

Pine trees—which are among the most heavily pruned of garden trees and are considered sculptural in their own right—are usually shaped into a triangular, or more properly, pyramidal form. The *tsukubai*—an arrangement of rocks found in the tea garden which includes a low water laver—is often designed so as to include, as a background element, a lantern, rock, or specimen plant. The relationship between the cluster of rocks forming the tsukubai and the background element is, again, a triangular form. Another triad used in garden design is the interplay of vertical, horizontal, and diagonal elements which are given the symbolic meanings of heaven, earth, and man, respectively. Rock arrangements, for example, deliberately include these three directional elements.

Grouping stones in threes not only provides visual balance and stability, it can also represent a religous metaphor—in this case a Buddhist triad.
Ryōtan-ji, Shizuoka

PLANES AND VOLUMES

Another aspect of balance used by garden designers is the relationship between two-dimensional, planar elements and those that are three-dimensional or volumetric. Perhaps this stems from one of the basic components of Chinese garden design; the harmonic relationship of Yin and Yang elements, such as water and mountains. Whereas the Chinese gardeners perceived a metaphysical meaning to this balance, it can also be said that the surface of the water is a plane and the rounded form of the mountains are volumetric, and the balancing of these has aesthetic meaning as well.

Japanese garden designers also work to balance planar and volumetric elements. This is most easily seen in the gardening style called *hira-niwa* or "flat garden." In the design of a flat garden, the key to a successful design lies in the treatment of the ground plane (*jiban*). This concept is revealed in an early expression for designing, *chi-wari*, which literally means to "divide the ground." In other words, the fundamental act of designing is deciding how to partition the ground plane. The

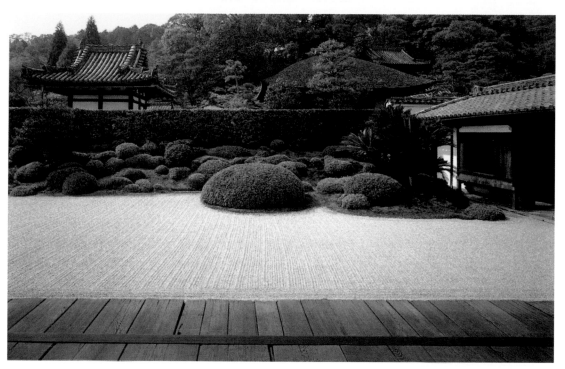

horizontal plane provides a stillness (*tomé*) that lends a peacefulness to the design.

In addition to the ground plane the designer also uses other planar elements: fences, walls, and hedges. These elements are used in two ways: as frames for the garden, in which case they act as a clean background for the details of the garden, or, they are interjected in between visually complex elements—plantings and earthwork "mountains"—in order to add depth to the garden through layering.

The planar elements are counterplayed against volumetric elements—stones, and clipped shrubbery—to create a unified composition. Nowhere is this more clearly

realized than in the design of *kare-san-sui* gardens in which rocks and tightly-clipped evergreens are used as foils against the stark surface of the raked sand, and the walls or hedges that enclose the garden. The reduction of the elements in kare-san-sui to their most simplified state—planes and volumes—is not unlike the sentiments of cubist art, and explains, in part, why these ancient gardens appear to be so "modern."

Planes and volumes: tightly clipped evergreens are used as foils against the stark surface of the raked sand and the hedges that enclose the garden.
Ikkyū-ji, Kyoto

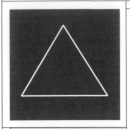

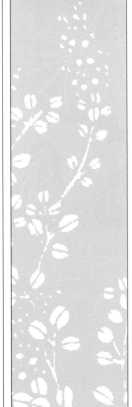

SYMBOLOGY

Beyond the aesthetic and spatial aspects of design, garden designers imbue their work with deeper meaning by interweaving symbolic images: allusions to religious, philosophical, or cultural ideas. In order for these images to have meaning, however, it is necessary that the owner of the garden has the same understanding of the symbols that the designer does.[4] In most cases these symbols are part and parcel of a society's collective heritage and so both the designer and client will take them for granted without explanation.

Symbology is a particularly common design technique in the Japanese garden and there are myriad types. The very fact that symbology plays such an important and ubiquitous role in the gardens suggests one way in which gardens were designed, specifically as metaphorical artworks. An understanding of these symbols gives insight into the meaning of the gardens. Although the symbols stem from societies and philosophies of the past, and at times seem trite or stereotypical, many hold lessons that are as relevant today as they were in the past.

RELIGION

Religious symbology in the garden is very common and incorporates both Shintō and Buddhist images—for instance, the triad of boulders used to create an image of Buddha and his attendants. Religious symbology culminates in designs in which the entire garden becomes representative of a religious ideal, as in the ancient paradise gardens. The garden built at Byōdō-in in the late-Heian period, which symbolizes the Western paradise of Amida Buddha, is a good example of this type.

GOOD FORTUNE / LONG LIFE

The most common symbols of felicity are the images of the island/mountain Hōrai (where the Immortals were said to live) and the associated tortoise and crane islands. The image of Hōrai is created by placing a solitary rock of unusual shape in a pond (or in the sand of a dry garden). The tortoise isle is a small mound in water or sand, that is usually planted with pines. A rock chosen for its resemblance to a turtle's head is placed at one end of the mound evoking an image of a turtle's snout poking up out of the water. Four other rocks are placed as the turtle's "feet" at the appropriate four corners.

The crane isle is also a small mound, again, planted with pines. To model the crane, a long rock is placed jutting out horizontally from the mound representing the crane's neck extended in flight, and prominent upright stones on the top of the mound are used to depict the wings of the crane drawn upward as it flies.

LANDSCAPE IMAGES

Garden designers also employ symbology in order to re-create an extensive landscape scene within the confines of a small garden. This technique is often talked about as miniaturization, but that term is misleading. The process of re-creating a landscape scene in the garden is not like model building where all elements are reproduced in miniature scale; rather, certain elements in the garden are used symbolically to represent parts of a natural vista. In this way mountain ranges become a group of upright boulders and the ocean is found in a sheet of white sand; one pine can represent the windswept bluffs along the ocean and a cluster of trimmed camellias depict the depth of a hidden valley.

LIFE LESSONS

At its best, the garden teaches us about life, revealing its lessons to the acute observer. For instance, *eternity* versus *the moment*—represented by the garden designer with the pine and the plum. The pine, as an evergreen tree with a noble stature, is representative of stability—those aspects of life that are eternal. In contrast, the plum, whose flowers briefly bloom in profusion and then scatter with the wind, is the quintessential image of the evanescent aspects of life.

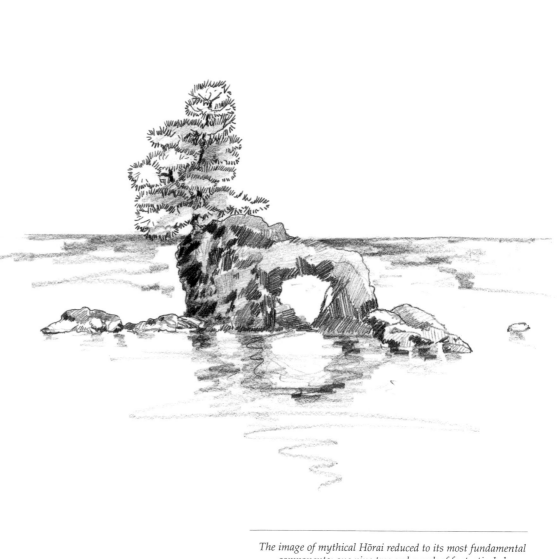

The image of mythical Hōrai reduced to its most fundamental components: one pine tree and a rock of fantastical shape.
Rikugi-en, Tokyo

139

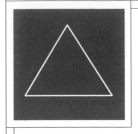

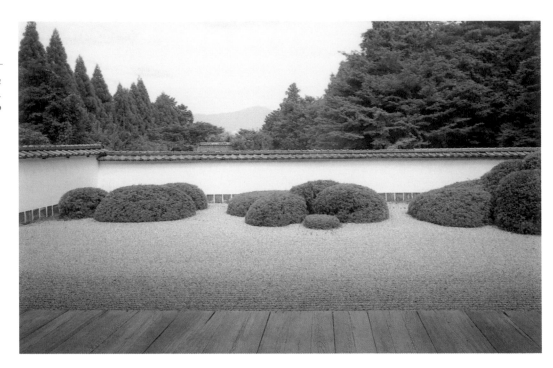

Hiei-zan, Kyoto's guardian mountain, used as borrowed scenery. Shōden-ji, Kyoto

BORROWED SCENERY

Borrowed scenery, *shakkei,* is a technique for enlarging the visual scale of the garden beyond its actual physical boundaries by incorporating a distant view as an integral part of the garden. Originally, this design technique derives from the religious master planning of some Muromachi-period Zen temples. At that time, the head priest of a temple or an advisor would select ten landmarks from the surrounding landscape and give them names (often Chinese), each containing a Buddhist message.[5] These landmarks—usually natural features, but sometimes built objects, such as bridges—were called the ten stages, or ten boundaries (*jikkyō*). By linking the temple

to the surrounding environment, the priests imbued the landscape surrounding the temple with Buddhist meaning and, in a sense, extended the domain of their temple to include the surrounding area. They perceived a religious or metaphysical dimension to this process—a quality that was abandoned during the Edo period as designers began to use the technique of borrowed scenery purely for its painterly qualities. Some of the views that had been originally incorporated as jikkyō—for instance, the summit of Arashiyama— would later be perceived in a painterly way.

Borrowed scenery, as applied to Edo-

period gardens, was a compositional technique derived from ink-wash landscape paintings of Sung-dynasty China and medieval Japan. Typically these landscape paintings included a scene of man in the foreground (minuscule in comparison to the vastness of nature), a majestic natural vista in the background, and a vague middle ground (clouds or mist) layered in between the foreground and background, lending perspective to the painting. Garden designers adopted this compositional technique, creating gardens that included a distant view as part of the composition of the garden. The whole design—garden and vista—was intended

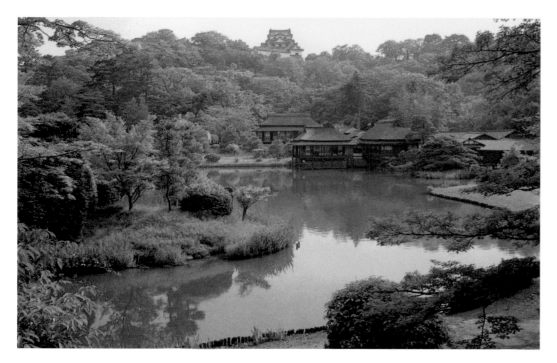

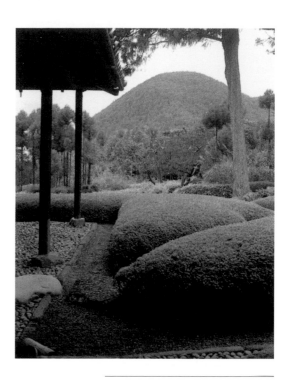

Above: Clipped azaleas mimic the
mountain form, linking the garden
to the background scene.
Kengei-in, Kyoto

Left: A castle as "borrowed
scenery" in a stroll garden.
Genkyū-en,
Hikone Castle, Shiga

to be appreciated as if it were a painting seen from one relatively fixed point, usually the veranda of a building overlooking the garden.[6] This perspective differs greatly from a "view from the garden" in which a distant object or vista is appreciated from within a garden as a beautiful thing "out there."

When designing a shakkei garden, the background already exists as a distant mountain, a waterfall, or even a large man-made object such as the sweeping roof of a temple. The middle and foreground are left to the garden designer to create. The foreground is the garden itself which the designer creates with the same rarefied palette as the paintings that inspired them. The design of the middle ground, however, is the key to creating shakkei. Skillfully eliminating unwanted details that exist in between the garden and the distant view, the designer achieves two things: the distant view is pulled forward and appears larger than it would otherwise, while the foreground (the garden itself) appears to deepen, pulling back toward the object in the distance. Whether a wall, fence, hedge, or grove of trees, this middle ground is a necessary linking element that the designer uses to unify the distant view with the garden in the foreground.

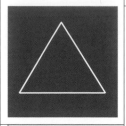

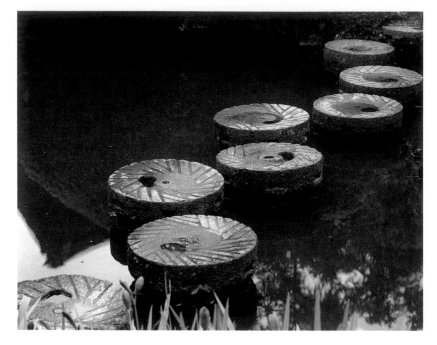

MITATE

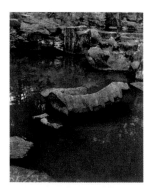

Mitate (pronounced *me-tah-teh*) is a design technique originally associated with the tea garden. Freely translated as "seeing anew," mitate is the process of finding a new use for an old object—objects themselves are called *mitate-mono*.[7] Some of the best examples of mitate-mono are the stone lavers (*chōzubachi*) found in the tea garden which guests use to purify their hands and mouth before entering the tea-room. Many chōzubachi are made from stones that were originally used for another purpose—a section of a multi-roofed stone stupa, a bridge pier, or the base of an old lantern.[8]

Another way designers commonly reuse old stone objects is as paving material, often combining cut stones with other natural stones into long, rectangular sections of paving that are called *nobe-dan* or *ishi-datami* (stone tatami). Mitate stones are also interspersed among natural stepping stones as a form of punctuation. Because of their breadth and flat surface they can be used as rest spots along a path where one stops to glance around the garden before continuing.

Garden designers also use old roof tiles as mitate-mono in a variety of ways. Inserted into the ground vertically in groups, they can be used to make a pathway or included as part of a nobe-dan. Tiles can also be used to line rain catches (*ama-ochi*), gravel-filled trenches that catch rainwater that falls from unguttered roofs, or to make the *chiri-ana*, the dust pits found in tea gardens.

Above: Old millstones given new form as stepping stones.
Isui-en, Nara

Left: A fragment of split granite becomes a boat.
Tōkō-ji, Yamanashi

THE PATH

In Kabuki theater the movement of an actor through space is a movement through time —a process called *michiyuki*.[9] Gardeners consider michiyuki in the design of the garden path. The path is created as a guide to the garden, revealing it in a succession of layers (*chōjō*), while regulating the timing of the experience as well.

For the garden designer, paths have a more important role than merely a design element. Through careful design of the paths, the gardener controls not only the cadence of motion through a garden but what is seen as well. Paths are not simply an element of the overall plan, but a technique the garden designer utilizes to control how the garden will be revealed. This technique was brought to its apotheosis in the tea gardens of the late middle ages, and designers have continued to use it in many styles of gardening ever since.

Take for instance the design of a stepping-stone path in a tea garden. Walking across uneven stepping stones (*tobi-ishi*), the guest is forced by the precariousness of the footing to look down and focus on the path. The designer has effectively stopped the guest from looking about at that time, but after a short run of stepping stones, the designer will invariably place a larger stone, perhaps at the junction of a second path or before the tsukubai. The larger surface of this stone allows the guest to stop comfortably, raise his head and look around at the garden. The designer has carefully chosen this spot for its view.

Another alternative the designer has to using a single large stone is create a large flat surface by combining smaller stones into a nobe-dan. The nobe-dan allows the guest to walk forward with his head up. The focus then shifts from his feet to whatever is at the end of the path. The designer has chosen the placement and direction of the nobe-dan in order to reveal some aspect of the garden in the distance —a lantern or the roof of a teahouse.

In larger stroll gardens the design of a path also includes determining the route. Invariably, the path through the garden is designed to move through a variety of spaces—some open, some introverted. As one moves around the garden, a series of "scenes" are alternately hidden and then revealed—a technique called *mie-gakure*.

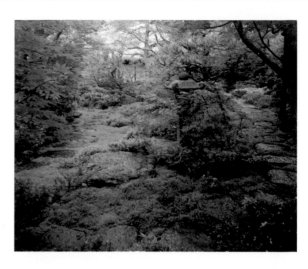

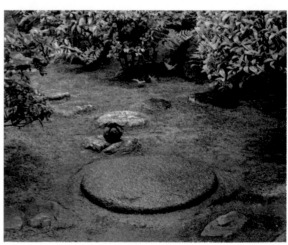

Above: Walking across uneven stones, the guest is forced by the precarious footing to look down and focus on the path.
Dokuraku-an, Tokyo

Below: A large stone (in this case a pillar base) breaks the rhythm of the stepping stones, and allows the guest time to view the garden.
Kankyū-an, Kyoto

143

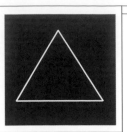

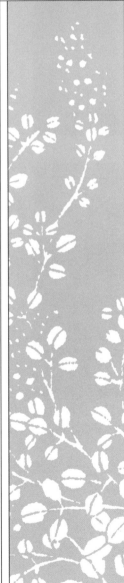

DETAILS vs MASTER PLANNING

It is common practice these days for designers to draw up a master plan for a garden before starting to build, especially true in the case of larger gardens. This is a Western approach which garden designers did not practice until very recently. In the past, inkbrush sketches may have been made to give an overall sense of the garden, but in most cases gardens were designed as they were being built. Certainly there was a general plan in the mind of the master gardener—the dimensions and shape of the pond, the position of major rock groupings—but all of these considerations were entirely subject to change as construction progressed.

Japanese gardens are made of natural materials each of which has a particular character all its own. In the past, materials were collected directly from the countryside while today it is more likely that they will be found in a gardener's private collection or a garden supply yard. In any event, all the materials are considered to be unique samples, each appreciated for their individual characteristics.[10] Rocks, for instance, are said to have a face (*kao*) and a top (*ten*, meaning heaven). The gardener places the rock with its face to the front of the garden and the top, as one might expect, is always set upwards. Trees and shrubs are selected for their individual shapes—the way the trunk bends or a branch angles off in a certain way.

The gardener gathers these sundry elements on site and sets them into place one by one. As each one is placed, the overall balance is affected and the next element is positioned accordingly. It is not uncommon for the gardener to reset plants or rocks that have already been positioned in order to obtain a better overall balance. Japanese gardens, therefore, are designed "up from the details" rather than "down from the master plan."

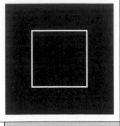

THE VARIOUS ELEMENTS THE JAPANESE GARDEN IS MADE OF—PLANTS, STONES, SAND, AND ORNAMENTS—HAVE BECOME SO WELL KNOWN THAT

THEY ARE NOW REPRESENTATIVE OF THE GARDENS THEMSELVES. HOWEVER, THE NOTION THAT JAPANESE GARDEN DESIGN IS ACCOMPLISHED SIM-

PLY THROUGH THE USE OF, FOR INSTANCE, PINE TREES, WHITE SAND, OR STONE LANTERNS BY THEMSELVES IS OF COURSE NOT TRUE AT ALL. WHAT IS

INTERESTING AND HELPFUL, HOWEVER, IS TO UNDERSTAND WHY CERTAIN STEREOTYPICAL ELEMENTS CAME TO BE INCORPORATED IN THE GARDENS,

AND WHAT PHILOSOPHICAL OR SYMBOLIC MEANINGS THEY HOLD, SO THAT THEY MAY BE USED MORE CONSCIENTIOUSLY.

ROCKS
I S H I

Japanese garden designers have used rocks in a variety of ways, some of them purely functional, like retaining walls or paths. In addition, there are at least four other ways in which rocks have been perceived by designers: animistically, as religious imagery, in a painterly manner, and as sculptural elements. In general, the perception of rocks shifted over the course of time: animistic in ancient times, this perception shifted to a religious one during the Heian period, and then to a painterly sense by the late middle ages. The use of rocks for their sculptural qualities existed in all ages, but can be said to be most indicative of the Edo period.

The perception of ancient *iwakura* and the geomantic use of rocks in the early classic periods were animistic—in both cases rocks were believed to contain a godspirit or supernatural power. "Spirit rocks" are sometimes found in later gardens, such as the *yōgō-seki* (shadow-facing stone) at Saihō-ji in Kyoto. It is unlikely, however, that garden designers put these rocks in their gardens. Instead, when a garden was to be built at a site that already contained one, the spirit of the stone was respected by incorporating it into the plan of the garden.

According to geomantic thought (which influenced garden design during the Nara and Heian periods), rocks of a particular shape or color possessed certain powers and were given names accordingly—Taboo Rock, Dragon's Abode Rock, Rock of the Spirit Kings.[1] Geomantic rocks were not perceived as containing a god, but rather as conduits or modulators of *ki*—life energy.

❶ Animism —
Godspirits are believed to dwell
in particular rocks:
the "shadow-facing stone."
Saihōji, Kyoto

❷ Religious images —
Religious mountain images are
ubiquitous in gardens;
in this case, Mount Shumisen.
Erin-ji, Yamanashi

❸ Painterly images —
Rocks mimic various elements
that were originally found in
monochromatic paintings
such as bridges and boats.
Itō Residence, Fukui

❹ Sculpture —
The large rock is called
eboshi-ishi *after the Heian-*
period headdress it resembles.
Jōju-in, Kiyomizu-dera, Kyoto

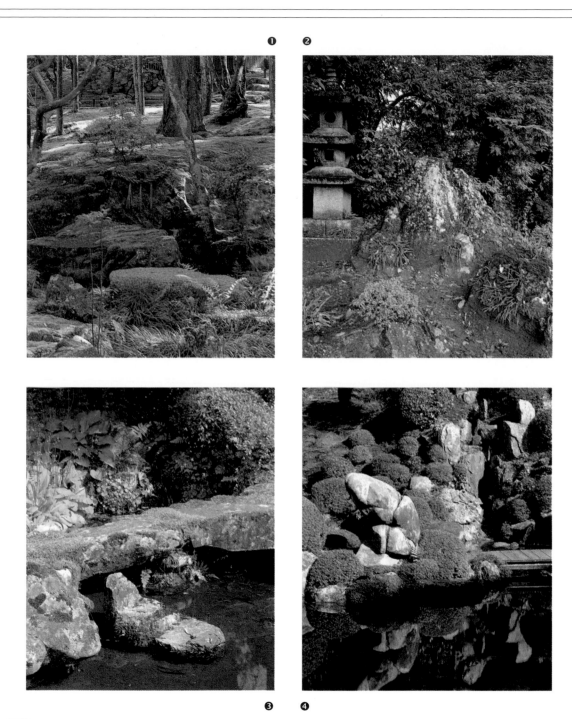

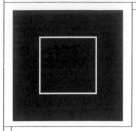

Religious ideals are the most common symbology assigned to rocks by Japanese garden designers. Religious mountain images are ubiquitous: Hōrai and Shumi-sen primary among them.[2] Rocks were also used by Zen priests to symbolize the philosophies of their religion: for instance, the carp stone, dragon's waterfall, and "deep mountains, mysterious valleys." Another Buddhist image represented in stone is the Buddha triad. An example of a stone with religious symbology that is not Buddhist in origin is the garden of the Katsura family in Yamaguchi Prefecture. Used for night-time lunar rituals, this garden contains a number of unusually shaped rocks that have been positioned with care so that they align with one another as well as with the direction of the rising moon.[3]

The painterly use of rocks in Japan was derived from ink-wash paintings of the medieval period. In this case the garden designer used rocks to mimic various elements that were originally found in those monochromatic paintings, for instance, mountains, bridges, and boats. Rocks that were shaped like boats were particularly valued. Most rocks, in the long process of weathering or tumbling down a river, end up in rounded, blocklike shapes. To find a rock that was not only long and narrow but curved like the hull of a ship was a rare thing indeed. In fact, many of the boat-shaped rocks in Edo-period gardens were not natural, but rather pieces that were found in stone yards, the discarded remains of the splitting process.

The sculptural qualities of rocks were undoubtedly always appreciated by garden designers, even if the rock was being used as a religious symbol or for its geomantic properties. In the Edo period, however, some garden designers used rocks primarily for their sculptural beauty. In the garden of Jōju-in (the main temple of the Kiyomizu-dera complex in Kyoto), a stone of the most unusual shape has been prominently placed in the garden. Shaped somewhat like a horn, and bulbous as if it had been made out of chunks of clay, this rock is called *eboshi-ishi* after the Heian-period headdress it resembles. The water laver in this same garden, also named after an article of clothing (a kimono sleeve—*taga-sode*), was also undoubtedly chosen for its sculptural qualities.

White sand has become synonymous with Japanese gardens. The earliest use of white sand may have been in the creation of the sacred spaces, *kekkai*, clearings made in the woods around particular trees or rocks. It is common for shrines today to spread sacred ground with white sand as a sign of purification—a practice which may have descended from ancient times.

In Kyoto, white sand was an easily available, local material. A large portion of the mountain range that flanks Kyoto's eastern side, Higashi-yama, is formed of white granite composed of three minerals: white feldspar, gray quartz, and black mica. When exposed to the elements, granite weathers and decomposes, breaking up into large, granular sand (*masago*) that runs off into the local streams and rivers. As a result the main river coming out of these mountains is called White River (Shira-kawa) and the sand is traditionally called *shira-kawa-suna* (the suffix *suna* means sand). While the stone is primarily white, the minor amounts of gray and black soften its visual effect, making it more complex and less tiring on the eye than, for instance, pure white marble.

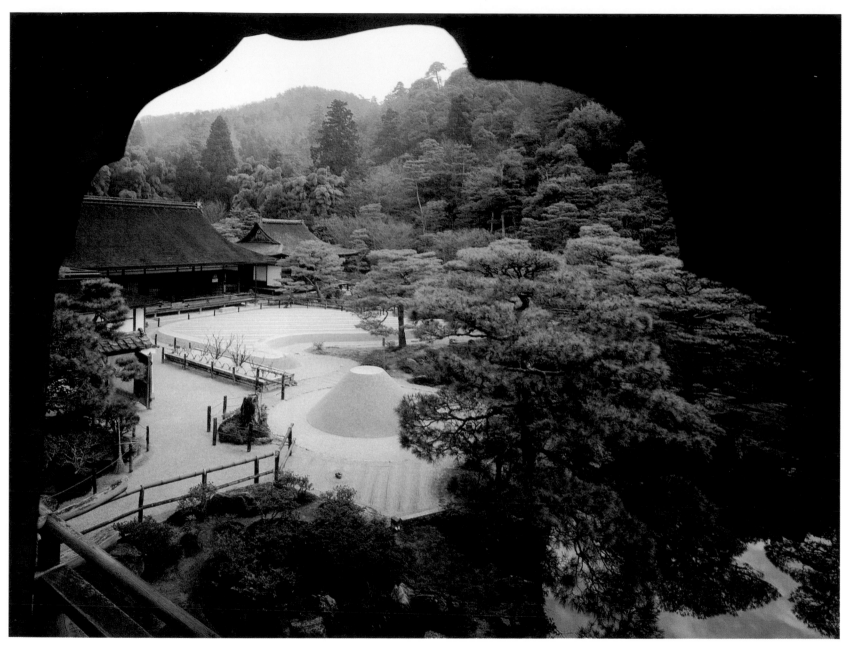

White sand turned out to be the perfect material to replicate the empty, white space of ink paintings.   Jishō-ji (Ginkakuji), Kyoto

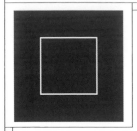

Japan is surrounded by ocean and blessed with rains that fill rivers and lakes. As a result, one of the most interesting aspects of the Japanese garden is the way in which water is sometimes portrayed through the use of sand, gravel, or small rocks, a concept unthinkable, for instance, for garden designers in arid regions. The luxury of substituting actual water with a "dry" symbolic element is affordable only in a country like Japan, which has such a dependable supply. The designers of the gardens in Zen temples were the first to use the technique of substituting sand for water. Whether this sand was originally white or not is speculative, but due to the local availability of white sand, and its appropriateness in mimicking the white spaces of ink paintings in favor at that time, it is more than likely that the original sand in many dry gardens was white. In these gardens, white sand takes on the meaning of streams, waterfalls, rivers, or the broad ocean. Lines raked into the flat expanses of sand mimic the rhythmic motion of the waves, ethereal when seen by moonlight.

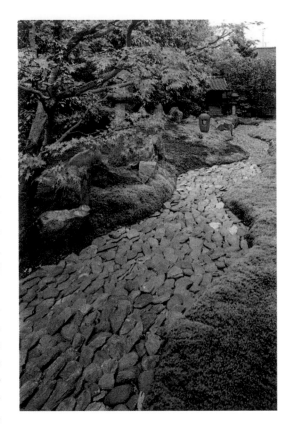

WATER
M I Z U

Water is sometimes portrayed through the use of gravel or small rocks: a concept unthinkable for garden designers in arid regions.
Shinnyō-in, Kyoto

Water is often used allegorically in the garden. Buddhists found the natural process of water springing from a mountain source, gathering strength as it rushes down a valley, and eventually dissipating calmly in the sea to be an apt metaphor for human existence. Birth, growth, death, and rebirth—Buddhism proposes that if one has lived purely, the last step, instead of rebirth, is an ascension to Nirvana and removal from the cycle of birth and death. The wide expanse of sand in contemplation gardens not only provides a visual tranquility, but also implies the peace of the afterworld.

Water. The coolness, the smell, the sound, the flickering of light on the surface. The sensory qualities of water are integral in the Japanese garden as they are in water gardens anywhere, but there is another aspect that is particularly important to the gardens of Japan—the visual space that a sheet of water provides. The landscape of Japan is confined: mountains are steep and packed closely together, the valleys are narrow with little breadth of view. Accentuating this is the effect rice farming had as paddies rapidly consumed most available flat land, resulting in densely populated communities. In light of this, to simply have a visual breadth of space in front of one, even if one can not enter it physically, is a precious luxury.

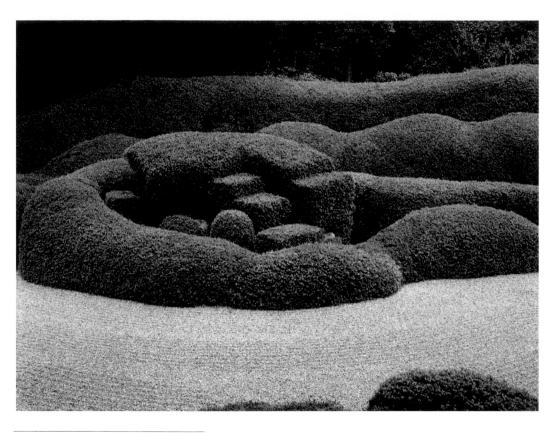

As garden designers began to create gardens in increasingly confined spaces, the custom of closely clipping shubbery into tight, rounded forms developed.
These represent the Seven Lucky Gods.
Daichi-ji, Shiga

PLANTINGS
SHOKUBUTSU

Plants in the Japanese garden have a variety of uses: hedges, seasonal flowers, shade, and so on. In the Heian period, garden plants contained both poetic and geomantic meaning, but these aspects are not stressed in garden building these days. In addition, Heian-period designers used a great variety of plants that are no longer used in the garden—especially flowers and grasses. The shift away from using perennial plants in gardens occurred during the medieval period under the influence of Zen Buddhism. The arts of that period are known for their rarefied palette, and landscape design is no exception. Although, in general, the variety of plant species (especially horticultural varieties) used in garden design steadily increased from the Heian period to the present, the austere gardens of medieval Zen temples used only a limited set of plants, referred to these days as *niwa-ki* (literally: garden plants)—pine, maple, azalea, and camellia, to name the best known. Also during the medieval period, as garden designers began to create gardens in increasingly confined spaces, the custom of closely clipping shrubbery (*kari-komi*) into tight-mounded forms developed.[4]

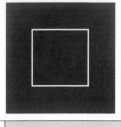

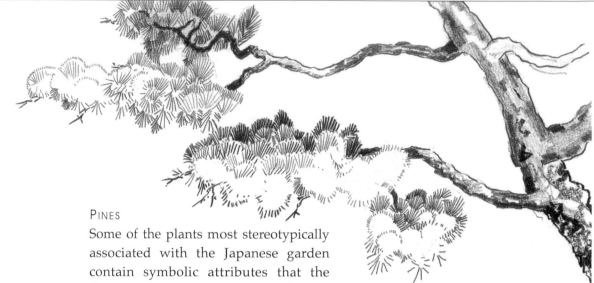

PINES

Some of the plants most stereotypically associated with the Japanese garden contain symbolic attributes that the designer uses to add meaning to the garden. Pines, for instance, are used as an image of longevity, which stems from the ancient image of pine-covered Hōrai island, more than the actual life span of pines in nature. Being evergreen, pines also represent permanence, in contrast to the ever-changing aspects of nature. In addition, the two most popular pines in the garden, the Japanese red pine and Japanese black pine, are symbolic of the mountains and the seashore, respectively. Reflecting their natural habitats, these pines are used intentionally in the garden to create an image of the seashore or a mountain scene. This technique is a good example of "learning from nature."

The red pine is also referred to as *men-matsu* (the female pine) and the black pine as *on-matsu* (the male pine) because of the respective masculine and feminine qualities perceived in their branching and needles. Both pines are pruned heavily to re-create the kinds of shapes that, in a natural setting, strong wind would create. This makes pines the most maintenance-intensive plant in the garden. In order to create and maintain the right shape, every needle on the tree must be trimmed at least once a year. This is usually done when the new growth (the candle) is emerging. By controlling how much of each candle remains, the shape and general direction of growth of the tree can be adjusted. Some of the larger pines trees will take several professional gardeners two or three days each to complete.

Bamboo

Bamboo is easily the most versatile Asian plant, although it is more likely to be used in garden design as part of a fence than as a living plant. Large bamboo is rarely used in gardens because it is simply too voracious; finer varieties are more easily controlled in height and form. Bamboo is an image of resilience, as is easily understood because of its supple nature. Although bamboo was used as a motif in ink paintings because its hollow trunk metaphorically depicted the Zen principle of an empty heart (*mushin*), it is difficult to say whether this image was deliberately integrated into the garden or not.

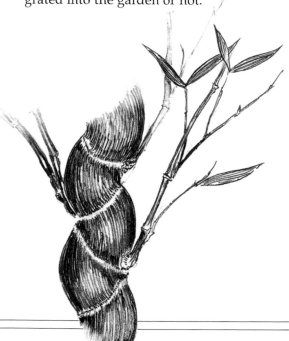

Plum and Cherry

Plums and cherries are both symbolic of evanescence and have been favorite garden plants since Heian times. In the Heian-period imperial palaces, the central stairs that led up from the southern court were flanked with one evergreen tree and one deciduous tree; the former was often a citrus tree or a pine and the latter a plum. In the middle ages the life of the samurai was equated with the brevity and grandeur of the plum flowers. Ironically, in medieval Japanese society the toughest of men would empathize with what, in the West, is considered a very feminine image. The plum and cherry differ, however, in the way they are usually used in the garden. The cherry is allowed to grow fully; in fact, trellises are used to extend the breadth of its branching beyond the normal limits. The plum, on the other hand, is often heavily pruned to effect an artful branching, reducing the tree to a gnarled old trunk and slender young shoots. This stems from the fact that plums can be heavily pruned while cherries do not prune well.[5]

Pine, bamboo, and plum, which form a classic botanical trio in Japan, often show up in paintings together and can also be used as a ranking system. Called *shō, chiku, bai*, they represent three good things in descending order, something like Best, Great, and Good. Gardens built for inns and restaurants will sometimes use a combination of these three plants as a symbol of felicity.

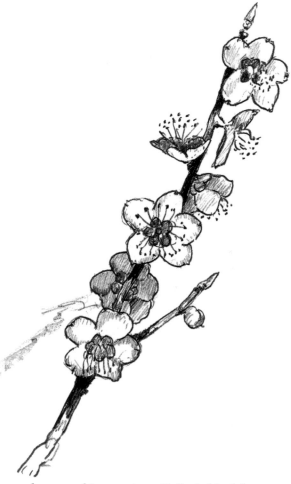

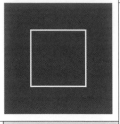

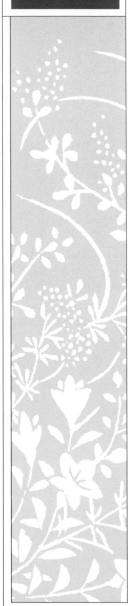

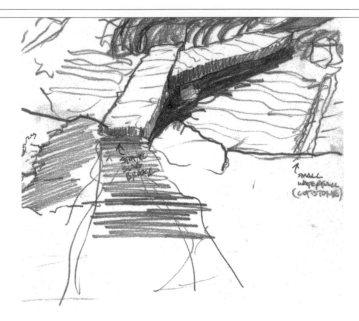

BRIDGES

HASHI

Bridges are used functionally for the purpose of crossing water but there is also a symbolic aspect to them as well. The word for bridge, *hashi*, is also a homonym with the word for edge. Symbolically, then, a hashi bridges the gap (ma) between one edge and another, linking two worlds: for instance, that of man and the gods.[6] In Heian-period pond gardens, the central island (*naka-jima*) in the pond, represented the Pure Land of Amida Buddha. A curved bridge (*sori-bashi*) was designed to connect the southern courtyard to the island, symbolically linking "this world" with "heaven"—inferring the possibility of rebirth in paradise.

In the case of the contemplation gardens in Zen temples, designers often set bridges over rivers of sand in miniature landscape scenes. These were the first stone-slab bridges used in gardens in Japan. Before the medieval period, bridges were wooden, at times painted with red lacquer. The contemplation gardens were modeled after Chinese-style landscape paintings which had as a central theme the contemplation of nature by a recluse philosopher in order to discover the inner meaning of life. Bridges in the paintings represented the passage out of the world of man and into the larger world of nature, implying, as well, the journey from an ordinary plane of consciousness to a higher one. The symbolic reasons for putting the bridge in the painting carried through to garden design as well.

SCULPTURAL ORNAMENTS
TENKEIBUTSU

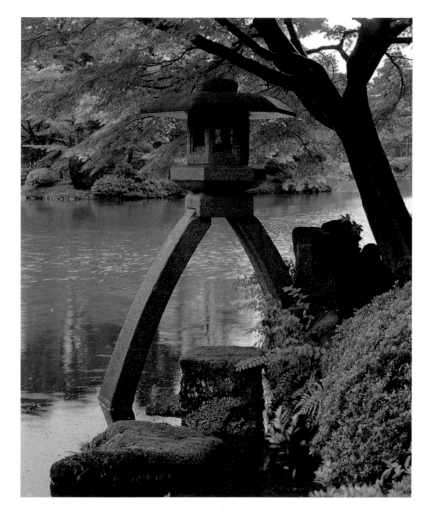

Stone lanterns are used primarily as sculptural elements; their function as lighting is secondary.
Kotoji-tōrō, Kenrokuen, Ishikawa

Although Japanese garden designers have always shunned the obvious use of sculpture in their designs, they have often included sculptural elements in understated forms.[7] Stone lanterns, for instance, are often used primarily as sculptural elements, their function as lights relegated to second place. In the past, before electric lighting, lanterns were undoubtedly lit more often than they are today, though even then the light from the lantern was feeble at best and did more to set the mood of a garden, or guide one dimly along a path, than to actually illuminate the garden as a whole. Lanterns were used first in gardens by the tea masters of the middle ages; before then their use was strictly limited to the entries of shrines or temples.

Stone stupas are another example of a garden element used for its sculptural quality, though the stupa's obvious Buddhist reference also lends a religious meaning to its use. Rocks have been used in gardens for their sculptural quality, as have trees and shrubs. Heavily-pruned pine trees are talked about in the gardening trade as having "artfulness" (*gei wo shiteiru*). Although Japanese gardeners are known for their avoidance of sculpture, the sensitive interplay of masses and volumes they create with stones, plants, or other materials is very close in spirit to that of a sculptor.

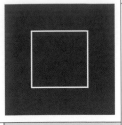

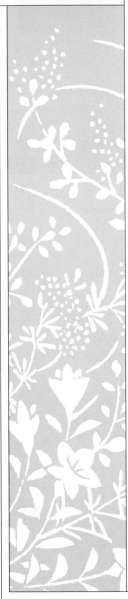

WALLS AND FENCES
KAKI TO HEI

The primary use of walls and fences by garden designers is for enclosure, or as dividers within a garden. The design of the wall or fence—the height, placement, and degree of transparency—will determine to what degree a view is obstructed or revealed. Japanese garden fences are often roofed to shield them from the deleterious effects of heavy rains. The roof, however, is usually built so that a small gap remains between it and the fence itself, which softens the visual impact of the fence by making the line between the fence and the view behind it less definite.

Solid, earthen walls are designed in a great variety of ways. Those within the gardens (as opposed to those that shield the garden from the outside) are often designed very low—just at eyeheight. This careful control of height allows a generous view of what lies beyond the wall while providing privacy at the ground level. Some fences are designed as partial screens, for instance those made from whole bamboo trunks tied to a wooden frame (*teppō-gaki*).[8] The slits between the uprights reveal what is on the other side of the fence to differing degrees, depending if one looks at the fence face on (greatest obstruction) or from an angle (most revealed). Because of this, as one passes in front of this kind of fence, whatever is beyond the fence is alternately revealed and then hidden. One particular variety of this fence has closely spaced bamboo on the top three quarters but the very bottom of the fence is left open so the ground beyond is revealed. The fence is designed this way to allow a view of something in particular—flowers, a brook, or a stone arrangement—while concealing the majority of the scene.

Another fence of particular interest is the "wing" fence (*sode-gaki*), which is designed to link architecture to the garden.[9] The wing fence is a small fence usually of shoulder height and slightly narrower than tall. Connected to a building on one side, it protrudes into the garden. The garden designer uses the wing fence, like the fabric wings on a stage set, to control how much of the garden a person will see when sitting on the veranda. By carefully controlling views, a garden

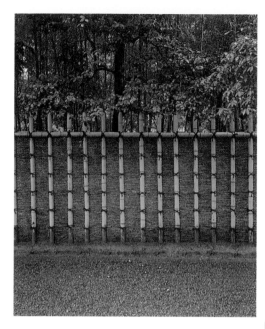

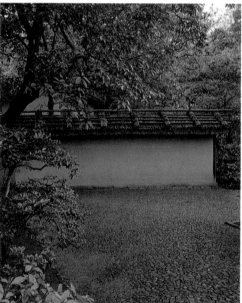

Above: Fences and walls provide an opportunity for the garden designer to display his sense of artistry.
Katsura Detached Palace, Kyoto

Right: Elegance enhanced by simplicity: this wall, made of clay and thatch, displays the refined taste of the designer.
Katsura Detached Palace, Kyoto

designer can give a sense of privacy to various rooms of a staggered building (for instance, a traditional Japanese inn) even if all the rooms look out onto the same garden.

Although Japanese garden design is usually noted for an understatement which hides the designer's hand, fences and walls are often highly decorative. More than any other garden element, fences and walls provide an opportunity for the garden designer to display his sense of artistry. There are over twenty-five varieties of bamboo fence alone, as well as wooden fences, twig-bundle fences, and earthen walls. Within each category the designer has infinite room for making variations on traditional themes.

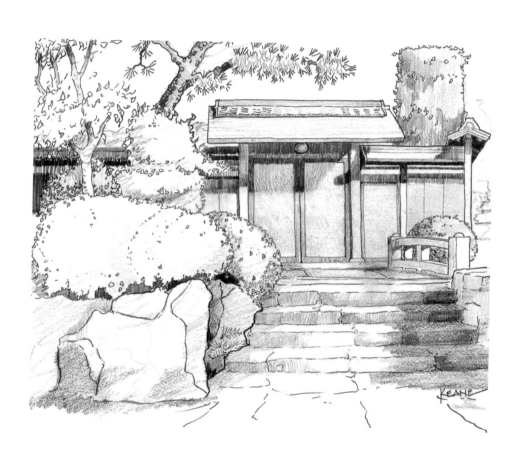

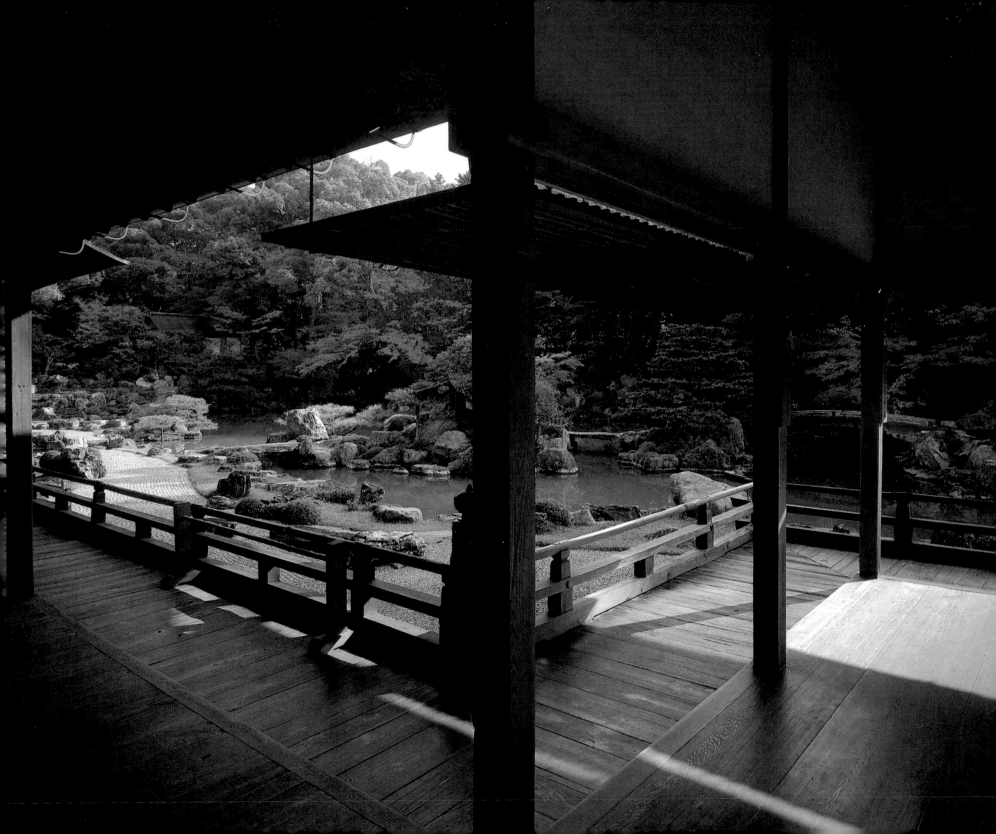

LOOKING FORWARD

Throughout the Edo period, Japan remained effectively closed to the outside world. With the opening of its borders during the Meiji period, Western ideas began to influence all aspects of Japanese society—government, education, industry, and of course the arts as well. The integration of these new ideas—so different and novel—was a difficult process, often guided by concession, as expressed in the contemporary term *wayō-secchū*; "a compromise between Japan and the West." Gardens began to show Western influences as well. In certain cases wholly Western style gardens were built at the homes of wealthy individuals and, on a broader scale, certain elements of Western gardens were incorporated as part of the general design palette—lawn for instance.

Today, designers are reexamining how the Japanese garden can exist within the framework of a modern city. As one small example of contemporary innovations in garden design, there is a trend among some "new garden" designers to use split granite stones in their gardens rather than the natural boulders of the past. This is caused by the rising costs and diminishing availability of natural stones as well as a shift in tastes, but it is also in part a response to modern architecture. Buildings of the past were made of subdued, natural materials, so rocks taken from rivers or mountains with a patina of age were suitable. Now steel, glass, concrete, and other processed materials dominate the architectural scene. The use of split granite reflects the feeling on the part of the designers that today's architectural design requires a new garden material that has the same sensory qualities as its surroundings.

How will the Japanese garden evolve into the future? The answer to this may well lie in gleaning lessons from the past—not simply with regard to the materials of the garden, or its form, but in perceiving what a garden *is*. For instance, an animistic perception, by which a garden is seen not simply as a pretty picture but as a living entity with a spirit, or by perceiving the garden as a painting, an object for contemplation, a spiritual passageway, or as a work of religious art. All of these perceptions from the past are still relevant today but only if those who design, build, and nuture gardens accept these views as meaningful. The future path for the Japanese garden may also lie in incorporating salient gardening ideas from outside the Japanese tradition, like "edible gardens" or horticultural therapy.

Gardens are essentially urban artforms—they were constructed, at first, by people in societies at the beginning stages of urbanization in an attempt to create environments that included elements of Nature they felt deprived of in the city. At the present time, forty-five percent of the world's population lives in urban areas—a proportion expected to rise to sixty percent by the year 2025. The need for gardens, therefore, will only become increasingly urgent. The gardens of Japan, for a number of historical reasons, are particularly well suited to the urban context. The way that Japanese garden designers have dealt with compressed spaces—the courtyard gardens of medieval Zen temples, the tea garden, and the tiny tsubo gardens of the urban merchants—holds invaluable lessons for designers today regarding how to incorporate elements of the natural world into the urban plan.

The Japanese garden will undoubtedly evolve in response to the changes of modern society—the forms and aesthetics designers express in the garden will be different. But, beyond the garden, imagine if the awareness of Nature and sensitivity to detail that is so evident in the gardens of Japan were expressed on a larger scale, by nations as a whole on their environments.

Utopia.

Notes

GODSPIRIT IN NATURE:
PREHISTORIC ORIGINS, page 3

1. Figures regarding volcanoes are drawn from *INFOPEDIA* (CD-ROM), San Diego; Future Vision Multimedia Inc., 1995.

2. Recent archeological evidence increasingly points to the existence of rudimentary agriculture in the late Jōmon period. For the sake of simplicity, in this book, the change from Jōmon to Yayoi is used to signify the shift from non-agricultural to agricultural societies. Although the Yayoi period did witness revolutionary changes in the development of agricultural skills and proliferation of fields, in fact the separation between the Jōmon and Yayoi periods is not so clear.

3. Nakamura Makoto. *The Twofold Beauties of the Japanese Garden, IFLA Yearbook*, 1986/87, pp. 195–98, and in conversation with the author.

4. Translation by author.

5. Kojima, Noriyuki. *Nihon koten bungaku zenshū, Man'yōshū*, poem no. 256.

6. Amino, Yoshihiko. *Nihon ron no shiza*, pp. 269–280.

7. The word *sono* means a bordered, restructured landscape. In this way, it is like the English word garden, which stems from ancient German and English words, such as *gart* and *geard*, which meant enclosure. In fact many other related English words—park, paradise, yard, and orchard—have similar etymologies.

8. Levy, Ian Hideo. *Man'yōshū*, poem no. 816.

9. Kojima, Noriyuki. *Nihon koten bungaku zenshū; Man'yōshū*, poem no. 816.

10. Shintō, literally: "The Way of the Gods," which began as a vague collection of religious practices, was formed into an institutionalized religion with dogma, literature, and architecture after the introduction of—and in reaction to—Buddhism.

11. Aston, W.G. *Nihongi*, pp. 60, 64.

12. Hasegawa, Masami. *nihon teien yōsetsu*, p. 160.

13. *Shime-nawa* means tied rope. The process of tying or binding was central to the act of demarcation—not only religious but for the marking of territory as well. Binding of grasses or ropes often plays a part in religious festivals in Japan. See Nitschke, Günter. "Shime; Binding /Unbinding." *Architectural Design*, December 1974.
   In order to allow people to pass into the sacred area, the shimenawa was most likely held aloft on a simple frame at one point to create a gateway. The frame itself outlasted the fragile straw rope and in time the frame, rather than the rope, came to symbolize the entry to the sacred area. These simple gates are now called *torii*. At some shrines, like *miwa jinja* south of Nara (which observes a pre-Buddhist form of the Shintō religion), it is still possible to see the shime-nawa held on poles used as a gate. This rope gateway is called a *shime-bashira*.

14. Masami Hasegawa refers to the sacred rings of stone as *himorogi*, while most other texts simply use the English words "stone circle." Hasegawa, Masami, *Nihon teien yōsetsu*, p. 164. Himorogi is a complex word with various meanings. At present it is used most often to mean an "offering to the gods" which these days is usually rice and saké, but was originally meat, cooked or raw.

*15. People had been coming from Korea to Japan, or through Korea to Japan, for millennia. "Korean community" here refers to recently arrived Koreans who still maintained their native language and customs.

POETRY IN PARADISE:
GARDENS OF THE HEIAN ARISTOCRATS, page 19

1. Morris, Ivan.*The World of the Shining Prince*, p. 153.

2. His surname, Kong, plus Fuzi, meaning Master, became latinized to Confucius—in Japanese he is known as *Kōshi*.

3. *Fūsui* in Chinese is *feng-shui*.

4. The two essential elements of the Chinese garden are mountains (Ch. *shan;* Jp. *san* or *sen*) and water (Ch. *shui;* Jp. *sui*). Mountains are masses (*yang* element); water is fluid (*yin* element). Dr. Evelyn Lipp. *Feng Shui Environments of Power*, p. 92. The Japanese, as well, used the expression "mountain-water" (*senzui*) to mean garden.

5. Aston, W.G. *Nihongi: Chronicles of Japan from the Earliest Times to AD 697*, Vol. 2, p. 65.

6. In full "Western Paradise Pure Land" *(saihō gokuraku jōdo)*.

7. Aston, W.G. *Nihongi: Chronicles of Japan from the Earliest Times to AD 697*, Vol. 2, p. 144.

8. In fact, there are several ways in which gardens are referred to in the early years of Japanese gardening history. The actual act of gardening is usually termed "setting stones upright" (*ishi wo taten koto*). The word used for garden is at times sono, though this is usually an agricultural garden. More often the words mountain (*yama* or *Sumi / Shumisen*), island (*shima*), pond (*ike*), or plantings (*senzai*) appear when referring to a garden.

9. The grid cities in China, one of which was the model for Heian-kyo, had high, strong defensive walls around them. Heian-kyo, being more of a bureaucratic city than a military one, had only a moderate rammed-earth wall (*dai-tsuiji-bei*) or embankment surrounding it.

10. Chang'an (present day X'ian) means Long Peace; Heian means Harmonic Peace, an obvious reference to its predecessor.

11. There was an extra row of blocks on the northern edge of Heian-kyō that was half the size of a standard *jō* in its north-south direction. This row was called a *kita hen*.

12. The use of the word wind (*fu*) in *fuzei* and *fūsui* is not referring to actual wind but something more like the ancient Greek concept of ether (Gr. *aitherios*)—an invisible element that permeates and binds all physical matter—or akin to the Latin and Greek roots of the English word air; sense, place, or disposition. From a lecture by Wybe Kuitert, Japan Foundation, Kyoto November 17, 1995, as well as his book *Themes, Scenes, and Taste in the History of Japanese Garden Art*.

13. These political intrigues may have, in a sense, been the cause of the cultural interest. Cut out from the possibilities of achievement in the political arena by the machinations of more powerful people, many courtiers found all they had left to do to occupy their time, and fulfill themselves, were artistic pursuits.

14. The process of transformation from life to death was graphically depicted in the painting *Kusōshi e-maki* and others. *Kusōshi e-maki* depicts the corpse of a beautiful woman (Ono no Komachi, one of the era's most renowned beauties) in nine stages of decomposition, from beauty to skeleton. These macabre paintings were common at the end of the Heian period and in the early Kamakura period.

15. Stylistic terms, for gardens or any other art, are usually assigned after the fact by following generations. Many of the terms for garden styles in this book—pond-touring gardens (*chisen shūyū teien*) for the Heian-period gardens, contemplation gardens (*kansho-niwa*) for those of the middle ages, and stroll gardens (*kaiyū shiki teien*) for the Edo-period gardens—are modern. Although these terms are descriptive of the gardens, and therefore informative, they were not used originally.

16. Ducks can be seen in paintings of ancient court life (i.e., *Kasuga gongen kenki e-maki*), crickets are mentioned in *The Tale of Genji*. The wide variety of plants are recorded both in contemporary writing, like *The Tale of Genji*, as well as archeological work which has identified the preserved seeds or leaves of at least 25 species, including conifers like pine, fir and hemlock; fruit trees like plums, cherries, pears, and peaches; broadleaf evergreens like bayberry, and evergreen oaks; deciduous trees like maples and the large growing Japanese hackberry; and spice plants like Japanese pepper. *Kyoto no teien: iseki ni mieru heian jidai no teien*. p. 61.

17. Izutsu, Toshihiko and Toyo. *The Theory of Beauty in Classical Aesthetics of Japan*, p. 18.

18. Kuitert, Wybe. *Themes, Scenes, and Taste in the History of Japanese Garden Art*. Part One:"Themes."

19. Shingon Buddhism is a branch of Mahayana or esoteric Buddhism—*mikkyō* (secret teachings) in Japanese. Shingon means "true word," which in Sanskrit is *mantra*.

20. The word *mandala* means "circle/disk" or "gathering" in Sanskrit, referring both to its shape, which at times contains circular forms, and also to the gathering of the universal forces it depicts. Mandala are pre-Buddhist in origin—the earliest forms depict Hindu gods.

21. At Tōji, the 21 Buddhist statues in the Hall of Teaching are arranged in mandalic order. Hempel, Rose. *The Golden Age of Japan*, p. 33.

*22. Many of these images are described in *The Tale Of Genji*, Edward Seidensticker or *Tales of Ise*, Helen Craig McCullough.

THE ART OF EMPTINESS:
THE GARDENS OF ZEN TEMPLES, page 45

1. *Kōan* are enigmatic statements, the most famous of which (and the first given to an initiate) is "what is the sound of one hand clapping?"

2. During the middle ages the Zen religion was still in its formative stages in Japan. As such, the term "Zen Buddhism" was apparently not used; the consciousness of Zen as a distinct entity not having fully developed. Instead the terms Rinzai sect or Sōtō sect were used.

3. The *hōjō* (not to be confused with the Hōjō family), is the abbot's residence and the name refers to the desire for a life of simplicity and detachment from the world as captured in *The Ten Foot Square Hut* (*Hōjō-ki*) written in 1212. Hōjō, means a square *jō*—a traditional measurement equal to 10 feet. A hōjō is, therefore, equal to about 100 square feet, and is often translated as "ten- feet square" to accentuate the sense of smallness.

4. Hall and Takeshi. *Japan in the Muromachi Age*, pp. 227–239.

5. In the case of Zen temples, another factor changing the way of entry was the shifting relationship with the imperial household. Official visits from the imperial household, which were frequent in the medieval period, became less so. For instance, at Daitoku-ji (Rinzai sect) the imperial visits were slowed to every fifty years, when a messenger from the imperial household delivers a new posthumous name, bestowed by the emperor on the patriarch founder of the temple. At that time the two piles of white sand in the garden, which are perfectly aligned with the pillars of the gate, are spread out to purify the garden for the visit. Other than these visits the garden is not entered, except for daily maintenance.

6. The waterfall arrangement—whether it contains running water or not—is usually formed with one or more central flat faced stones over which the water falls and large rounded boulders on either side built up to visually frame and physically support the central ones. At the bottom of the waterfall, in the center of the "stream," is a single upward facing stone, that represents the struggling fish, called a carp stone (*rigyo-seki*).

7. Meditation in front of a garden is a regular experience only for young initiate priests, called *unsui* (cloud-water), who live together in a special temple complex (*senmon dōjō*) that is used exclusively for Zen Buddhist training. Training for all initiates is not identical—at Daitoku-ji training includes: rising early to do chores (at 2 or 3 A.M. depending on the season), begging for alms, and receiving religious training, which in the case of

NOTES

the Rinzai sect includes the zen *mondō*. Then in the evening, starting at dusk, initiates begin communal meditation in the zendō hall. After perhaps three hours of zazen, the initiates then go and sit on the veranda of a nearby hall and meditate in front of a garden (*yaza*). Whether the garden can actually be seen depends on the moonlight. After initiates leave the training temple to become priests, meditation in front of a garden is no longer a regular part of their religious life.

8. Zen meditation can be divided into two groups: meditation performed while still and meditation that is performed while in motion. Zazen is of the former type, also called the "stillness method" (*jōchū no kufū*). In contrast, daily chores, including garden maintenance, is considered meditation while in motion, and is known as *samu* or the "moving method" (*dōchū no kufū*).

9. Photographs from the early part of this century show the garden east of the hōjō at Daisen-in to be twice as wide as it is now and covered with moss, not sand. In terms of using the garden as a religious teaching tool, though, the historical authenticity of the garden is secondary to the ability of the resident priest to homilize.

10. Insofar as they are artworks that express religious values the *kare-san-sui* can be compared to, for instance, totem poles of the Northwest American Indians, icons of Russian Orthodox Christianity, or Tibetan sand mandalas.

*11. *Senzui narabi ni yagyō no zu* has been translated into English by David Slawson in *Secret Teachings in the Art of Japanese Gardens*.

*12. The *kawara* (riverbank) was uncontrolled by government regulations. As such, entertainers could set up temporary theaters there without permission. Due to this, the *kawara-mono* also became associated with the entertainers among them. Kabuki theater is said to have its origins in such a community.

*13. Hall and Toyoda. *Japan in the Muromachi Age*, p. 144.

SPIRITUAL PASSAGE: THE TEA GARDEN, page 67

1. These aesthetic advisors were known communally as *dōbōshū*. Low-ranking courtiers, in an attempt to raise their status in society, would often take priestly vows, becoming *tonsei-sha*. Although the term tonsei-sha literally means "recluse hermit," many initiates used their new status to gain acceptance in the dōbōshū circles. Among the tonsei-sha, many were members of the Ji sect of Buddhism, and consequently added *a* or *ami* to their names—for instance Nōami, Geiami, and Sōami, advisors to Ashikaga Yoshimasa, builder of the estate now known as the Silver Pavilion (Ginkaku-ji). Hall & Toyoda. *Japan in the Muromachi Age*, pp. 186–191.

2. Known as the Time of Warring States (*sengoku jidai*).

3. Nowadays this kind of ceiling material costs more per square foot (sometimes ten times more) than the average per square foot cost of a building itself, and it may well have been comparatively expensive in the Momoyama period as well.

4. Gardens are also broken down into categories of *shin-gyō-sō*, but this categorization is found primarily in texts from the late Edo period, during which all matters were systematized, and the examples often seem forced.

5. Contemporary records state, for instance, that Sen no Rikyū disliked flowering plants in the tea garden for two reasons: the effect of the simple flower arrangement placed in the *tokonoma* of the teahouse would be weakened by abundant flowers outside; also, the *wabi* mood would be destroyed by having too lavish a display of seasonal color. Some other tea garden designers, however, did not follow this wabi-cha trend. Apparently there was even one tea garden—at the Fushimi Castle—planted entirely with cycads (*sotetsu*—a palm-like tree).

6. "Passage six parts, landscape four" (*watari rokubun, kei yonbun*): this phrase also expresses

Rikyū's feeling that the *roji* (and *cha-no-yu* in general) should be weighted slightly in favor of function rather than artistry. Other tea masters, like Oribe and Enshu, saw things the other way around.

7. Not all tea gardens are divided into an inner and outer roji; some are smaller and simpler. Those that do have two sections are called *nijū roji* (two-layer roji) or *tajū roji* (multi-layer roji).

8. From the memoirs of the monk Nanbō, a contemporary of Sen no Rikyū. Izutsu, Toshihiko, and Toyo. *Theory of Beauty in the Classical Aesthetics of Japan*, p. 144.

9. There is also, a kind of middle gate called a *naka-kuguri* that looks as if one wall of a teahouse has been constructed separately mid-way through the garden. It often has a window and a small doorway (like a *nijiri-guchi*) that one passes through.

10. The word *tsukubai* derives from the verb *tsukubau* that means to kneel, suggesting the low-set nature of the arrangement of stones. Previous to the introduction of the tsukubai, most people of rank would have used a standing water basin (*tachi-bachi*) for cleansing their hands and mouth. The low position of the tsukubai enforced humility by requiring one to bow before receiving water.

PRIVATE NICHES: TSUBO GARDENS, page 83

1. The annual Gion Festival in Kyoto—begun in the tenth century—was revived in the late Muromachi period by *machi-shū* communities with each group building a decorative carriage (*yama* or *hoko*) for the event.

2. There were other classes recognized by the government including, priests, nobles, and outcasts. The outcasts included the *eta* (full of pollution) of whom the kawara-mono were considered a part, and, at the very bottom, the *hinin* (non-humans).

3. The merchant areas of the other towns and

cities of the Edo period, not having as long a history of formal town planning as Kyoto, did not go through such an evolution—their merchant quarters developed spontaneously from scratch and usually show their organic growth in the random patterning of their streets.

4. Hisamatsu, Sen'ichi. *The Vocabulary of Japanese Literary Aesthetics*, pp. 63–66.

A COLLECTOR'S PARK: EDO STROLL GARDENS, page 97

1. The title *daimyō* was bestowed on those who had lands worth 10,000 *koku* or more. A koku (180 liters) was the quantity of rice that could feed a retainer for a year. The wealthiest of the daimyō, the Maeda's, controlled lands worth over one million koku and there were another 22 daimyō with large fiefs. Although the bulk of the daimyō had smaller fiefs, a daimyō's wealth could easily be enough to feed the entire population of his lands—not that he would—simply that he could.

2. As many as three residences were required of the daimyō within Edo alone—*kami-yashiki*, *naka-yashiki*, and *shimo yashiki*. Shirahata, Yozaburo. *Edo no daimyō teien*, p. 4.

3. Shirahata, Yozaburo. *Edo no daimyō teien*.

4. Shirahata, Yozaburo. *Edo no daimyō teien*, and in conversation with the author.

5. Hisamatsu, Sen'ichi. *The Vocabulary of Japanese Literary Aesthetics*, p. 20.

6. McCullough, Helen Craig. *Tales of Ise*, p. 74.

7. The Western Lake is Lake Xi-fu, Hangzhou, Zheijiang Provence, China.

*8. *Ueki-ya* (literally, tree planters) seems to be the oldest term for this group of professional gardeners. Another term is *niwa-shi*. The origin of the term niwa-shi has not been pinned down very accurately. According to the *Nihon kokugo daijiten*

the first usage is attributed to Kunikida Doppo, a poet active during the Meiji period. The Edo period also witnessed a boom in horticulture (*shugei, jugei*, or *geishoku*) and plantsmen (*uekiya, geika*, or *kako*); *Nihon nōsho zenshū*; *Kadanchi kinshō*. Shadan Hōjin, Nōsan Gyoson Bunka Kyōkai, p. 6.

*9. Trade specialization is indicative of the Edo period in general. Woodblock prints, for instance were produced by at least three trades: the artist responsible for the design, the woodblock carver, and, finally, the printer. Carpentry also had a similarly hierarchical structure: the owners or caretakers of the forest (*yama-nushi*), those who collected wood from the mountains and sawed it into lumber (*kobiki*), those whose business it was to stock and sell wood (*zaimoku-ya*), and the carpenters themselves (*daiku*).

DESIGN, page 115

1. The physical spaces and culture of modern day Japan are, in many ways, as different from premodern Japan as, for instance, America and Japan are different today. In light of this, modern Japan is as "alien" an environment for the traditional Japanese garden as Los Angeles would be.

DESIGN PRINCIPLES, page 117

1. Translation by author, after modern Japanese transliteration in *Sakuteiki: gendaigo taiyaku to kaisetsu*, Takei, Jiro.

2. Some *chōzubachi* are natural stones which have basins already carved into them by the eroding effects of water. In addition, not all chōzubachi, are made from natural stones. Some are created from old found objects, such as parts of stupas or bridge pilings.

3. The lotus rises from the muck at the bottom of a pond and lifts its flower head up above the surface of the muddy water, opening to reveal a flower of incomparable beauty. Buddhists see this as analogous to man's ability to rise above his

sordid, earthly existence and attain Buddhahood, a state of purity symbolized by the silvery pearls of rainwater that get caught in the cuplike lotus leaf.

Fringed pink, in Japanese, *nadeshiko*, literally meaning pampered (caressed) child, refers to young girls.

4. The landscapes of northwest Kyoto are famous for their cherries and maples. It is interesting to note that these are not all indigenous but, instead, were planted during ancient and medieval times by people who wanted to "improve" the view, raising the question of what is a "natural landscape." As early as the thirteenth century we find a note by Emperor Gosaga on cherries being moved from Yoshino (near Nara) to Arashiyama, see *Process Architecture #116*, p. 18.

5. After the Heian period, grasses all but disappeared from the Japanese garden, partly a result of the reduced size of the later gardens but also due to a general trend that began during the medieval period of using sculptural woody plants, predominantly evergreens.

6. Translation by author, after modern Japanese transliteration in *Sakuteiki: gendaigo taiyaku to kaisetsu*, Takei, Jiro.

7. Paraphrased from *Form, Style, Tradition*, Kato, Shuichi, p. 4.

8. Translation as found in *This Moment: A Collection of Haiku*, Margaret Chula, closing page.

9. Record of the monk Nanbō (*Nanbō roku*). Itsuzu, Toshihiko and Toyo. *Theory of Beauty in the Classical Aesthetics of Japan*, pp. 136–158.

DESIGN TECHNIQUES, page 129

1. Entry in Japanese gardens can happen physically, as it does in expansive stroll gardens or diminutive tea gardens, or, in the case of contemplation gardens, entry can be restricted to an exclusively mental exercise.

NOTES

2. In addition to aesthetic reasons for avoiding centering, there is also a rule against planting a single tree in the center of a court because this pictorially represents the Chinese character for distress, *komaru*, which is written with the character for tree inside a box. For similar reasons a *bonsai* tree is never planted in the center of a pot.

3. The art of flower arranging started with offerings before Buddhist altars. Here, too, there were three components (*mitsu-gusoku*), namely, a incense burner, candlestick, and vase of flowers.

4. In some cases, the sensory quality of the design will convey a symbolic message even if the underlying philosophy is not known. For example, the raked white sand found in the gardens of Zen temples speaks eloquently of paucity and purity even if one hasn't been informed of the Zen precept of emptiness (*mu*).

5. The first such advisor on record was a high-priest from Sung-dynasty China, who introduced the concept of *jikkyō* at the temple Higashiyama Kennin-ji in Kyoto during the Muromachi period. *Process Architecture #116*, p. 20.

6. *Shakkei* was at times incorporated in Edo-period stroll gardens. In this case the view had to work as seen from a number of vantage points. In effect these scenes become several shakkei using the same distant view in one garden.

7. The opposite of *mitate-mono* would be "*sōsaku-mono*," something designed specifically for use in the garden.

8. For a detailed description of many different types of chōzubachi (in English and Japanese) see: Yoshikawa, Isao. *Chōzubachi; teienbi no zōkei*, Graphic-sha.

9. A particularly well-known expression of *michiyuki* in Kabuki theater is the procession of two young lovers—disparaged with the world and bent on double suicide (*shinjū*)—along the long entry walk (*hanamichi*) that leads to the stage.

10. Recently, garden ornaments, like lanterns, and stepping stones, are being mass produced for the trade. In this case, there are many that are almost identical, and their value is consequently low.

DESIGN ELEMENTS, page 145

1. For a full description of the various named stones see *Secret Teachings in the Art of Japanese Gardens*, Slawson, David.

2. Shumisen is clearly a Buddhist/Hindu image; Hōrai, stemming from ancient Chinese legendry, is not as easy to categorize.

3. Ohashi, Haruzō, and Saito, Tadakazu. *Nihon teien kanshō jiten*, p. 146.

4. Topiary work was also undoubtedly encouraged by advances in metalworking techniques which allowed for the development of better gardening tools. By the Muromachi period, it is most likely that metal shears or scissors were in use both by the practioners of bonsai and ikebana as well as gardeners. Hida, Norio. *Teien shokusai rekishi (muromachi jidai no shokusai)—nihon bijutsu kogei*.

5. Japanese gardeners have an expression: "The fool cuts the cherry but not the plum," (*sakura kiru baka, ume kiran baka*).

6. In Noh theater, the mirror room (*kagami-no-ma*)—where the performer dons his mask and takes on the spirit of his role—is linked to the stage (*butai*) by a bridge/passageway called a *hashi-gakari*. The entrances to Zen temples were often marked by a bridge that crossed a pond (*han-chi*) symbolic of the threshold between the "outer world" and that of the temple. Also, in the prototypical architecture for shrines, the entrance to the shrine was connected to the ground by a long flight of wooden stairs called a bridge (*hashi*) or ladder (*kake-hashi*).

7. It should be correctly stated that there are some extant outdoor sculptures from pre-Heian times.

These include a sculptural representation, carved in stone, of Shumisen. This sculpture was also a fountain, and water could be caused to flow from it in four directions (a reference to the legends of Shumisen which say it has four rivers running from it in the four cardinal directions). There are also some other garden sculptures from this ancient time that are representative of male, distinctly non-Japanese, figures. The designers of these sculptures, both the figures and the Shumisen image, were most likely foreign craftsmen.

8. Fences designed as screens are called *shahei-gaki*. Those intended as only partial screens are generically called *sukashi-gaki*—open-worked fences or see-through fences.

9. In Japanese, *sode* means sleeve (*gaki* or *kaki* means fence). *Sode-gaki* refers to the shape of these little fences which resemble that of a woman's kimono sleeve if her arms were held out and the sleeves draped down.

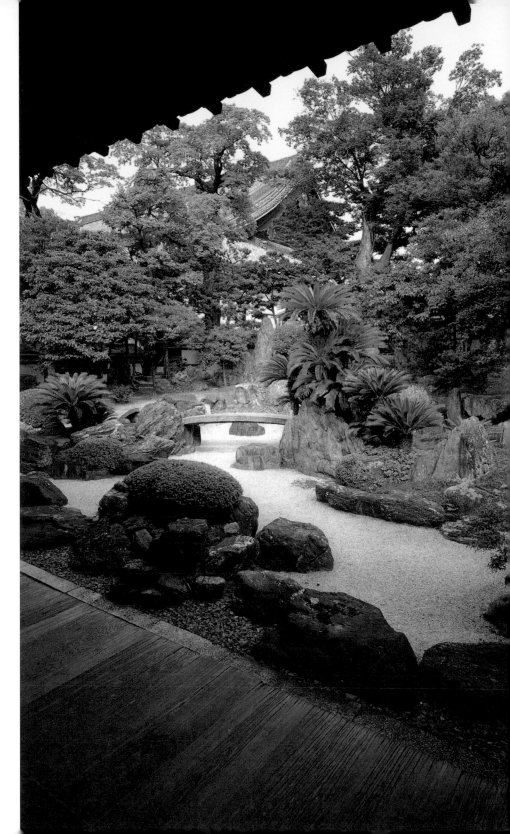

*The large, sweeping temple roof
replaces the usual mountian scene
in this shakkei garden.*
Tiger Glen Garden
Nishihongan-ji, Kyoto

TIMELINE

DATE	PERIOD	JAPANESE GARDENS	JAPANESE CULTURE	WORLD HISTORY	WORLD GARDENS
10,000 B.C.	JŌMON 10,000 B.C. –300 B.C.	PRE-GARDEN: ANIMISTIC PERCEPTION OF THE NATURAL WORLD. RELIGIOUS PRACTICES TAKE PLACE WITHIN NATURE: SACRED STONES AND PONDS (IWAKURA AND KAMI-IKE)	HUNTER/GATHERER SOCIETY LATE JŌMON: SLASH & BURN AGRICULTURE, PIT-DWELLINGS	C.3000 BC: EGYPTIAN KINGS C.1800 BC: BABYLONIA C.500 BC: CONFUCIUS, BUDDHA (SIDDHARTHA GUATAMA)	C.3000 BC: EARLY AGRICULTURAL GARDENS IN EGYPT C.2000 BC: STONEHENGE, CARNAC ASSYRIAN ORCHARD GARDENS IN MESOPOTAMIA
300 B.C.	YAYOI 300 B.C.– A.D.300		WET RICE CULTURE DEVELOPS RAPIDLY BRONZE & IRON IMPLEMENTS WHEEL-THROWN POTTERY	A.D. 317-589: NORTHERN AND SOUTHERN DYNASTIES IN CHINA	C.1000 BC: CHINESE IMPERIAL PARKS C.600 BC: PERSIAN PARADISE GARDENS
300 A.D. 400 500	KOFUN 300–552		CONSTRUCTION OF LARGE BURIAL MOUNDS; SOCIAL ORDER BASED ON CLANS; IMPERIAL LINE EMERGES FROM ONE SUCH CLAN		C.200 BC: ROMAN GARDENS
600	ASUKA 552–710		BUDDHISM & CHINESE CULTURE IMPORTED INTO JAPAN	C.500: DARUMA TO CHINA C.600: MUHAMMAD: ISLAMIC RELIGION 607–907: T'ANG DYNASTY	C.600 AD: BYZANTINE: HORTICULTURAL GARDENS CHINA: PHILOSOPHER RETREAT GARDENS EUROPE: MONASTIC CLOISTER GARDENS
700	NARA 710–794	INTRODUCTION OF GARDEN ART FROM KOREA AND CHINA: GARDENS DESIGNED BY FOREIGN CRAFTSMEN; MODELED AFTER CONTINENTAL FORMS.	C.700: MAN'YŌSHŪ & CHRONICLES OF JAPAN (NIHONGI) DEVELOPMENT OF SHINDEN ARCHITECTURE		
800 900 1000 1100	HEIAN 794–1185	NEW FORM: POND & ISLAND STYLE OF SHINDEN RESIDENCES PRIMARY INFLUENCES: GEOMANCY (FUSUI) POETIC IMAGERY (FUZEI) PARADISE IMAGES (E.G. JŌDŌ) DESIGNERS: ARISTOCRATS SHINGON PRIESTS (ISHI-TATE-SŌ)	C.1000: TALE OF GENJI MID 1000S: BOOK OF GARDENING (SAKUTEIKI)	960–1127: NORTHERN SUNG 1127–1279: SOUTHERN SUNG	C.800: MOORISH GARDENS IN SPAIN C.1000: GARDENS IN CHINA INFLUENCED BY PAINTINGS

DATE	PERIOD	JAPANESE GARDENS	JAPANESE CULTURE	WORLD HISTORY	WORLD GARDENS
1200	Kamakura 1185–1333	NEW FORM: Dry landscape gardens of Zen Temples & samurai residences	Early 1200s: Zen Buddhism to Japan from China		c.1200s Italy: Early botanical gardens North America: Religious earthwork (serpent mounds)
		PRIMARY INFLUENCES: Culture of Chinese Literati Ch'an/Zen Buddhism	Development of Castle Towns	1274: Mongol invasion of china	
1300	Muromachi 1333–1568		c.1300s: Ink painting becomes popular in Japan	c.1300: Rise of Ottoman Empire	
1400		DESIGNERS: Zen priests (ishi-tate-sō) Riverbank people (kawaramono)	Late 1300s: Shoin style of architecture	1368–1644: Ming Dynasty	
1500			Mid 1400s: Garden text: (Senzui narabini yagyō no zu)	c.1500: European Global Exploration; Italian Renaissance	c.1500s India: Mogul water gardens England: Knot gardens Italy: Renaissance villa gardens
1600	Momoyama 1568–1600	NEW FORM: Tea garden Stroll garden Machiya Tsubo garden	Development of wabi tea ceremony	1600: Baroque period in Europe; Colonization of N. America	c.1600s: Portugal: Pool gardens
	Edo 1600–1868	PRIMARY INFLUENCE: Tea ceremony	Development of machiya architecture Kabuki Theater Woodblock prints (ukiyo-e) Grandmaster system (iemoto) Way of Tea (Sadō, Chadō)		Mid 1600s India: Apex of Mogul gardens France: Vista gardens
1700		DESIGNERS: Teamasters (Cha-no-yusha) Professional gardeners (Ueki-ya)	Way of the Flower (Kadō) Way of the Sword (Kendō) Way of the Bow (Kyudō) Etc.		c.1700 England: Landscape gardens
1800				Mid 1800s: Industrial Revolution Late 1800s: French & American Revolutions	Mid 1800s: Europe & America: Public arboretums & parks
1900	Modern Era: Meiji 1868–1912 Taisho: 1912–1926 Showa: 1926–1989 Heisei: 1989 ~	PRIMARY INFLUENCE: European gardens DESIGNERS: Professional gardeners (Niwa-shi) Many stroll gardens become public parks (c. 1870)	Westernization of Japan	Digital Revolution	c.1900: Profession of landscape architecture formalized

PLANTS MENTIONED IN THE TEXT

ENGLISH	JAPANESE	LATIN
EVERGREEN TREES		
Bayberry	*yamamomo*	Myrica rubra
Japanese black pine	*kuromatsu*	Pinus thunbergii
Japanese fir	*momi*	Aibes firma
Japanese hemlock	*tsuga*	Tsuga sieboldii
Japanese red pine	*akamatsu*	Pinus densiflora
Japanese white oak	*shirakashi*	Quercus myrsinaefolia
Japanese white pine	*goyōmatsu*	Pinus pentaphylla
Mandarin orange	*tachibana*	Citrus tachibana
Ring-cupped oak	*arakashi*	Quercus glauca
DECIDUOUS TREES		
Cherry	*sakura*	Prunus spp.
Japanese hackberry	*enoki*	Celtis sinensis var. japonica
Japanese maple	*momiji, kaede*	Acer palmatum
Magnolia	*mokuren*	Magnolia liliflora
Northern Jap. magnolia	*kobushi*	Magnolia kobus
Peach	*momo*	Prunus persica
Pear	*nashi*	Pyrus pyrifolia
Plum	*ume*	Prunus mume
Weeping willow	*shidare yanagi*	Salix babylonica
EVERGREEN SHRUBS		
Azalea (satsuki)	*tsutsuji, satsuki*	Rhododendron indicum
Camellia	*tsubaki*	Camellia japonica
Gardenia	*kuchinashi*	Gardenia jasminoides
Japanese pepper	*sanshō*	Zanthoxylum piperitum
Sweet daphne	*jinchoge*	Daphne odora
Sweet osmanthus	*kinmokusei*	Osmanthus fragrans

ENGLISH	JAPANESE	LATIN
DECIDUOUS SHRUBS		
Bush clover	*hagi*	Lespedeza bicolor
Hollyhock	*aoi*	Asarum spp.
Japanese snowflower	*unohana, utsuki*	Deutzia crenata
Japanese witch hazel	*mansaku*	Hamamelis japonica
Kerria	*yamabuki*	Kerria japonica
HERBACEOUS PLANTS		
Bellflower	*kikyō*	Platycodon grandiflorum
Chrysanthemum	*kiku*	Chrysanthemum spp.
Fringed pink	*nadeshiko*	Dianthus superbus
Japanese iris	*ayame, kakitsubata*	Iris spp.
Japanese pampas grass	*susuki*	Miscanthus sinensis
Lotus	*hasu*	Nelumbo nucifera
OTHER PLANTS		
Bamboo	*take*	Phyllostachys spp.
Cedar moss	*sugi koke*	Pogonatum spp.
Japanese wisteria	*fuji*	Wisteria floribunda

For a more complete list of Japanese plants see
Richards & Kaneko, *Japanese Plants, (Japanese, English, and Latin names)*
and *Zōengaku yōgoshū, Yōkendō (Japanese, English, and Latin names)*

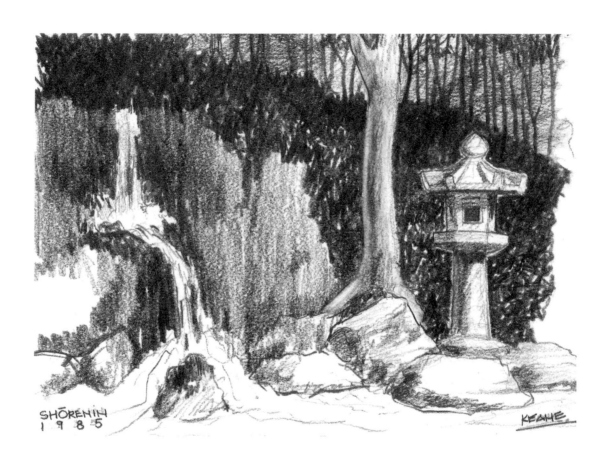

SHŌRENIN
1 9 8 5

KEAHE

GLOSSARY

( ) = Chinese character
bold = in glossary

aida (間) An interval, a space between two things. One of the pronunciations of the character **ma.**

ama-kudaru-kami (天下る神) Gods that descend from above, heaven, or the mountaintops; according to one theory, one of the two types of ancient gods. See **tōrai-kami.**

Amida (阿弥陀) Amitabha Buddha; one of the various incarnations of Buddha; overseer of the Western Paradise (**jōdo**) into which the souls of the pure can be reborn.

asobi (遊び) Playfulness; an aesthetic term from the Edo period.

awaré (哀れ) [ah-wa-reh] An intense emotion felt in response to beauty, especially one of a subtle, ephemeral nature or in response to the inherent sadness of life itself; an aesthetic term from the Heian period.

bakufu (幕府) Military government of the medieval period; literally, curtain government: a reference to the custom of delineating an area of a military encampment with long cloth curtains the height of a man to act as screened meeting places for the upper eschelon of the army.

bō (坊) The large north-south divisions of the original grid plan of the Heian capital.

bonsai (盆栽) A dwarfed shrub or tree planted on a shallow tray; introduced to Japan from China in the early medieval period.

bonseki (盆石) A miniature landscape built on a tray; similar to a **bonsai** but featuring rocks in order to compose a scene.

buke-yashiki (武家屋敷) Warrior's residence; a style of architecture that developed during the medieval period as an outgrowth of the earlier aristocrats' residences (**shinden**).

bushi (武士) A warrior, a **samurai**; in the Edo period, denoting a member of a specific social class.

bushidō (武士道) The way of the warrior; a social institution that developed during the Edo period emphasizing chivalry and obediance to superiors.

cha-ji (茶事) A gathering (usually with few guests) for an elaborate tea ceremony, during which whipped green tea (**koi-cha**, thick tea, and **usu-cha**, thin tea) a meal (kaiseki), and sweets are partaken, and various artworks are viewed.

cha-kai (茶会) A gathering (often with many participants) for a simple tea ceremony, during which whipped green tea (**usu-cha**, thin tea) and sweets are partaken and various works of art are viewed.

cha-no-yu (茶の湯) The proper term for the "tea ceremony"; literally, "hot water for tea"; the term expresses the understatement inherent in the tea world.

cha-no-yusha (茶の湯者) A master of the tea ceremony; one who has the aesthetics and tastes promoted in **cha-no-yu.**

chadō (茶道) The way of tea; see **cha-no-yu.**

chigai-dana (違い棚) A set of staggered shelves found in the tearoom next to the tokonoma; used for the display of artwork.

chiriana (塵穴) A small disposal pit found in the tea garden (**roji**); originally used as a place for the temporary disposal of garden waste; in **cha-no-yu**, symbolic of the preparations the host has gone through for the guest.

chisen-shūyū-teien (池泉周遊庭園) Heian-period pond gardens; literally, "pond-touring gardens."

chi-wari (地割) An early term (perhaps from the Edo period) for garden design; literally, "dividing the ground."

chō (町) One of the sub-divisions in the grid plan of the Heian capital; one chō (120 x 120 meters) was the size usually alloted for an aristocrat's residence (**shinden**).

chōjō (重畳) Accmulated layers in the garden; sensory experiences or scenic views layered in space.

chōnin (町人) Townsfolk of the medieval period onward; refers especially to tradesmen or merchants.

chōzubachi (手水鉢) A water laver; sometimes part of a **tsukubai** arrangement; originally used for the functional purpose of washing hands (as after going to the toilet); in the tea garden it is incorporated as a symbol of spiritual purification.

chū-mon (中門) The middle gate; a simple gate in the middle of the tea garden (**roji**) that separates the inner and outer tea garden;

passing the middle gate is symbolic of entering a deeper state of consciousness.

daimyō (大名) A feudal lord; during the early medieval era, the daimyō were warlords who attained and preserved their domains through military conquest; during the Edo period, at the top of a rigid class structure they built many large stroll gardens.

dharma (Sanskrit) True eternal law, or the true nature of life; understanding dharma is a central pursuit of Buddhism.

dhyana (Sanskrit) Meditation; a central focus of Buddhist religious life.

dō (道) A "way," a school of thought; a term from the Edo period when many previously existing arts (both aesthetic and martial) became codified and institutionalized into a strictly hierarchical system.

dōbōshū (同朋衆) Artistic advisors; often lay-priests of the Ji sect of Buddhism; served medieval daimyō as arbiters of tastes.

domin (土民) Heian-period serfs who did sundry earthwork; therefore, the actual builders of Heian-period gardens.

Edo (江戸) The former name of Tokyo; seat of the military government from 1600–1868.

eki (易) Divination; in Chinese, *yi*; the changeable state of things and interaction of positive and negative aspects of nature; see **geomancy.**

Fujiwara-kyō (藤原京) Capital of Japan from 694 to 710; the first large-scale capital built in Japan; laid out on a grid with wide avenues in imitation of the Chinese capital Chang'an.

fukan-bi (俯瞰美) Bird's-eye perspective; in the garden, fukan-bi refers to the emphasis of designing of the groundplane (**chi-wari**) as if in plan view.

fūsui (風水) **Geomancy**; literally: wind-water.

fuzei (風情) Taste, sensibility towards design; a term applied to garden design, especially during the Heian period; written with the characters for wind and emotion, fuzei is an emotional response to nature.

genkan (玄関) Entrance hall; an outgrowth of the cusp-gabled carriage approach (*karahafu*) found in early samurai residences.

geomancy • A theory of the structure of the universe; Chinese in origin; based on the opposing yet complimentary principles of *in* (the negative, passive force) and *yō* (the positive, active force), and their mutual effects on the five basic elements: wood, fire, earth, metal (gold), and water; a pseudo-physical science drawing on aspects of climatology, ecology, and geophysics (i.e. magnetism); applied in the planning of cities, buildings, and gardens; Jp: **fūsui**, Ch: *feng-shui*.

gōsō (豪壮) Splendor, grandeur; an aesthetic term from the Edo period with Chinese overtones.

gyoen (御苑) An imperial garden.

haha-guni (妣国) Ancestral land; literally, the mother country; refers to a mythical island across the ocean; the abode of ancestral gods.

hana-mi (花見) Flower watching; usually refers to the yearly event of viewing cherry blooms.

hanchi (泮池, 畔池) Pond at the entrance to Zen temples; symbolizes the threshold between sacred (inside) and profane (outside) spaces.

hashi (橋) Bridge; homonymous with edge, bridges are seen as linking two edges— opposite shores of a river, or "this world" and the "afterworld."

hatsu-hana (初花) First flowers of the year; refers not to actual flowers but to snow tufted on the branches of deciduous trees in late winter.

Heian-kyō (平安京) The imperial seat from 794–1868; known as Kyoto since the medieval period; Heian-kyō was the grandest of the ancient capitals built after the example of the Chinese capital Chang'an (長安).

henushi (戸主) The smallest partition in the grid plan of **Heian-kyō**; approximately 15 x 30 meters; the lot size granted to a commoner.

himorogi (神籬) An offering made to the gods; originally meat, recently rice or **saké.**

hira-niwa (平庭) A flat garden; made without creating artificial mountains (**tsuki-yama**).

hō (保) Largest sub-division in the grid of the Heian capital; subdivided into four **chō.**

hōjō (方丈) Head abbot's residence within a temple; often translated as "ten-foot-square hut," a jō is about three meters, thus a hōjō (square jō) is roughly nine meters square.

honcha (本茶) "True" tea; tea produced from the original strain brought to Japan in the late twelfth century by the Buddhist priest Eisai.

Hōrai (蓬莱) Mythic mountain of Chinese legendry; believed to be the abode of the immortals, Hōrai images were built into gardens to entice the immortals to visit and, in doing so, infuse the household with longevity.

ike (池) Pond; one of the earliest terms used to mean garden.

iki (粋) Chic; an aesthetic term from the Edo period.

ishi (石) Rock.

ishi-datami (石畳) A type of paving in which a variety of flat-topped stones are composed into one rectangular strip; literally, stone **tatami**.

ishi-tate-sō (石立て僧) Garden-building priests; originally used in conjunction with priests of the Shingon sect (notably from Ninna-ji in Kyoto) during the Heian period; later, during the medieval period, the term became widely applied to priests of the Zen sect.

ishi-wo-tatsu (石を立つ) Garden building; literally, setting stones upright; a term that originated during the Heian period, if not earlier.

iwa (岩) Boulder.

iwakura (磐座, 岩座) Boulders used since ancient times as prayer sites; the iwakura are seen as containing a god (**kami**) or as being a link to the world of the gods.

iwasaka (磐境) A form of sacred boulder, similar to the **iwakura**; twin rocks evoke the image of the female sex; one theory sees the iwakura as a place to pray to ancestral gods and iwasaka for prayers for progeny.

izumidono (泉殿) The well-spring arbor; built in the garden of the Heian-period **shinden** residences.

jiban (地盤) Ground, groundplane.

jikkyō (十境) Ten stages, ten boundries; ten landmarks in the environment surrounding a temple given names with Buddhist meaning, thereby incorporating them into the extended masterplan of the temple.

jiriki (自力) Self aid / strength; a precept of Zen Buddhism that enlightenment is available only through one's own efforts, for instance perserverance at meditation; see **tariki**.

jō (条) The large east-west divisions of the original grid plan of the Heian capital.

jōdo (浄土) The Pure Land; a paradisiacal heaven described in Amida Buddhism; properly *saihō-gokuraku-jōdo* (西方極楽浄土); the Western Paradisiacal Pure Land.

jōdo-teien (浄土庭園) A Pure Land garden; a gardening style from the Heian period in which an image of **Amida** Buddha's Pure Land (**jōdo**) was reconstructed; jōdō was usually represented as an island in a pond connected to shore by a bridge, implying the potential of salvation.

jōka machi (城下町) Castle towns; developed during the medieval period.

kaiyū-shiki-teien (回遊式庭園) A stroll garden; a style that developed during the Edo period on the large estates of the daimyō; incorporating a number of "scenes" in the overall plan, which were revealed as one strolled about the garden on a meandering path.

kake-kotoba (掛詞) A pun; a literary technique used extensively in Heian-period poetry; standard images found in the puns (often nature images) were also used as motifs in garden design.

kami (神) God, godspirit.

kami-ike (神池) Ponds used in ancient times as prayer sites; islands built in the ponds, representative of the **haha-guni** or ancestral land, were the object of worship; also pronounced *shinchi*.

kanshō-niwa (観賞庭) Contemplation garden; a form of garden that developed during the medieval period; not intended to be physically entered, but rather, contemplated upon from the rooms of an adjacent building.

kare-san-sui (枯山水) Literally, dry-mountain-water; a style of garden which creates the image of mountains and water through the use of sand, stone, and at times, sparse plantings. The term is found in Heian-period gardening texts, but kare-san-sui gardens are usually associated with Zen Buddhist temples of the Muromachi period.

kare-taki (枯れ滝) Dry waterfall. See **ryū-mon-baku.**

karei (華麗) Magnificent, gorgeous; an aesthetic term from the Edo period.

kari-niwa (狩庭) Hunting range.

kawara-mono (河原者) A pejorative term for an underclass in Japanese society to whom undesirable tasks —butchering, tanning, heavy construction—were assigned; literally, riverbank people; see **senzui-kawara-mono.**

kekkai (結界) A sacred space; in ancient times, before religious architecture developed, kekkai were used as sites for prayers.

ken (間) The basic modular measurement used in Japanese architecture; approximately 1.8 meters (six feet).

ki (気) Life energy (also spirit; mind; soul); according to Eastern medicine and geophysics, all matter is imbued with ki, the study and manipulation of which was central to **geomancy.**

kimochi-ga-yoi (気持ちが良い) Pleasant, comfortable; an aesthetic term from the Edo period.

kimon (鬼門) In **geomancy**, the northeast quadrant; the direction from which evil (unfavorable **ki**) is most likely to enter.

kirei (綺麗) Beautiful; an aesthetic term from the Edo period.

kōan (公案) An enigmatic statement; presented by a Zen master to a disciple, the pondering of a kōan is intended to break down dualistic thought, leading to self-realization.

koi-cha (濃い茶) Thick green tea; powdered green tea that is whipped with hot water to the consistency of cream.

koshi-kake-machiai (腰掛け待合い) Roofed waiting bench; in tea gardens, used as a place for spiritual preparation before entering the tea house.

kū (空) Nothingness, emptiness (Sanskrit: sunyata); a teaching of Zen Buddhism.

kūkan (空間) Space; a three-dimensional void.

kyoku-sui (曲水) A winding stream; a feature of some Heian-period gardens; also called **yarimizu.**

kyoku-sui-no-en (曲水の宴) The Feast by the Winding Stream; a poetry event held in Heian-period gardens.

kyaku-shitsu (客室) Guestroom; most gardens in private residences are associated with this room.

ma (間) Space; depending on its use, ma can represent linear, planar, volumetric, temporal, or social spaces.

machiya (町家) Town house; any of a number of styles of wooden residences built within the precincts of a town or city.

makura-kotoba (枕詞) An epithet; literally, pillow word; a standard literary technique in Heian poetry.

mappō (末法) The latter days of Buddhist Law; a degenerate age.

masago (真砂) Sand composed of decomposed granite.

matsu (松) Pine tree.

michiyuki (道行) Progression through space and / or time; movement through various "layers" of a garden; A Kabuki actor's movement through space expressing story development in time.

mitate (見立て) The reuse of old objects in the garden; originally associated with the tea garden; *mitate-mono* = reused objects.

miyabi (雅び) Elegant, refined; an aesthetic term associated with the Heian-period aristocracy.

mizu (水) Water.

mono-no-awaré (物の哀れ) A sensitivity to beauty found in the pathos or evanescence of life; an aesthetic associated with the Heian-period aristocracy.

mu (無) Nothingness, emptiness; a teaching of Zen Buddhism.

mujō (無常) Transience, mutability; expressed in the emotion mujō-kan.

naka-jima (中島) The central island in a pond garden; often representative of an afterworld, such as **jōdō,** the Pure Land of **Amida** Buddha; also used as a stage for musicians.

nantei (南庭) The open, flat area directly south of a **shinden** residence; literally: southern garden; covered with sand for formality and ease of function; used for events and gatherings.

nijiri-guchi (躙口) The small door in a tea house used as the guest's entrance; from the verb *nijiru*, to edge forward.

niwa (庭) Garden; in ancient times contained the meaning of territory or a place for events to take place.

niwa-ki (庭木) Gardening plants; referring to a limited palette of plants that are used for gardening, see **zōki.**

niwa-saki (庭先) Garden.

niwa-shi (庭師) Gardener; a term originating in the Meiji period referring to professional gardeners.

nobe-dan (延段) A type of paving; contains a variety of flat-topped stones that are arranged together in a long, rectangular strip.

nōson fūkei (農村風景) A pastoral, agricultural landscape; included as part of the overall plan of large Edo-period stroll gardens.

omoteya-zukuri (表屋造り) A form of urban architecture that developed during the late medieval and early Edo periods; consisting of a deep, narrow dwelling that has a shop in the front (*omote-ya*) and multi-generation residences towards the rear.

on-yō-ryō (陰陽寮) The Bureau of Yin and Yang (in Japanese *on-yō* or *in-yō*) established in the ancient capital, **Heian-kyō**; responsible for matters dealing with geomantic divination.

ri-gyo-seki (鯉魚石) A carp stone; part of a waterfall arrangement (**ryū-mon-baku).**

rittai-bi (立体美) Sculptural or volumetric beauty; as opposed to planar beauty; expressed through garden rocks and masses of clipped plants.

roji (露地) A tea garden; literally, dewy ground; originating from a homonym (路地) that means alleyway.

ryū-mon-baku (龍門瀑) An arrangement of stones made to appear as a waterfall, often without any actual water; containing Chinese / Zen Buddhist symbolism.

sabi (寂び) A weathered patina; an elegant simplicity; an aesthetic quality in artwork and tea utensils appreciated by tea masters from the Momoyama period onward.

sadō (茶道) The Way of Tea. See **cha-no-yu.**

saké (酒) Japanese rice wine.

sakui (作意, 作為) Personal creativity; literally, to make (something) for the sake of it.

Sakuteiki (作庭記) An eleventh century gardening text; purportedly written by Tachibana no Toshitsuna, the son of a Fujiwara nobleman.

samurai (侍) A warrior; in early medieval times a fighting soldier; later, during the Edo period, samurai were the highest class in a strict caste system.

sa-niwa (清庭, 斎場, 沙庭) A purified space used to pray to, and receive divine messages from, godspirits.

san-sui (山水) An early medieval term meaning garden; literally, mountain-water; also pronounced *sen-zui.*

san-sui-ga (山水画) A type of inkbrush painting depicting natural landscapes; literally, mountain-water-painting.

sanzon-ishi-gumi (三尊石組) An arrangement of three stones in a triangular form that represent a Buddhist trinity.

seii-tai-shōgun (征夷大将軍) See **shōgun.**

sentei (剪定) Garden; a term used in provincial areas rather than Kyoto or Tokyo; literally, to prune.

senzai (前栽) A small garden associated with the townhouses (**machiya**) of Kyoto.

senzui (山水) An alternative pronunciation of **sansui**.

senzui-kawara-mono (山水河原者) A class of gardeners from the medieval period; originally members of the **kawara-mono** class.

shahei-gaki (遮蔽垣) A fence intended as a screen.

shakkei (借景) Borrowed scenery; a gardening technique in which a distant view is incorporated as an integral part of a garden, the whole scene being composed as if it was a painting.

sharé (洒落) [*sha-reh*] Fashionable; an aesthetic term from the Edo period.

shibumi (渋味) Quiet, somber; an aesthetic taste associated with the Edo period **chōnin.**

shiki (四季) The four seasons.

shima (島) island; one of the original terms meaning garden.

shime-nawa (注連縄) A rice straw rope ritually

tied around an area or object to demarcate it as sacred.

shin-gyō-sō (真行草) Formal, semi-formal, informal; a ranking system first applied to design styles by the tea masters of the medieval period.

shinden (寝殿) The main hall of the residences of the Heian-period aristocracy; from which derives the term *shinden-zukuri* denoting that style of architecture in general.

shi-nō-kō-shō (士農工商) The social caste system of the Edo period; respectively samurai, farmer, craftsman, merchant.

shinrin (神林) A sacred forest; the forested area surrounding a shrine.

shintō (神道) Native Japanese animistic religion; literally, the Way of the Gods.

shinzan-yūkoku (深山幽谷) The mystery of wild nature; literally, deep mountains, mysterious valleys; an image associated with Zen Buddhist priests and recluse philosophers who find the meaning of life in the study of nature.

shira-kawa-suna (白川砂) White sand; the material that has become most associated with the design of **kare-san-sui**.

shō, chiku, bai (松竹梅) Pine, bamboo, plum; used as a ranking system; respectively—best, great, good.

shōen (荘園) An estate, a manor; large tracts of land held by aristocrats or temples, especially during the Heian period.

shōgun (将軍) A general or commander; head of state from medieval times through the Edo period; an abridged version of **seii-tai-shōgun** —barbarian-subduing generalissimo.

shoin (書院) A writing alcove; an architectural feature found first in the Zen temples and warrior residences of the Muromachi period; thus the architectural style *shoin-zukuri*.

shokusai (植栽) Plantings.

Shumisen (須弥山, 須彌山) The central, immovable mountain of Buddhist cosmology; expressed in Japanese gardens by setting a singular rock upright; one of the first religious images incorporated in Japanese gardens.

sōan (草庵) A teahouse; literally, grass-roofed hut; the representative architecture of the wabi-cha tea culture which began in the Momoyama period.

sode-gaki (袖垣) A wing-fence. A small fence extending outward from a building that limits the view (to the right or left) of a garden as seen from a first-floor room.

sono (園) Garden; often with agricultural connotations.

sōsaku-mono (創作物) A "designed object": a lantern, laver, etc., that is specifically designed for use in a garden.

soto-mon (外門) The outer gate of a tea garden that separates the garden from the outer world.

soto-roji (外露地) The outer part of the tea garden.

sui (粋) Worldly, knowing; an aesthetic term from the Edo period.

sukashi-gaki (透かし垣) A see-through fence; open, lattice-work fence.

suki (数寄) Artisticness; an aesthetic term from the Edo period.

sukiya (数寄屋) A form of residential architecture influenced by the understatement and naturalness of the **sōan**; in this style the designer's tastes are expressed in a variety idiosyncratic details, for example transoms (*ranma*), nailcovers (*kugi-kakushi*), and the display alcove (**toko-no-ma**).

suna (砂) Sand: see **shira-kawa-suna**.

tainoya (対屋) Subsidiary halls in a **shinden** residence; built to the east and/or west of the main shinden hall; tainoya were connected by roofed corridors to garden arbors.

tanka (短歌) Japanese verse form with 31 syllables; standard poetic form of the Heian period.

tanoshimi (楽しみ) Fun, playfulness; an aesthetic term of the Edo period.

tariki (他力) External aid/salvation; calling, through prayer, for the intercession of a superior being to save one's soul as practiced by certain Buddhist sects, i.e., **Amida** Buddhism; see **jiriki**.

tatami (畳) Straw matting; used as flooring in Japanese architecture from the medieval period onward; one mat is approximately 1.8 x 0.9 meters.

GLOSSARY

teien (庭園) Gardens; in the ornamental sense.

tenkei-butsu (添景物) A garden ornament; for instance, lanterns, bridges, and water lavers.

teppō-gaki (鉄砲垣) A type of bamboo fence; unsplit sections of bamboo are tied to a horizontal wooden frame in vertical ranks; *teppō* means rifle, which the regular uprights resemble.

tōcha (闘茶) Tea-tasting competition; a pastime of the medieval samurai elite; the overt intention of the competition was to discern true tea (**honcha**) from others, in reality it also involved copius quantities of **saké.**

toko-no-ma (床の間) An alcove used for the display of artwork.

tokoyo-shisō (常世思想) The concept of a paradisiacal afterlife, eternal life, or immortality. Early Japanese gardens were designed to evoke the image of such paradisiacal worlds.

tomé (止め) [toe-meh] Stillness; in the garden the surface of a body of water, a flat expanse of raked sand, or flat-topped rocks positioned so that their upper surfaces are level.

tōrai-kami (到来神) Those native Japanese gods believed to come from an ancestral land (**haha-guni**) over the sea.

tsū (通) Connoisseurship, professionalism; an aesthetic term from the Edo period.

tsubo-niwa (坪庭, 壺庭, 経穴庭) A tiny, enclosed garden; as found in the town houses (**machiya**) of the Edo period.

tsuki-yama (築山) An artificial "mountain"; in actual size anything from a one-meter berm to a small hill; created with soil and, for larger hills, rock infill.

tsuiji-bei (築地塀) A rammed-earth wall; used for the outer, defensive walls of cities and some residences.

tsukubai (蹲踞) An arrangement of stones found in a tea garden that includes a water laver used to purify hands and mouth before entering the tearoom.

tsuridono (釣り殿) The "fishing" arbor; built in the garden of the Heian-period **shinden** residences.

ueki-ya (植木屋) Gardener; the first class of professional gardeners, stemming from the late medieval or early Edo periods.

usu-cha (薄茶) Thin green tea; powdered green tea that is whipped with hot water to create a frothy surface.

utsukushii (美しい) Beautiful; an aesthetic term from the Edo period.

wabi (侘び) Subdued taste; an aesthetic of the Momoyama tea culture; often used in the combined expression wabi-sabi; an appreciation of things that have or express **sabi.**

wabi-cha (侘び茶) The rustic tea culture that developed during the Momoyama period.

wa-fū (和風) Japanese style.

wa-shin (和心) Japanese spirit.

yama (山) Mountain; one of the earliest terms used to mean garden.

yarimizu (遣水) A garden stream; typically found in the garden of Heian-period **shinden** palaces.

yaza (夜坐) Evening **zazen**; meditation in front of a garden is often associated with yaza.

yohaku-no-bi (余白の美) The beauty of paucity; a medieval aesthetic appreciating the unstated or unexpressed portion of a work of art.

yōjō (余情, 餘情) Spontaneous artistic effect; associated with Heian-period poetry.

yūgen (幽玄) Subtle profundity, mysteriousness; an aesthetic from the medieval period.

yu-niwa (斎庭) A purified space used to pray to, and receive divine messages from, godspirits.

zazen (坐禅) Seated meditation; as practiced in Zen Buddhism.

zendō (禅堂) A meditation hall; the center of communal meditation in the Zen sect; often dark and introverted, eliminating external distractions.

zōki (雑木) Miscellaneous trees; plantings associated with the tea garden; using a wide variety of naturalistic planting rather than a strict set of horticultural species; see **niwa-ki**.

ACKNOWLEDGMENTS

I must begin by thanking all the people at the Charles E. Tuttle Company for seeking me out and supporting me in the creation of this book. Thank you, too, Professor Nakamura Hajime, for giving me my start in Japan, and Wybe Kuitert, for your friendship and many insightful comments that made this a better book. To Kinoshita Ryoichi, many, many thanks for your constant support. Also, I am very grateful to Monica Bethe, Richard Tanter, Tacy Apostolik, Andrew Hare, and everyone else who opened up new worlds to me by lending me your books. Yoshiko Mastubara is owed special mention for her ink brush characters which complement the pages on aesthetics. There are three people without whom this book would not be what it is and to whom I owe a special debt of gratitude:

Ōhashi Haruzō, for his beautiful garden photographs. Mr. Ōhashi, who started taking photographs just about the year I was born, has made photographing Japanese gardens his life's work and has at least thirty books on that subject.

John Einarsen for giving form to my words. A resident of Kyoto for the last fifteen years, he is best known as the chief editor and art director of *Kyoto Journal*, an excellent quarterly magazine on Japan and Asia.

Preston L. Houser for his clear, editorial insight. Mr. Houser is author of *Invitation to Tea Gardens: Kyoto's Culture Enclosed* and the CD-ROM *Kyoto Gardens: A Virtual Stroll Through Zen Landscapes*.

This book is the result of eleven years of research and design work. It is impossible to list all the many, many people who have helped me along the way: the scholars who shared their thoughts with me and the gardeners who gave me insights into their world. I am very grateful to all of you.

And, most of all, to Momoko and Kai, who made it all worth it just by being there.

BIBLIOGRAPHY

BOOKS IN ENGLISH

Addiss, Stephen. *The Art of Zen*, New York: Harry Abrams, Inc. Publishers, 1989.

Aston, W.G. *Nihongi: Chronicles of Japan from the Earliest Times to A.D. 697*, Tokyo: Charles E. Tuttle Company, 1972.

Awakawa, Yasuichi. *Zen Painting,* Tokyo and New York: Kodansha International Ltd., 1970.

Carter, Dr. Jon and Covell, Alan. *Japan's Hidden History: Korean Impact on Japanese Culture.*, Elizabeth, NJ, Seoul: Hollym International, 1984.

Elison, George, and Smith, Bardwell L., editors. *Warlords, Artists, and Commoners*, Honolulu: University of Hawaii Press, 1981.

Engel, Heinrich. *The Japanese House.*,Tokyo: Charles E. Tuttle Company, 1964.

Hall, John W. and Takeshi, Toyoda, editors. *Japan in the Muromachi Age.* , Berkley, Los Angeles, London: Unversity of California Press, 1977.

Hempel, Rose. *The Golden Age of Japan 794-1192*, New York: Rizzoli International Publications, Inc., 1983.

Hisamatsu, Sen'ichi. *The Vocabulary of Japanese Literary Aesthetics*, Tokyo: The Centre for East Asian Cultural Studies, 1963.

Houser, Preston. *Invitation to Tea Gardens*, Kyoto: Mitsumura Suiko Shoin, 1992.

Itoh, Teiji (translated by Friedrich, Ralph and Shimamura, Masajiro). *Space and Illusion in the Japanese Garden*, New York, Tokyo, and Kyoto: Weatherhill/Tankosha, 1983.

Itsuzu, Toshihiko and Toyo. *The Theory of Beauty in the Classical Aesthstics of Japan*, The Hague, Boston, London: Martinus Nijhoff Publishers, 1981.

Kane, Daniel R. "The Epic of Tea: Tea ceremony as the Mythological Journey of the Hero," *Kyoto Journal, Vol. #1*, 1987, pp. 12-22.

Kato, Shuichi. *Form, Style, and Tradition*, Tokyo, New York and San Francisco: Kodansha International Ltd., 1971.

Kodansha Encyclopedia of Japan, Tokyo, New York: Kodansha, 1983.

Koren, Leonard. *Wabi-Sabi for Artists, Designers, Poets, and Philosphers*, Berkley: Stone Bridge Press, 1994.

Kuck, Loraine. *The World of the Japanese Garden*, New York and Tokyo: Weatherhill, 1984.

Kuitert, Wybe. *Themes, Scenes, and Taste in the History of Japanese Garden Art*, Amsterdam: J.C. Gieben, Publisher, 1988.

Levy, Ian Hideo. *Man'yōshū: Volume One*, Princeton, NJ: Princeton University Press, 1981.

Lip, Dr. Evelyn. *Feng Shui; Environments of Power*, London: Academy Group Ltd., 1995.

Mason, Penelope. *History of Japanese Art*, New York: Harry N. Abrams, Inc., Publishers, 1993.

McCullough, Helen Craig. *Tales of Ise.* ,
Tokyo: University of Tokyo Press, 1968.

Morris, Ivan. *The World of the Shining Prince*, England: Penguin Books Ltd., 1964.

Murakami, Hyoe, and Seidensticker, Edward G., editors. *Guides to Japanese Culture*, Tokyo: Japan Culture Institute, 1977.

Nakamura, Makoto. *The Twofold Beauties of the Japanese Garden*, International Federation of Landscape Architects (I.F.L.A.) Yearbook, 1986/87, pp. 195-198.

Naito, Akira. *Katsura; A Princely Retreat*, Tokyo, New York and San Francisco: Kodansha International Ltd., 1977.

Nelson, Andrew Nathaniel. *The Modern Reader's Japanese-English Character Dictionary: Second Revised Edition*, Tokyo: Charles E. Tuttle Company, 1974.

Nishi, Kazuo, and Hozumi, Kazuo, translated by Horton, H. Mack. *What is Japanese Architecture?* Tokyo, New York: Kodansha International Ltd., 1983.

Nitschke, Günter. *The Architecture of the Japanese Garden: Right Angle and Natural Form*, Köln: Benedikt Taschen, 1991.

Okakura, Kakuzo. *The Book of Tea*, Tokyo: Charles E. Tuttle Company, 1956.

Richards, Betty W., and Kaneko, Anne. *Japanese Plants: Know Them & Use Them*, Tokyo: Shufunotomo Co. Ltd., 1988.

Rodd, Laurel Rasplica. *Kokinshu*, United Kingdom: Princeton University Press, 1984.

Sansom, G.B. *Japan; A Short Cultural History,*

Tokyo: Charles E. Tuttle Company, 1931.
The Tale of Genji, translator, Seidensticker, Edward G.. Tokyo: Charles E. Tuttle Company, 1976.

Sakuteiki; The Book of Garden, translator, Shimoyama, Shigemaru. Tokyo: Town and City Panners, Inc., 1976.

Slawson, David. *Secret Teachings in the Art of Japanese Gardens*, Tokyo and New York: Kodansha International Ltd., 1987.

Stanley-Baker, Joan. *Japanese Art*, London: Thames and Hudson,1984.

Treib, Marc, and Herman, Ron. *A Guide to the Gardens of Kyoto*, Tokyo: Shufunotomo Co. Ltd., 1980.

Ueda, Makoto. *Literary and Art Theories in Japan*, Ann Arbor, Michigan: Center for Japanese Studies, The University of Michigan, 1967.

Varley, Paul H. *Japanese Culture; A Short History*, Tokyo: Charles E. Tuttle Company, 1973.

Wright, Tom. *Zen Gardens*, Kyoto: Mitsumura Suiko Shoin, 1990.

Yamazaki, Masafumi, editor. *Process Architecture #116; Kyoto; Its Cityscape Traditions and Heritage* (Japanese and English), Tokyo: Process Arcitecture Co., Ltd., 1994.

Yoshikawa, Isao. *Chōzubachi; tienbi no zokei* (Japanese and English), Tokyo: Graphic-sha, 1991.

Yoshikawa, Isao. *Zendera no niwa* (Japanese and English), Tokyo: Graphic-sha, 1991.

BOOKS IN JAPANESE

Amino, Yoshihiko. *Nihonron no shiza*, Tokyo: Shogakkan, 1991.

Hasegawa, Masami. *Nihon teien no genzō*, Kyoto: Shirakawa Shoin, 1978.

Hasegawa, Masami. *Nihon teien yōsetsu*, Kyoto: Shirakawa Shoin, 1983.

Hida, Norio. *Teien shokusai rekishi; Nihon bijutsu kōgei,* 1990–1991.

Hisayama, Kikuo. *Fiirudo gaido: daimonji yama*, Kyoto: Nakanishiya Shuppan, 1991.

Kanji-gen, Tokyo: Gakken, 1988.

Kogo daijiten, Tokyo: Shogakken, 1983.

Kojima, Noriyuki, et al. *Nihon koten bungaku zenshū: Man'yōshū*, Tokyo: Shogakkan, 1990.

Kyoto no meien: Sono kachi to hensen, Kyoto: Kyotoshi Bunkazai Bukkusu Dai 9 Shū, 1994.

Kyoto no teien: Iseki ni mieru heian jidai no teien, Kyoto: Kyotoshi Bunkazai Bukkusu Dai 5 Shū, 1990.

Kyoto rekishi atorasu, Tokyo: Chūō Kōronsha, 1994.

Meien wo aruku; Vols. 1-8, Tokyo: Mainichi Shinbunsha, 1990.

Nakane, Kinsaku. *Meitei no kansho to sakutei*, Osaka: Hoikusha, 1972.

Nihon kokugo daijiten, Tokyo: Shogakken, 1946.
Nihon nōsho zenshū: Kadanchi kinshō, Tokyo:

Shadan Hōjin, Nōsan Gyoson Bunka Kyokai, 1995.

Niwa zukuri yōgo jiten, Tokyo: Kenchiku Shiryo Kenkyusha,1987.

Ōhashi, Haruzō. *Niwa no rekishi wo aruku*, Tokyo: Sankosha, 1992.

Ōhashi, Haruzō and Saitō, Tadakazu. *Nihon teien kanshō jiten*, Tokyo: Tokyodo Shuppan, 1993.

Shirahata, Yozaburo. *Edo no daimyō teien*, Tokyo: INAX, 1994.

Takei, Jirō. *Sakuteiki: Gendaigo taiyaku to kaisetsu.*, Kyoto: Kyoto Geijutsu Tanki Daigaku, 1995.

Zōengaku yōgoshū, Tokyo: Yōkendō, 1979.

ABOUT TUTTLE: "Books to Span the East and West"

Our core mission at Tuttle Publishing is to create books which bring people together one page at a time. Tuttle was founded in 1832 in the small New England town of Rutland, Vermont (USA). Our fundamental values remain as strong today as they were then—to publish best-in-class books informing the English-speaking world about the countries and peoples of Asia. The world has become a smaller place today and Asia's economic, cultural and political influence has expanded, yet the need for meaningful dialogue and information about this diverse region has never been greater. Since 1948, Tuttle has been a leader in publishing books on the cultures, arts, cuisines, languages and literatures of Asia. Our authors and photographers have won numerous awards and Tuttle has published thousands of books on subjects ranging from martial arts to paper crafts. We welcome you to explore the wealth of information available on Asia at **www.tuttlepublishing.com**.

INDEX
Boldface type indicates an illustration